MIRRORS OF MEMORY

MIRRORS

OF MEMORY

Culture, Politics, and Time in Paris and Tokyo

James W. White

UNIVERSITY OF VIRGINIA PRESS | CHARLOTTESVILLE AND LONDON

University of Virginia Press
Printed in the United States of America on acid-free paper

First published 2011

9 8 7 6 5 4 3 2 1

Library of Congress Cataloging-in-Publication Data
White, James W., 1941–
    Mirrors of memory : culture, politics, and time in Paris and
Tokyo / James W. White.
        p. cm.
    Includes bibliographical references and index.
    ISBN 978-0-8139-3070-1 (cloth : alk. paper)
    ISBN 978-0-8139-3079-4 (e-book)
    1. Architecture and society — France — Paris.   2. Archi-
tecture and society — Japan — Tokyo.   3. Sociology, Urban
— France — Paris.   4. Sociology, Urban — Japan — Tokyo.
5. Paris (France) — Civilization.   6. Tokyo (Japan) —
Civilization.   I. Title. II.   Title: Culture, politics, and time
in Paris and Tokyo.
    NA2543.S6W495   2011
    307.760944´361 — dc22   2010021798

Illustration Credits: Fig. 1, Eckhard Pecher; *figs. 2, 6, 8, 9, 24, 25, 26, 29,
33,* author's photographs; *fig. 3,* Bibliothèque Historique de la Ville de
Paris, adapted by Michael Southern; *fig. 4,* Chūō Kōron Sha, adapted
by Michael Southern; *figs. 5, 7, 12, 13, 14, 15a, 15b, 21,* Erin S. White;
figs. 10, 19, La Documentation Française, adapted by Michael Southern; *fig. 11,* John Murray Rare Book Collection, University of North
Carolina at Chapel Hill; *fig. 16,* Jean-Pierre Verney © Établissement
de Communication et de Production Audiovisuelle de la Défense,
France; *figs. 17, 18, 28,* Collection of the Pavillon de l'Arsenal, City of
Paris; *fig. 20,* Wikipedia; *fig. 22,* "Rama Neko," via Wikipedia; *fig. 23,*
Louis-François Delannoy, via Wikipedia; *fig. 27,* David C. Moore,
2005; *fig. 30,* Mathieu Pernot; *fig. 31,* Chikuma Shobō, Inc.; *fig. 32,*
Michael Southern; *fig. 34,* © Allan A. Philiba; *fig. 35,* Stéfan Le Dû,
via Wikipedia.

CONTENTS

TABLES AND FIGURES

PREFACE

This work represents for me a departure from a scholarly career hitherto spent almost exclusively in, and on, East Asia. In its pursuit I have therefore, far more than has previously been the case, relied on the kindness of strangers. Many old colleagues did give me advice and encouragement along the way, including Henry D. Smith, Kurasawa Susumu, William LaFleur, Muramatsu Michio, Kawamura Nozomu, and the late Charles Tilly. Along the way I have also made the acquaintance, virtual or personal, of Augustin Berque, John Merriman, Henry Millon, Josef Konvitz, Toriumi Motoki, Guy Burgel, Maurice Aymard, Sophie Body-Gendrot, and Christian Sautter, all of whom opened many doors (and, on occasion, my eyes). The staff at the library of the International House of Japan, the National Diet Library, and Kris Troost of the Duke University Library East Asian Collection all helped me run down sources of one kind and another, and Allan Philiba, Mathieu Pernot, and Erin White shared their photographs with me.

But the really gratifying thing about this project was the unfailing generosity and cooperation I encountered when coming unannounced into a variety of public institutions, searching with my limited linguistic skills for data or visual images of the city. The staff at the Bibliothèque Historique de la Ville de Paris, Antonella Casellato and Christine Hoarau of the Pavillon de l'Arsenal of the Prefecture of Paris, the Institut d'Aménagement et d'Urbanisme de la Région Île-de-France, the Edo-Tokyo Museum, the Maison Européenne de la Photographie, the Bibliothèque Jacques Doucet, Pascale Tresserre and Elisabeth Szlezys of ECPAD (Établissement de Communication et de Production Audiovisuelle de la Défense), La Documentation Française, and Tokyo City Hall, even when they did not have the materials I was seeking, were without exception open-armed and -minded. Neither the Japanese nor the French are famed for their receptivity to strangers; I finished this project mystified by the origin of these stereotypes.

Another pleasant surprise was my discovery of the intellectual free market of Wikipedia. I have always cautioned my students about using this source in their research, but in my case it was photographic images of Paris and Tokyo that I sought, and many of the entries in Wikipedia are accompanied by high-quality images, all in the public domain. Not all of the contributors can be traced through their pseudonymous user names, but I was able to track down Stéfan Le Dû, Eckhard Pecher, David C. Moore, "Rama Neko," and Louis-François Delannoy, all of whom graciously confirmed the availability of their work to my purposes.

In getting from research to manuscript to book, I have profited from the skilled assistance of several people. Laura Oaks gave the manuscript a thorough edit and, with Katie Haywood, produced the final electronic version; Boyd Zenner and Angie Hogan of the University of Virginia Press shepherded it through the editorial process; Michael Southern expertly contributed several maps; and Roberta Engleman did the index. None of the people or institutions mentioned above, of course, is responsible for any errors of fact or interpretation in this book.

One stylistic note: I have given Japanese names in Japanese order (surname first), except in the case of authors of English-language works.

INTRODUCTION

A Parisian in Tokyo, or a Tokyoite in Paris, will find much there that is
familiar. Huge cities, embedded in yet bigger metropolitan regions, both
are busy, vibrant, clearly prosperous, stimulating, and at the cutting edge
of modernity, or postmodernity. Both are capitalist cities, brimming with
consumer goods and leisure opportunities; both are "global cities": cosmopolitan nodes in the web of global commerce, communication, human
movement, finance, and corporate governance. Both are dominant, their
countries' capitals and largest cities by far, and home as well to disproportionate shares of their nations' educational, economic, and cultural resources. They have long been so, as their nations' capitals for several centuries. And they *work:* trains and subways hew to a tight schedule; streets are
cleaned; and urban decay, crime, poverty, and economic polarization[1] are
relatively uncommon.

A more searching look reveals more parallels. Both have dominated their
countries economically, politically, and demographically for centuries now,
and for at least the last century or two have been subject to dirigiste rule,
under the state's firm grip. Though democratic in the present day, both
Paris and Tokyo have been shaped by states which have tried to compensate
in many spheres for the vagaries and brutality of the market, and to aid the
weak and unproductive.[2] The state is a large contributor to the revenues of

both cities;[3] Japanese and French political cultures recognize a large public sphere and the legitimate pursuit of a wide variety of collective goals by the state.

Yet despite the supposedly homogenizing forces of modernity, capitalism, globalism, democracy, and dirigiste states, no one would ever mistake Tokyo for Paris — even with a (slightly taller) copy of the Eiffel Tower looming over Shiba Park. One may argue that world cities like Tokyo and Paris resemble each other more today than they do the rest of their respective countries,[4] but arguments for "convergence" among postindustrial capitalist cities seem at best inadequate when one contemplates the apparently formless, seething social and physical magma of Tokyo against the fixed baroque elegance and calculated social savoir faire of Paris.

"Well, of course," is the easiest response: Japan and France are a *mikan* and a *pomme*. Two different cultures, two different developmental paths, two entirely different historical trajectories — what would one expect? But this assessment seems wanting. It is too broad; indeed, the cultural brushstroke explains everything, and thus nothing. It begs the question, *What* in the culture — or elsewhere — explains the differences we see? A culture is not a unitary essence. And *how* might "culture" — hardly a tangible actor — have exerted an influence on the city? Culture is not destiny — it is contingent, and mediated by human agency.

Initially, space and built form are just a matter of visual impression. In a first step toward understanding how this form came to be, one can examine how others have seen the city, and in so doing, the differences multiply: perceptions of the capital by its own people, its recorders and observers, and the state vary dramatically between Paris and Tokyo. Both positive and negative evaluations of Paris far outstrip those of Tokyo (and its predecessor, Edo), achieving a level of passion only rarely matched by the chroniclers of the latter city. Again, why? And different perceptions — mediated over centuries through the agencies of rule — have contributed to quite different relationships between the capital and its provinces, its suburbs, and its national government. And, to complete the circle, perceptions and relationships have through time powerfully influenced the built environment of the city in the ways we see today. Or so I shall argue.

What follows is an exercise in the reconstruction of history, an attempt

Fig. 1. Tokyo Tower.

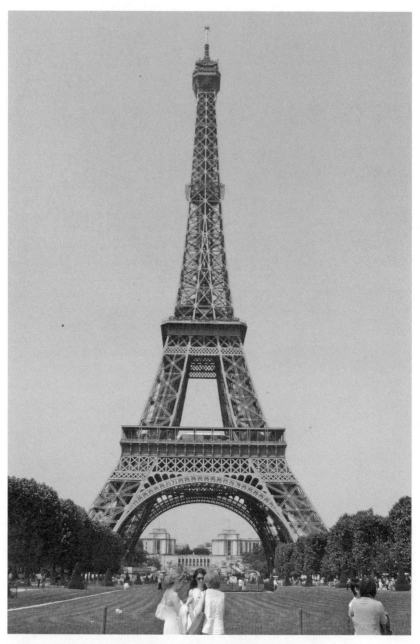

Fig. 2. Eiffel Tower. Or perhaps this is Tokyo, and the other is Paris.

to suggest how the physical, perceptual, and relational differences between contemporary Paris and Tokyo have come to pass through the interaction of the particularities of ecology, culture, politics, and time. I could have chosen different cities, in different countries, but the payoff from these two is particularly great. I began with Tokyo, where I have focused during much of my career. But a treatment of one city doesn't necessarily tell us anything about urban development in general. So the question was, To what other global city shall I compare Tokyo? American and German cities were out: both countries have federal, not unitary, national governments, and their political and economic capitals are different. London, in the 1980s and 1990s ruled by Parliament, had no real city government at all. Of the world's other truly global cities, only Paris seemed to provide the combination of comparable traits sketched out above and intense contrasts that any visitor will feel upon first emerging from the subway at Châtelet or Nishi Ginza.

TWO PATHS TO PRIMACY

In the succeeding chapters, I discuss in detail a wide variety of historical developments in Paris and Tokyo, in an attempt to explain such feelings. First, I supply a brief history of each, to provide some context for those less familiar with one city or the other.

From Parisii to Predominance

Paris, as a site, has been meaningfully inhabited for far longer than has Tokyo.[5] Paleolithic remnants have been found in the area dating back perhaps forty thousand years, and a fixed settlement, Lutetia (in French, Lutèce), was on the spot during the third century B.C., at the strategically and commercially significant junction of a north-south land trade route and an east-west riverine route, where the Île de la Cité facilitated crossing the river, in the heart of the Parisian basin, with its fertile soil, quarries, and forests. Its inhabitants — the Parisii — however, burned the settlement and fled before the Romans in roughly 50 B.C. The Romans rebuilt, on the left bank and then the Île, a standard provincial Roman town with intersecting *cardo* and *decumanus* (main roads), forum, and bath (see fig. 3). In its early years, Roman Lutetia had no fortifications.

The town grew to several thousand inhabitants, but its path was rocky. It was pillaged and burned in the third century A.D., but recovered — with fortifications now, and referred to increasingly as Paris — to become the capital under King Clovis around 500. With Clovis's death, however, Paris suffered further reversals. As the capital of a fragmented and decentralized kingdom with an itinerant monarch, the town saw violence on several occasions between the fifth and tenth centuries and was also the target of a variety of barbarian attacks and sieges. Its history as capital really began around A.D. 1000 with the Capetian kings, who nursed national ambitions and increasingly focused their attention on the Île-de-France region, despite friction with the bishop of Paris, an ecclesiastical power already entrenched on the Île de la Cité. Perhaps the most significant of these kings, at least from the standpoint of the form of the city, was Philippe Auguste, who in the early thirteenth century built the first major city wall, initiating a historical tendency to envelop the city in a physical straitjacket. By this time, Paris had become, although not the nation's capital once and for all, a major city, as table 1 indicates. But in that age, such a size was only barely sustainable. The king's absence, famine, and pestilence (especially the Black Death of the mid-fourteenth century) all drove the population down.

So did violence. The years between 1350 and 1600 saw recurrent conflict: sometimes it was foreign invasion, with the English attacking and occupying Paris in 1422–36; sometimes it was French against French, as in the St. Bartholomew's Day sectarian massacre of 1572 and other wars of religion. And sometimes it was the people against the monarchy, as Paris acquired a reputation for insurrection. In the 1350s, the city leader Étienne Marcel led a coup against the king, and the period of violence ended with the assassination of Henri IV in 1610. This lesson was patent to the young Louis XIV, who, having survived the rebellion of the Fronde in the 1640s, decamped, court and all, for Versailles.

But Paris survived this exodus, and indeed thrived. During the seventeenth and eighteenth centuries, the city continued to grow — by 1789, it

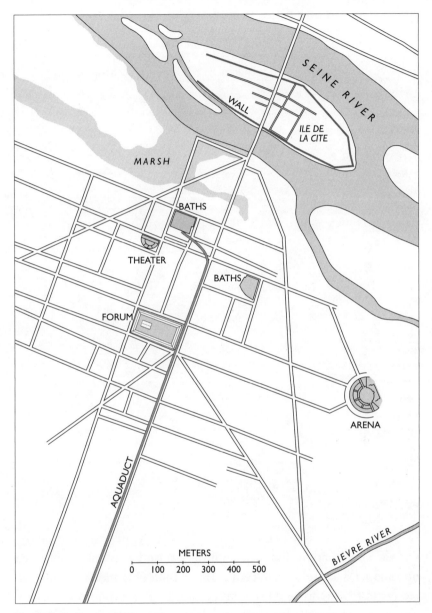

Fig. 3. Gallo-Roman Paris.

Table 1. Population of Paris

Year	Approximate population	
	Paris	Suburbs
Under Rome	8,000	
1200	100,000	
1300	200,000–250,000	
1450	100,000	
1550	250,000	
1580	350,000	
1650	430,000	
1684	480,000	
Early 18th century	500,000–600,000	
1789	600,000–650,000	
1801	550,000	
1817	714,000	
1850	1,000,000	
1870	2,000,000	
1880	2,300,000	450,000
1886		600,000
1901	2,700,000	1,000,000
1921	2,900,000	2,000,000
1931	2,900,000	2,000,000
1936	2,800,000	
1970	2,600,000	5,600,000
1976	2,300,000	7,600,000
2002	2,100,000	8,900,000
2007	2,200,000	9,400,000

Sources: Jones 2005; LeClère 1985; Noin and White 1997; Bergeron 1989; Mollat 1971; Evenson 1979; Cornu 1972; Roche 1987; INSEE, various years.

was the largest city in Europe — and to burnish a cultural luster it had not enjoyed since its brilliant turn as the epitome of Gothic art and architecture in the twelfth and thirteenth centuries. But such growth was not universally admired: increasingly people in the provinces began to regard Paris as too big, too overpowering, too voracious.[6] And too threatening: all France was terrified by the revolutionary passions which poured forth from Paris in 1789. The city itself benefited in some ways from the Revolution and its aftermath, as the centralizing efforts of the both Jacobins and Napoleon concentrated ever more power in the capital. But such state power came at the price of Paris's long-prized municipal autonomy, which was lost — until the late twentieth century — as Napoleon firmly subordinated the city to two state-appointed prefects, one in charge of administration and the other (who remains today) in charge of the police.

The nineteenth century was for Paris an era of transformation, transcendence, and (further) turmoil. Industrial and demographic growth continued, as did the weight of Paris within the nation: in 1800, it was four times as large as the next biggest city in France; by 1900, it was eight times as large.[7] The Industrial Revolution was in full swing, and Paris became not only the political capital but the nation's economic capital as well, which led, toward the end of the nineteenth century, to the emergence of a sprawling working-class *banlieue* (suburb or outskirts) around the city. This transformation was partly spontaneous but — France being France — partly determined by dirigiste regimes and rational planners. There were three major actors in this drama: the first was Napoleon I, who bedizened the city with monuments and a few boulevards. Second was Adolphe Thiers, who in the 1840s promoted the construction of a new wall around Paris. This immense project — an earthwork wall supplemented with seventeen outlying forts — never thwarted an aggressor but has left an enduring physical and psychological mark on the city, as we shall see. The third city-builder was Napoleon III, who in the 1850s delegated to his prefect of the Seine, Georges-Eugène Haussmann, the wholesale demolition of central Paris and its redevelopment with plazas, boulevards, parks, and streetscapes, creating the gem of a city we see today.

The nineteenth century was as well the age when one might rightly refer to Paris as the "Capital of the World,"[8] an unparalleled center of cultural opulence, consumer sophistication, international magnetism, and transcendent modernity. But the shadows remained, too, and the nineteenth century saw unprecedented violence in the city. The long-running leitmotif of Parisian contention rose in pitch in 1830, as Charles X abdicated amid rioting in the city. His successor, Louis-Philippe, was dethroned by the even larger Revolution of 1848, which, followed by Louis Napoleon's coup and Second Empire, left Parisians and provincials locked in mutual hostility. In

1871, following the French military debacle against Prussia, the leitmotif crescendoed as the Paris Commune essentially declared its independence from France. The state responded with a bloodbath the likes of which the nation had never witnessed.

In subsequent years, the traumatized capital turned away from politics. Industrialization and demographic growth continued, although, as one sees in table 1, now mostly at the margins of the city: in the suburbs and in the arrondissements just within the wall.[9] The central arrondissements began to depopulate, enhancing anxiety about the working-class "Red Belt" surrounding the city. In time this belt became restive once again; the early twentieth century was characterized by increasing labor strife, peaking in the 1930s with violent clashes between leftists and rightists in the Parisian streets — and by more suburban sprawl, while the population of Paris proper peaked and began to decline. Nor did the removal of the long-obsolete fortifications in the 1930s integrate the metropolis: a new buffer zone of open spaces, apartment buildings, slums, and athletic facilities replaced it.

Paris escaped World War II relatively unscathed; the postwar years saw — at long last — recovery of both prosperity and municipal authority. Paris basked in thirty glorious years of economic growth which followed the war. The metropolitan region continued to grow, and although the separation of the suburbs endured (a new peripheral highway was begun in 1957 along the old lines of the wall), their "redness" began to fade. And Parisian autonomy began to be restored. In 1964, the city of Paris became a single *département*, and in 1975, the state took a deep breath and allowed the city to elect a mayor of its own, for the first time in more than 150 years.

The bloom came off the economic rose in the 1970s, as it did in much of the industrial capitalist world. Paris was no exception, but throughout subsequent decades it has managed to retain its position as France's premier city and, to much of the world, the City of Light. During this period, a number of trends took shape which continue today. First, Paris has continued to grow in size, with its greatest population and employment growth in areas ever more distant from the city center.[10] Second, Paris has ceased to dominate the nation economically and demographically quite as much as previously. Although its precise share of economy and populace has fluctuated, the city no longer raises the specters of parasitism and predation that it once did.

Third, despite these changes, Paris continues to prosper — indeed, perhaps too much. Much hand-wringing has taken place over the perceived trend toward the concentration of an ever higher social class in the city and the concomitant rise in rents and housing prices. But this trend is unlikely to reverse since, on the one hand, Paris has an enduring housing shortage, and, on the other, the city was embellished lavishly toward the end of the twentieth century by a series of grand presidential projects which have marvelously enhanced its cultural, architectural, and athletic assets. Paris is not, like Tokyo, one of a small number of "global cities" by whose multinational corporations and financial institutions the international economy is shaped.[11] Nonetheless, few would deny its eminence among the great cities of the world.

Metropolitan Phoenix

While the Romans were busily turning Gaulish Lutetia into an orderly, checkerboard provincial town, much of what is today's Tokyo was under the sea.[12] Urban development in Japan in general came late, impeded for several centuries by the custom of moving the capital whenever a new monarch took the throne. In the second half of the first millennium A.D., the imperial capital of Heian-kyō (now Kyoto) grew large, but it, too, underwent reversals as real power moved away during the feudal period which began in the twelfth century. There was by the fifth century a town in the region in which Tokyo now stands, but it was the provincial administrative center of Fuchū, about 25 kilometers west of where the Imperial Palace sits today.

During the feudal era, the strategic significance of a coastal location increased as main roads between western and northeastern Japan converged on the Musashi plain at the western end of Tokyo Bay and periodic fortifications were built at a variety of spots on the alluvial delta at the head of the bay. But the real history of Tokyo began in 1456, when Lord Ota Dōkan built a "modest castle" near the village of Edo,[13] and a "small town" grew up to its east.[14] Feudal rule had by this time deteriorated into a state of civil

war, and Ota's rule did not last long, but a series of vassals of the major warring clans maintained an armed presence in and around Edo thereafter.

In 1590, Tokugawa Ieyasu, the leading vassal of Japan's newly hegemonic
lord, was assigned to Edo (see fig. 4). He might well have been appalled by
the state of disrepair of the castle,[15] but he applied himself immediately to
its improvement. He established himself as Japan's new hegemon, or shogun, after his victory at the Battle of Sekigahara in 1600, and inaugurated
an age of urban development the likes of which the world had never seen.
In Edo itself, he built a vast castle (16 kilometers in circumference) and
created a city from scratch: rivers were diverted and turned into canals and
moats, streets were laid out, the bay was reclaimed, radial highways and
aqueducts were built, and a mountain was leveled for landfill.[16] Between
1600 and 1700, the population went from essentially zero to perhaps 1 million, far outstripping the population growth of Paris during its period of
most rapid expansion.[17]

Edo was first and foremost the shogun's capital. The administrative center was the castle; between its three concentric rings of moats, lords and
their retinues were given land for their villas. Outside the castle grounds, a
grid street pattern was laid out for the commoner quarters on the flat land
to the east, while the nobility were given additional lands on the highlands to the west for large residential estates. The entirety was divided up
according to the feudal class system, with those of similar status grouped
together. Commoner neighborhoods were mutually separated by gates and
internally responsible for their own administration and civil order. This is
not to say that Edo was a tranquil place: crime and fighting were endemic,
and in the later years of the era, economic decay led to food shortages and
widespread food riots.[18] But anxieties like those of the French state in the
face of the population of Paris are not to be found there.

The city's growth was partly calculated and partly natural. The lords
and their families and retinues were required to spend certain terms in
Edo, resulting in a warrior population of perhaps a half million; this had
the consequence of attracting a huge commoner population to satisfy the
warriors' needs. Table 2 shows only the commoner population for the
Tokugawa era (1600–1868), but the total population of Edo is generally es-
timated at about 1 million, and population estimates for "Greater Edo" by

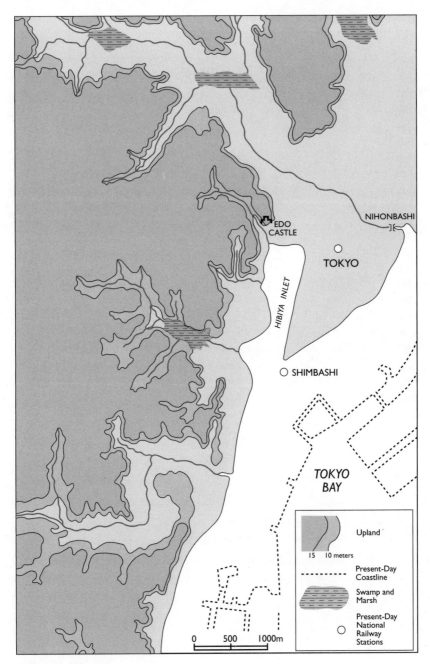

NIHONBASHI

EDO
CASTLE

TOKYO

HIBIYA INLET

○ SHIMBASHI

TOKYO
BAY

	Upland
15 10 meters	
	Present-Day Coastline
	Swamp and Marsh
○	Present-Day National Railway Stations

0   500   1000m

Fig. 4. Edo, about 1600.

Table 2. Population of Edo/Tokyo

Year	Approximate population	
	Edo/Tokyo	Suburbs
1721	500,000	1,900,000[*]
1747	500,000	
1750		1,800,000[*]
1804		1,700,000[*]
1810	500,000	
1828		1,700,000[*]
1840	550,000	
1846		1,800,000[*]
1850	550,000	
1867	540,000	
1872		1,900,000[*]
1876	875,000	
1877		2,100,000[*]
1884	1,000,000	
1900	2,000,000	
1920	3,700,000	3,900,000[**]
1930	5,400,000	4,600,000[**]
1940	7,400,000	5,400,000[**]
1945	3,500,000	5,900,000[**]
1955	8,000,000	7,400,000[**]
1965	10,900,000	10,200,000[**]
1975	11,700,000	15,300,000[**]
1985	11,800,000	18,400,000[**]
1997	11,800,000	20,800,000[**]
2002	12,200,000	21,600,000[**]
2007	12,800,000	22,100,000[**]

[*]Musashi Province, including Edo/Tokyo
[**]Kanagawa, Saitama, and Chiba prefectures

Sources: White 1992; Masai 1989; Tokyo-to 1971; Nakamura 1968; Sōmu-shō Tōkei-kyoku, various years; Sekiyama 1958; Yano, various years.

the mid-nineteenth century run from 1.3 million to as high as 2 million,[19] making Edo the world's largest city.

Exactly what "Greater Edo" might have been, however, is hard to say: although the city was dominated by the huge castle, it was unwalled and essentially unbounded. A variety of administrative jurisdictions were specified over time, but according to one foreign observer,[20] the only way to tell that one had entered Edo was that the streets were more regular and the crowds larger. Over the era, Edo sprawled incorrigibly, and physical clarity of the kind imposed by the walls and gates of Paris was utterly lacking.

Throughout the Tokugawa era, Edo prospered, but its prosperity was an artifice, the result of the compulsory presence of the nobility and their needs. Occasional famines and plagues, plus frequent fires, kept the city in a race to sustain itself. As the shogunate decayed in the nineteenth century, the economic basis of the nobility shrank, and economic vitality drifted from the cities to rural towns. Edo's regulatory power declined also, and when it relaxed the system of compulsory residence (ca. 1860), a mass exodus by the warrior class ensued. In 1868, the feudal state was overthrown in the Meiji Restoration, and a new, centralizing regime took power. Even more of the former nobles left town; the city's population crashed by perhaps half, its built-up area shrank dramatically, and many buildings fell apart. It would be twenty years before the city regained a population of 1 million,[21] even though, as table 2 shows, the capital region came through the crisis relatively unscathed.

The new regime was intent on centralization and modernization, and Tokyo — the Eastern Capital, as Edo was renamed — was part of its plan. Numerous administrative reorganizations took place on all levels of local government,[22] but throughout that process the capital was kept firmly in the hands of state-appointed governors — not so much out of fear, as in France, but because Tokyo was intended to be the urban face of the new, modern Japan, and this was too important a role to be entrusted to the city itself. Authoritarian dirigisme was the spirit of the day. Old shogunal buildings and warrior quarters were confiscated by the new government, foreign architects and urban planners were brought in, grandiose foreign-inspired buildings sprang up hither and yon, and Tokyo multiplied its political centrality both functionally and visually.[23] Business and then industry — reliant on state assistance for success — were drawn to the flame, outlying areas were annexed, and modern Tokyo grew great from the remnants of Edo.

Growth continued into the twentieth century; in 1920, Greater Tokyo accounted for 14 percent of the nation's population and, by 1940, 18 percent. But Tokyo did not dominate Japan as Paris did France: Osaka remained an economic rival, and Kyoto Japan's cultural heart. Tokyo was on the cutting edge of modernity, but it was not seen as a threat. There were riots in 1905 and 1918, but nothing that shook the regime or identified Tokyo with insurgency. What shook Tokyo the most — literally — in the years before World War II was the earthquake of 1923, which destroyed most of the central city. Whatever vestiges of Edo had survived the Restoration now vanished, and Edo was destroyed psychically as well.[24] The city revived (the data in table 2 for 1920 and 1930 suggest that it never missed a beat), but it was a different city. Central Tokyo began to depopulate, and people moved to the suburbs in an ever increasing stream, facilitated by new commuter rail lines. But, unlike workers in Paris, they were predominantly white-collar and middle-class, and Tokyo never saw itself as besieged by a cordon of hostile proletarian suburbs.

World War II saw Tokyo reduced to rubble once again, but as soon as the dust settled, the people again poured back in from their rural retreats, and the city regained its prewar population high by 1953. But, again, it was a different city that entered the postwar era: ramshackle at first, gradually transformed into more lasting concrete, and then, as economic growth accelerated in the 1960s, blossoming into a major international metropolis which no longer simply summoned foreign architects to help it realize its own self-image but produced its own architects of international renown.

And it was a city in a different country. Japan democratized after the war, and Tokyo was headed by a popularly elected governor and assembly. Central constraints over local government remained, but the degree of autonomy was dramatically enhanced, and the city has taken full advantage of it. Some governors have embraced the state; some have confronted it. Most of the city's physical transformations have required state permission, and some have enjoyed state sponsorship. But the transformation of Tokyo by and for itself has surpassed what has occurred in Paris: the most impressive additions to the Tokyo skyline and urban space since the war have been the work of private enterprise and city hall, not — as in France — of the state executive.

Part of Tokyo's postwar revival was, of course, demographic. But the metropolis also came to draw disproportionate shares of other national resources — cultural, financial, and commercial — as well. At first the concern was that the national economy and population were becoming overconcentrated in the zone along the Pacific coast; then "unipolar concentration" in Tokyo and the "Tokyo Problem" became buzzwords. But, paradoxically, although Tokyo's dominance in Japan has increased at the same time that Paris's has diminished in France, Tokyo has never been seen as the threat that Paris has. A threat to itself, yes: the government flatly stated in 1973 that if demographic and functional trends were not interrupted, the city would be "paralyzed" by 1985.[25] Oh, well. But whereas Paris today accounts for 3.5 percent of the French population and the Île-de-France for 19 percent, the equivalent figures for Tokyo (prefecture and region) are 10 percent and 27 percent, and, if the larger "Capital Region" (including more prefectures) is considered, 32 percent.[26] Clearly the link between perception and reality differs in France and Japan.

Two Megacities

But before turning to differences in perception, past and present, and their implications for the shape of the city, I would like to offer one last joint snapshot of Tokyo and Paris today. As noted, each dominates its society in a variety of ways, but not in the same ways. Both are typical of contemporary world cities with their demographically stagnant centers and growing, doughnut-shaped peripheries.[27] Tokyo is more dominant, almost four times larger than the next largest Japanese city, Yokohama, whereas Paris is only one and a half times larger than Lyon, France's number two. Why Tokyo's dominance seems less worrisome is unclear, although it might have something to do with the overall number of kindred urbanites: 86 percent of the Japanese population lives in communes comprised of more than twenty thousand people, whereas only 38 percent of the French do.[28]

Precisely comparable economic data are hard to come by. Both cities account for slightly less than one-third of their national GDPs, and both are home to between two dozen and three dozen home offices of multinational corporations.[29] Slightly more than one-third of those employed in managerial and "superior intellectual professions" in France are in Île-de-France; slightly less than one-third of Japanese managerial personnel are in the Tokyo region.[30] Roughly one-third of the university students (in Japan) and "university populations" (in France) are in the capital region.

Aside from economic indicators, a few statistics suggest a slightly better quality of life in — surprise, surprise — Tokyo.[31] Among a group of world cities, Tokyo ranked fourteenth, while Paris came in twenty-fifth (just ahead of New York and London). Tokyo bettered Paris in public safety and crime rate, public health, noise, and traffic; Paris had cleaner air and more living space (fewer people per room; but Tokyo actually had more space per residence). But in all instances except traffic, the differences were small; the far different historical trajectories that the two cities have followed up to the present day have eventuated in cities which, on many dimensions, appear to have more in common than in contrast.

THE PLAN OF THIS BOOK

This book is an exploration of why Paris and Tokyo, cities with so much in common, look and feel so different. I advance a number of explanatory propositions, but I am less interested in formal explanation than in gaining insights into these cities and countries. In causal terms, I have tried to induce some possible explanations from a visual and felt urban setting, that is, I have conjured possible causes from visible characteristics. Then I examine these "explanations" to see which appear most valid.[32] My goal is plausibility, not proof: if characteristic A of the contemporary city is consistent with or reflects historical or cultural element B, it does not mean that B caused A at all; if, however, a reasonable or logical connection between B and A can be shown, this "empirical plausibility" will suffice.[33] I am looking for consistency between historical element X and the appearance or feel of Paris today, versus consistency between historical element Y and Tokyo, and for evidence that the differences between Paris and Tokyo are congruent with the differences between X and Y. Alternative "explanations" may not be excludable, but some are more plausible than others. My arguments are relative throughout — there is no unique or unchanging Japanese or French cultural "essence." If I say that the French are hostile to Paris, I mean only that more of them feel negatively toward their capital than the Japanese do toward theirs. I do *not* mean that all French are hostile, or that all Japanese are fond of Tokyo.

Given the softness of this approach, comparison is essential. Some may see this study as serial anecdote rather than real comparison, but until one compares one society, or city, with another, one cannot say with any assurance that what one sees or feels is specific or universal, unique or common: "what appears self-evident . . . in one context is a problem requiring explanation in another."[34] I have already cited a number of Tokyo phenomena which resemble those of Paris — and London and New York — and "a phenomenon that is global in scope cries out for comparative discussion."[35] I have managed to hold a number of global factors constant in choosing Tokyo and Paris — size, political economy, modernity, dirigiste and centralized regimes — and the different ways each city mediates its legacy will illuminate the way each looks, and is looked at, today.

*Significance **and** the City*

So why cities? Because of their role as windows into, or mirrors of, their societies. A city is the reflection, or distillation, of "the dreams, the possibilities, indeed sometimes the failures of our forebears,"[36] of "different conceptions of man's destiny."[37] It is a refraction of the "collective will" of a society.[38] "In the city, time becomes visible," and this past "teaches us the possibilities for the conduct and co-ordination of our actions"; that is, the city is a means of communication between the past and the present, and a "precondition imposed by the present on the future."[39] "Cultural memory . . . lies stored and encoded in the city's built environment," and so we can read a city like any text, in it understanding an entire culture, just as we may understand the city by reading the culture.[40]

A city, especially an old one, does not signify simply adaptation to an ecological setting; centuries of different settlements superimposed in a single site indicate rather societies' "truly infinite capacity" to inform their universes; cultures in general and cities in particular are determined less by "exterior givens" than by "the way people arrange the material means at their disposal."[41] And a capital city provides us with yet more intellectual mileage. The "look and feel [of cities] reflect decisions about what — and who — should be visible and what should not, on concepts of order and disorder, and on uses of aesthetic power."[42] Societies build cities reflecting ruling-class values and interests, and thus capitals in particular are physically legible symbols of state unity, authority, values, policy preferences, resources, and aspirations.[43]

There is an additional reason to focus on the city, to believe that place matters. Physical places and spaces not only reflect culture, economy, and politics — they influence them as well.[44] Place influences behavior both indirectly, by influencing people's identities, and directly, as a physical setting. Baron Haussmann, for example, clearly thought that Parisians would behave differently on broad boulevards than in the rabbit warrens of Belleville. Place structures social behavior; "political behavior is intrinsically geographical"; and some settings "are much more conducive to the formation of a group outlook and collective action than others."[45]

Much of modern social science has nonetheless focused almost exclusively on individual-level characteristics in the explanation of behavior; collectivities as actors and the causal potential of physical settings have been underemphasized. But both will loom large in this study — how could it be otherwise, when neighborhoods in Edo typically and frequently acted almost as unitary organisms, and when one of the primary rationales for capital-building in history has been the impact of architecture and urban form on the thoughts and behavior of an elite or mass audience?[46] Certainly a group shapes its setting, but the relationship is reciprocal: it then "becomes enclosed within the framework it has built."[47]

Significance in the City

In this study I am less interested in the influence of Paris and Tokyo on their people. But I do expect, through an examination of capital cities of long standing like Paris and Tokyo, to learn about France and Japan in toto, and about power and esthetics; and religious, economic, and social values, hopes, and fears. But where should we look in the city, and for what? The impetus to this study came from simply walking in Paris and Tokyo, and then reading what observers over the centuries have had to say about them. Thus I emphasize the city materially and socially, especially as a conscious or unconscious consequent, or symbol, of antecedent forces and ideas and events. Cities are "symbolic landscapes," full of physical and behavioral images which inspire nostalgia and anticipation, hope and fear, celebration and commiseration; they can legitimize and delegitimize leaders; and they can show the strength of some and the weakness of others.[48]

Thus I have spent a lot of time trying to infer the symbolism of buildings, places, ceremonies, forms, and relationships which distinguish Paris from Tokyo. I am interested more in memory than in anticipation, and memory — revealed in physical form and behavior — is a key theme here.[49] A city is a repository of memories — some purposely kept alive, some stifled, some lively and some moribund. Some of these memories are spaces, like the Tomb of the Unknown Soldier, while some are patterns of behavior, like a neighborhood festival. Many are fixed, but they are empty vessels: when time and change produce new wine, it is often made sense of and legitimized by decantation into old, familiar symbolic bottles.

In a social setting like the city, a particular type of memory is of interest: "remembering in common," or commemoration.[50] Communities evolve their own memories for their own ends; thus the physical and ritual environment of a community reflects its preferred, or mythic, history. Such histories may be imposed, as by the first leader who said "seeing is believing" and built his palace accordingly. Or they may be insurgent, as when opposition groups take to the streets of eastern Paris on July 14 to challenge the establishment's story of 1789. They may last, like the pyramids, or not, like the works of Ozymandias. In this book, I am most interested in physical commemorations, in "places in which the collective heritage" of the city is encapsulated,[51] although one of the arguments I shall make is that Japan and France differ markedly in their preferences for tangible/material or intangible/nonmaterial commemorations. Tokyo is notably bereft of physical monuments. Collective memories, yes; monuments, no.

As noted, I focus initially on what strikes any pedestrian in the city: the built environment. And my strongest impressions — contradictory and begging explanation — have included these:[52]

» Tokyo appears unorganized, chaotic, and disorderly in form; Paris appears organized, harmonious, and orderly.
» Paris's built environment appears unchanging and constructed to last for ages; Tokyo's is fluid and impermanent, and manifestly built for the moment.
» Tokyo's physical form lacks a sense of overall plan; Paris appears carefully laid out in accord with some superordinate Cartesian will.
» Paris is a voluntaristic work of artifice and distinction; Tokyo has grown and sprawls today like a natural, holistic organism.
» Tokyo — unwalled, uninvaded, and unrevolutionary — seems to be much less the physical product of fearful authority than does Paris.

Such are my overall visual impressions. There are, in addition, specific aspects of the cityscape which have intrigued me:

» Tokyo's center has been famously described as "empty" (Barthes 1982), a term one would never attach to Paris's.
» No one has any doubts as to exactly where Paris begins and ends; at its margins, Tokyo is fuzzy and ambiguous.
» And yet Tokyo has fewer misgivings about its margins and marginals: they have never been regarded with the fear and contempt that Paris's banlieues and lower classes have received.

Finally, Paris and Tokyo appear to reflect very different orientations toward the city as an object. Specifically,

» Paris looks as if it has historically been the object of authoritative, planned manipulation; Tokyo appears to be the consequence of unplanned fatalism.
» Consequently Tokyo is a strikingly nonmonumental city, and the monumentalism that exists is less physical, less political, and less public than in Paris. The Japanese do commemorate, but in a very different way.

These observations are gleaned simply from walking the city, and they may well be false, based on inaccurate impressions, or — within each city taken alone — true but commonplace. Therefore I have also looked not just *at* each city but *into* the city, into its history and its relationships with its own setting, and at them together. I have been interested in the origins of these cities. Historians have argued that different origins — religious, political, cultural, or economic — have different consequences.[53] And what then were their subsequent developmental sequences? Edo was created in order to be a capital; Paris, by contrast, was a city long before the state took up residence there. Might this account for differences such as whether only the capital's center was fortified, or the city as a whole?[54] And in general, what was the interplay of economic and political power in each city's history: did the state shape the city, or did capital shape the capital?[55] What was the interplay of state power and its rivals, especially clerical or noble rivals, popular political contenders, and foreign states?

Origins and sequences, then, are one shaping force; perceptions — gleaned from literary records — are another. Both Edo/Tokyo and Paris have long been the focus of literary attention, and this literature enables us to see the cities as both outsiders and insiders have seen them. I especially consider two impressions:

» The literary history of Edo and Tokyo reveals far fewer acutely negatively perceptions of the city than does that of Paris.
» Paris, among both its lovers *and* its haters, has inspired far more passion than has Edo/Tokyo.

In the eyes of state officials, such perceptions directly inform decisions about the form imposed on the city. And such decisions, and the political arena where they are taken, are the final focus of our attention, the final lens through which we hope to find significance in the city. Thus we shall focus on the city's relationships with the rest of the nation, the state, and the suburban and regional context. (The global environment will enter the discussion, but to a lesser extent, for reasons given below.) And when one does, again, impressions of difference emerge:

» Paris has been regarded by provincial France with a greater degree of fear and loathing than has Tokyo by the Japanese.

» Provincial France's greater parliamentary voice has translated into a more adversarial and punitive state posture toward the capital than has been the case in Japan.

» Tokyo has regarded its suburbs with far greater equanimity and far less condescension than has Paris.

These three dimensions of impression — physical, perceptual, and relational — are of course closely and reciprocally related. Perceptions influence relationships which influence city form, form influences relationships and perceptions, and so on. My main aim is to seek factors outside these three dimensions which help account for them as a whole. I do so inductively, investigating first the accuracy of the impressions themselves and then the plausibility of the different explanations available for those that do seem accurate.

Along the way, however, there are three paths that I do not take, but that are popular enough in urban studies to merit mention. The first is the path of convergence, which argues that as societies modernize they become more and more similar. Cities have been part of human society for more than four thousand years, but in the same way that there was never a single type of "premodern city," there is not today a single form of modern, or postindustrial, city.[56] There are different paths to modernity, and vastly differing starting points, and different modernities as a result. Skylines and transportation systems and neon do not even look the same in Paris and Tokyo — even the gutters are different. Clearly modernity has not led to convergence.[57]

The second road not taken is the Marxian one. Marxism is unsatisfactory because it is unfalsifiable. Additionally, since both Paris and Tokyo are advanced capitalist cities in a global capitalist economy, it cannot explain their differences. Third, it unrealistically privileges economic causation over the political,[58] and class and class consciousness over, for example, community and nonclass social structures and motivations.[59] Finally, it invites a narrow emphasis on domination and oppression. Of course, the city mirrors the efforts of rulers at control, self-defense, self-aggrandizement, and legitimacy. But neither the city nor the citizens are impotent victims, as both French monarchs and Japanese shoguns learned to their chagrin.

The third path I glance down but largely avoid is that of globalization. Like modernization and Marxism, the globalization approach posits a degree of convergence among cities which I find at odds with what I have seen in Paris and Tokyo. The ever faster movement, across ever greater distances, of ever greater volumes of commodities, communications, people, ideas, and financial instruments is one of the more impressive, and undeniable, phenomena of our time. But, as I have argued elsewhere,[60] it does not mean that economic causation is all that matters in the form and function of cities, or that states are no longer masters in their own territories, or that global cities like Paris and Tokyo must inevitably become "dual cities," bifurcated between a growing upper class of professional, technological, and corporate elites and a growing subproletariat of service workers. This does not mean that I should, or do, overlook globalization entirely here. Despite the cosmopolitanism of Paris and the famed insularity of Japan, I see Tokyo as having been impacted more heavily by globalization. The question is, again, Why? — which leads us in some of the same directions that different spaces, perceptions, and relationships do.

CONCLUSION

Paris and Tokyo today are cities whose sums are different but whose parts are often similar. That is, there is little distinctive to Paris which cannot be found in Tokyo, and vice versa. Walls and wars, fears and hopes, pragmatics and esthetics, authority and insurgency, will and fatalism, elitism and populism, permanence and evanescence, exclusion and inclusion, order and chaos, clarity and ambiguity, nature and artifice — all can be found inscribed on the faces of both cities, and none essentializes either city. Broad plazas, city walls, monuments, even baroque cities — the Japanese can do all that. Exquisite nooks and crannies, serpentine streets, dramatic urban transformation, amorphous suburbs — the French can do all that too. And they both have, at certain times and in certain places. Yet both peoples seem not really to have had their hearts in certain types of urbanism. Thus the degree of each characteristic varies, as does its frequency of occurrence and its impact on the appearance, imagery, and position of the city today.

To introduce what is to come in chapter 2, I venture here some conclusions which may seem surprising. It is Tokyo which is the City of Light, shaped by peace and order, confidence and reassurance, progress and inclusion. Paris is more a City of Darkness, formed by rebellion and war, threat and fear, and reaction, invidious distinctions, and marginalization. The Abbey of Thélème may well be French, but it is Tokyo which has enjoyed the greater degree of *vouloir libre*. Despite Restoration, earthquake, and war, Tokyo has (relatively) built upon its past, while Paris — despite a heritage of splendor and a beautiful cityscape more than a century old — has spent much more time and effort overcoming its own. History is not destiny, but the inscriptions of the past on the present take a bit of the bloom off the Parisian rose, while they make the chaotic, congested Ugly Duckling by the Bay begin to look as if it might just be a swan. But, paradoxically, behind these contemporary manifestations of the past lie possibly contradistinguished futures: less "globalized" and more governmentally put-upon Paris is better poised both to maintain its international renown and to achieve a position of equipoise which benefits both itself and France, while more globalized and governmentally favored Tokyo may have already missed its chance to fulfill its international potential, at the same time that it flows ominously toward the engulfment of Japan.

1

VIEWS OF THE CAPITAL
WALKING AND READING THE CITY

In this chapter, I spin out descriptively some of the impressions offered in the introduction. Most of them will not surprise those who have visited either Tokyo or Paris, although most visitors will also be able to cite exceptions to the differences between the two cities. So can I. As noted in the introduction, anything visible in or said of Tokyo can probably be seen in or heard about Paris as well. Many of these observations might also strike one as self-evident, and indeed, many are. But why are they what they are, and why do the cities differ?

WALKING THE CITY

Liquid City, Crystal City

Tokyo resembles a giant amoeba — nebulous, amorphous, and heterogeneous. The question is how such a tightly wrapped society produced such "bewildering diversity," where the "surface appearance is jagged and disturbing, a riot of free enterprise and often unconstrained growth."[1] Paris, by contrast, while lavishly baroque and art deco in its parts, perhaps, is orderly and patterned — somewhere René Descartes is smiling. Streetscapes are often classically harmonious wholes, whereas Tokyo's architecture

⌃ Fig. 5. A Tokyo streetscape.

⌄ Fig. 6. A Paris streetscape.

generally totally ignores its context — statement buildings abound, as do striking (if not beautiful) parts, but coherent large-area wholes are rare.[2] Paris enjoys visual "continuity, with many distinctive parts clearly interconnected,"[3] whereas Tokyo is a mishmash, with oddly incompatible architectural pieces juxtaposed everywhere, with little but the subway system holding it together.

This lack of firm spatial form in Tokyo is partnered with a lack of temporal stability. Like Rome, Paris has "seemingly traversed the centuries without rupturing the continuity of life; great upheavals may severely shake society without altering the appearance of the city." But Tokyo is a city of "plasticity and fluidity," "never finished," "always in flux," "in a permanent state of construction."[4] Built almost from scratch in the 1590s, it was rebuilt in large part after the Meireki Fire (1650s), the Ansei Earthquake (1850s), the Restoration (1868), the 1923 earthquake, and World War II — and, some would add, during the period of high-speed economic growth in the 1960s and 1970s.[5] The scope and speed of change have been breathtaking, unrestrained by almost any preservationist impulse. City planning did appear, 1,500 years ago — and then disappeared. It reemerged in the castle towns of the sixteenth century — and disappeared again. In the last century, it has tried to reassert itself, with — at least as compared to Paris — very limited success: Tokyo seems to obey no rules, no rigor, no plan; it is "overflowing with the spirit of freedom" in a way which would appall Baron Haussmann.[6] Not that this is necessarily a bad thing — one person's symmetry is another's straitjacket.

In general, then, Edo and Tokyo have placed less emphasis on the built dimension of the city than has Paris. But cities also have a natural dimension and a social dimension, and it may be argued that Tokyo has historically emphasized both of these more than has Paris. Tokyo is a "stage," "a place for performance," whereas in Paris the city itself is a statement, a sort of inanimate performance in stone, metal, and glass.[7] Parisians are the audience; Tokyoites are the cast. French authorities are in a position to alter the appearance of the city, at least partly *in order to* influence its social dimension. But in Edo and Tokyo, the social dimension itself is the direct object of regulation, and the built city itself seems less used to this end.

The Capital, Inside Out

One aspect of the built city which strikes the flâneur in contrasting ways in Paris and Tokyo is its center. Paris's is "an organized space, where nothing is left to chance."[8] Tokyo's is at first glance almost nothing *but* space — an empty center, in Roland Barthes' words.[9] There is the Imperial Palace, unseen behind low walls and moats, and some parks and encircling avenues, but that's it. One could argue that this is broadly civilizational: Western cities have been described as centripetal and dense at the core, whereas Asian cities are more centrifugal, suburbanized, and sprawling.[10] I prefer to think, however, that it is more distinctively Japanese, and that Barthes was simply wrong. Tokyo's center may be closed and invisible, but empty it is not, and just because this escapes the foreigner's notice does not mean that it is not there.

When one moves from the center to the periphery, however, even a foreign newcomer to Paris and Tokyo cannot miss the differences. The edges of Paris are crisp and clear, those of Tokyo "vague" and "soft."[11] "There is never any doubt as to where Paris ends or begins. Paris begins at the gates of Paris, and nowhere else."[12] Paris is an extreme case: "there is virtually no parallel for this distinction [between inside and outside] in any other major European city."[13] But so is Tokyo: "Even locals seem to understand Tokyo more as a series of train stops than as a unified whole,"[14] and would be hard put to trace the city's border. It cuts through city blocks, divides either side of narrow lanes, runs across vacant lots, and is generally physically — and psychologically — invisible. From Tokyo Tower, "as far across the city's plain as the eye can see . . . there is nothing but city!"[15] And it has been forever thus: the Tokugawa government adopted various administrative definitions of Edo, but they contradicted each other; to say that today's borders "create confusion"[16] would elicit nods of commiseration from city magistrates of two hundred years ago. Tokyo likewise fades into indefinability psychologically. There are at least four Tokyos: the central twenty-three-ward area, Tokyo Prefecture, the four-prefecture Tokyo Region, and the seven-prefecture Capital Region. And in common parlance there are also "Saitama Tokyoites," "Chiba Tokyoites," etc., that is, "Tokyoites" who do not live in Tokyo at all.

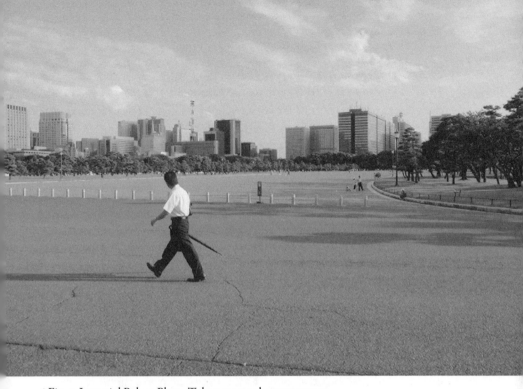

⌃ Fig. 7. Imperial Palace Plaza, Tokyo: vacant but not empty.

⌄ Fig. 8. Central Paris: the Place de la Concorde, fully embellished.

We shall return to the psychological. For the moment, sticking to the visual, I am impressed by the greater homogeneity of Tokyo's suburbs and the greater polarization of Paris's. Certainly property prices indicate the presence of high-income and low-income suburbs in Tokyo, but overall they are a formless sprawl, with fewer slums, fewer ghettoes, and less visible poverty than in Paris. Tokyo's suburbs, like its population in general, are overwhelmingly middle class, both in their self-perceptions and in their visible residential situations. Thus the margins, and the marginals, of Paris appear more problematic in a variety of ways than those of Tokyo.

Free Will and Force of Will

One possible reason why the boundaries of Paris seem clearer than those of Tokyo is that this unguided definition of the latter appears to reflect a more general political absence of will when it comes to shaping the city. "Paris is in itself a work of art";[17] for centuries it has been a canvas upon which monarchical, bureaucratic, ecclesiastical, and architectural egos have painted with broad strokes. This is not to deny the force of economics and spontaneity in shaping the city, but it *is* to surmise that esthetics and voluntarism — the imposition of will or intention on surroundings or experience — have both played a larger role in the evolution of Paris than of Tokyo.

If Paris has been a canvas, Edo/Tokyo has with a few exceptions been no more than an easel: rulers have set it up and let private and spontaneous forces paint the picture. City planning, as noted, had a vogue in the middle of the first millennium A.D., and again around 1600, but faded; modern city planning did not really take hold until the twentieth century, and the production of a host of plans has done little more than suggest that successive Japanese states have simply not cared as much about the shape of the capital as have those of France.

A similar lack — or difference — of emphasis lies in the area of esthetics. The Japanese are often cited as having an exquisite esthetic sense, but it is hard to see in Japan's cities. Exciting as they may be, it is hard to keep the word "ugly" from coming to mind. Production and consumption are on full display — indeed, nighttime Tokyo in all its neon-lit glory is a spectacle which can hardly be imagined — and they "powerfully order the manage-

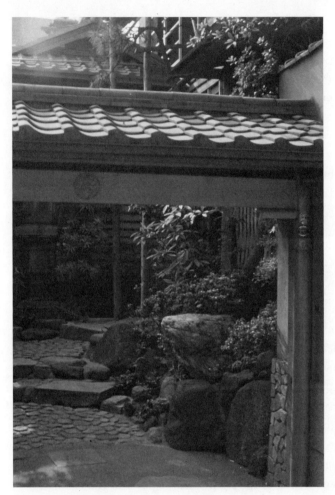

Fig. 9.
Hidden order:
the entryway
to a home on
a downtown
Tokyo street.

ment of space,"[18] but at first glance there is virtually no evidence of an esthetic impulse behind the form of the city. Esthetics is alive and well in the
built setting of Tokyo, but it is an esthetic of parts, not wholes, an esthetic
of a tiny garden in a house's entryway on a featureless street, or a lovingly
preserved wooden storefront next to a glass-and-steel high-rise.[19]

All Monuments Great and Small

But it is not a *combination* of authority and esthetics; for evidence of this
we must look to Paris, specifically, to its monuments, its landmarks, and

its public spaces. A traveler in Paris is struck by the sheer monumental-ism of the city. Governments in general tend to boast, impress, and try to legitimize themselves through the built environments of their capitals — palaces, churches, parliament buildings, arches, fountains, memorials to heroes, and so on.[20] But this tendency is in Paris overwhelmingly on view; the city has become "a place charged with symbols, a space replete with signs and historical and political significances that have interwoven the destiny of a city with that of a country."[21] The symbolic reach of these monuments is breathtaking. Such treasures as the Louvre, Notre-Dame, and the Eiffel Tower are "simultaneously Parisian, ecumenical, national, and international."[22] Sometimes it seems "as if . . . everything must become a center and a monument."[23]

The spaces of Paris also set it apart: wide boulevards, broad plazas, and dramatic vistas. These are equally monumental and commemorative, but they are more: they constitute arenas in which the powerful can assemble and awe the people, and some of them serve also to control the people by making the transit of soldiers and artillery easier, and the construction of barricades harder. Certainly the people are not powerless; rulers shape the environment, but the people often take it over for their own purposes. But the original shaping has remained the prerogative — and the impulse — of centuries of French rulers.

The visitor to Tokyo, by contrast, will look long and hard for built monuments, great public spaces, or other evidence of the hand of author-ity manipulating the city for either political or esthetic ends. This is partly because the center of Tokyo has changed so much, and so little of anything is left from past centuries. But it is more: Japanese rulers seem not to have cared to exercise power by either accommodating or impressing the people; consciously created loci of memory — or *lieux de mémoire* — are rare.

This is not to say that the Japanese *cannot* "do" monumentalism. They have built palaces, castles, whole planned cities, arches, buildings, and temples. But the monumentalist impulse does not seem to come naturally to them. Past monuments have often been left to decay, and contempo-rary monuments are often foreign in both inspiration and incentive — foreign designs to impress foreigners — and more often private than pub-lic in execution.[24] Nor do the Japanese "do" public spaces often or well.

Not only is monumental architecture lacking, but so are "any of the urban features — broad streets, crescents, plazas — in which monumental buildings are seen to advantage."[25] Again, there are exceptions. But wide streets are few and "range from featureless to ugly," and public spaces tend to be small, local, and scattered.[26] There are vistas, but — in sharp contrast to Paris's intra-urban vistas — they involve tailoring the urban setting to incorporate views of mountains *outside* the city.

If the Japanese do not tend toward monuments and great public spaces, they still manage to commemorate and symbolize. Few Japanese streets have names, but those that do often commemorate — as, for example, Ginza (Silver Guild), once home to the eponymous association. Far more common are names for neighborhoods, stations, and places: some commemorate persons, but most are named for long-gone communities and natural features, including more than eight hundred named hills.[27] There are a few public statues of individuals, but many more privately erected stone markers along roadsides, memorializing past events.[28] Buddhist temples and Shinto shrines commemorate deities and natural features, and some are dedicated to the memory of individuals like the Meiji emperor, but few of monumental size remain. (A major exception to this generalization is, of course, the Yasukuni Shrine, in which the souls of Japan's war dead are enshrined.)

Like Paris, Tokyo commemorates, but without the monuments. Tokyo, too, creates "symbolic landscapes," but without the grand spaces. The term refers to markers which "are fondly regarded, evoke positive images about the places where they are set, and often are part of the iconography of a nation."[29] Those of the Edo era are mostly gone. Some Meiji-era landscapes came and went, like the Ginza's brief incarnation as a Western-inspired "Brick Street" and the Nihonbashi Victory Arch. Postwar Tokyo possesses many, from the humble (Shibamata in Katsushika Ward) to the pretentious (the Tokyo Waterfront City Subcenter). And there is, of course, the Imperial Palace.[30] Thus the symbolic landscapes of Tokyo do not need monuments or grand spaces to make their point. They may have them — the growing subcenter in Shinjuku ("Tokyo's Manhattan") features the colossal New City Hall and the Citizens' Plaza inspired by St. Peter's Square — but most do not.

READING THE CITY

But landscapes of all kinds are easier to interpret if war, fire, natural disaster, and the developer's wrecking ball do not carry them away. And in this, one is handicapped in Tokyo, whose history is far less visible than Paris's. One suspects that some of the difference is simply that between an architecture of wood and an architecture of stone, but I suspect a difference in attitude toward the past, and toward the built city, as well as in the way the capital relates to its national and regional environment. So a walking tour of the city will reveal very little from this standpoint, especially in Tokyo; a deeper look at what these attitudes and relationships might in fact be is called for. And when one looks, differences do emerge, differences which we may provisionally imagine are linked to the cityscape differences we can see ourselves.

In the Eye of the Beholder

There are three things that leap to the eye when one examines historical and literary perceptions of Tokyo and Paris: Paris is viewed far more problematically, especially negatively; it is also viewed as being more politically dangerous; and it is viewed — both by its lovers and its enemies — far more passionately than is Tokyo. This is not to say that Edo/Tokyo is never criticized or attacked; indeed, one may find in many bookstores a whole shelf devoted to the "Tokyo Problem." But there is a difference as to what *kind* of problem Tokyo is imagined to be, in ideas about what to *do* about it, and in the low intensity of feeling focused on Tokyo (as city and as capital).

Rather than saying that Paris is viewed with more hostility than is Tokyo, one should perhaps say "ambivalence." Victor Hugo may have seen Paris as the "focal point of civilization," but authors in more recent times have been writing books with titles like *Paris and the French Desert; Paris: A State within the State?* and *Fear of the Suburbs.*[31] And if "it is bred into the Parisian that the superiority of Paris, like the goodness of God, is self-evident," to others the city has seemed a leviathan, a vampire "nourishing itself on the living flesh of France."[32] And there is nothing new about this ambivalence. Paris has had its champions — Philippe Auguste, Henry IV, Louis XIV (although he didn't want to *live* there), and Napoleon I and III —

but also its zero-sum, Malthusian detractors: Henry II, Louis XIII, the Jacobins, and the Third and Fourth Republics.

In the nineteenth century, this schizoid uneasiness took full form. Hugo's paeans nicely complemented the glorification of Paris by Persigny, Napoleon III, and Haussmann, but Paris-as-Hell had already become a cliché by the 1830s, and as industrialization accelerated in the second half of the century, it was easy to see the capital as a devourer both of the *naïfs* who moved there and of the provincial France they left behind.[33]

The Belle Époque produced its full share of lovers of Paris; literarily it was followed in the 1920s by, among others, a generation of Americans for whom it was near Paradise. But among the French, views remained intensely mixed.[34] Paris was seen as both an economic-demographic danger and a moral-political one, and a zero-sum view of capital and country was common throughout the prewar period. This view acquired its modern champion in 1947 with the publication of *Paris and the French Desert,* by Jean-François Gravier, "the cantor, if not the theoretician, of anti-Parisian policy."[35]

The book was in fact part of a significant postwar genre which included such titles as those noted above. Obviously this genre does not exhaust the field of Parisian literature — the encomiums far outpace it, and visitors have voted overwhelmingly (by returning time and again) in the city's favor. The genre does seem to have faded in recent decades. But it is still significant, in two ways. First, this view has had a powerful impact on those who have until recently made the decisions which influence the form of the city which we see today.[36] And, second, although a genre in French literature, it is a lacuna in the Japanese. Criticism of Edo and Tokyo has simply never approached the level of vituperation seen in Paris.

From its beginnings, Edo was big — very big. It drew to itself a horde of nobles, and commoners to satisfy their needs, and soon produced a booming consumption-based, commoner-dominated society wholly at odds with the aristocratic, agrarian ideology of the Tokugawa government. The common people loved it, and throughout the era, plebian authors and woodblock-print artists celebrated the raucous, competitive, carpe diem pursuit of pleasure and wealth by the citizenry.

All this, of course, did not sit well with the physiocratic elites, especially as it began to infect the warrior class, and a number of critics of Edo emerged.[37] Edo was too big and sprawling, too commercial, and too mobile, and city dwellers were too materialistic, too clever, too rootless, too criminal, and too individualistic. But despite the wide-ranging criticism, there is a tone about their writings which differs from that of their French contemporaries. The warriors should be removed from the corrupting money pit of Edo and returned to the land — this done, there was nothing intrinsically wrong with the city. That is, many critiques in fact presupposed city life.[38]

Observers of the capital after the Restoration continued much in this vein: lots of emphasis on the attractiveness of Edo — now Tokyo — and critiques which, while frequently sharp, were often derivative of other concerns and so fell short of demonizing the city. Modernization and industrialization both came under fire from certain quarters. The Meiji state preached the virtues of rural simplicity and honesty and innocent love of emperor and country, but without direct attack on the capital,[39] and no one actually proposed to restrict Tokyo's growth or economic development.

There were, of course, those — like Nagai Kafū in the early twentieth century — who loved the city, but rarely with passion. Warm views of Tokyo as often as not were actually more nostalgic for vanished Edo than appreciative of the contemporary city, and *angst* might even be a better term than *love*.[40] We have seen ambivalence in the case of Paris, but this is different: whereas French views of the capital have been practically apocalyptic, both pro and con, Tokyo simply does not seem to inspire.[41]

After World War I, Japan experienced a wave of cosmopolitanism; the modern vogue (most in evidence in Tokyo) provoked an antimodern reaction which swept Tokyo into its net. And the Great Depression hit rural Japan hard, reviving anti-urban, agrarianist sentiments in which urbanization and industrialization were blamed for the "ruination" of the countryside.[42] But even though the militarists who took over Japan in the 1930s (and their intellectual supporters) rhetorically promoted agrarianism, they for the most part accepted commerce, industry, capitalism, and urbanism — and Tokyo.[43]

After the war, Japan's economic recovery was centered at first along the Pacific coast, but gradually the center of economic and demographic gravity moved toward Tokyo. This entailed some jealousy, but, in general, feelings of inferiority, defensiveness, dependency, and attraction have out-weighed hostility.[44] Tokyo was, and is, a "problem" but not a curse, a given to be worked around rather than an evil to be confronted.[45] Anti-urban and zero-sum views of the urban-rural relationship, though they do exist,[46] have hardly generated their own genre. Indeed, it has been argued that there is no Tokyo genre, that "a literature of Tokyo scarcely exists."[47] Perhaps it is the tepidity of this regard which is inscribed across its face.

In the Eye of the State

Neither have observers of Edo and Tokyo been inspired by the potential of the capital — despite all the usual stereotypes of urban crime and violence — to cause trouble. Trouble there has been, but it has never been as crimi-nal or violent as Western perceptions suggest is the case in European cit-ies.[48] Thousands rioted and burned in 1905 and 1918, mobs murdered Ko-rean residents in 1923, coups d'état were attempted in the 1930s, hundreds of thousands demonstrated against the U.S.-Japan Mutual Security Treaty of 1960, and the late 1960s and 1970s saw a wave of homicidal ultraleftist violence. But the state has not for four hundred years regarded the capital as a threat. It has taken nothing for granted: Edo was highly organized and regimented, at least in its first century or two, and the criminal justice system was draconian. The modern Japanese police have acquired a reputa-tion for high effectiveness. But fears of revolution, or even of destabilizing unrest, are simply not in surface evidence.

The contrast with Paris is stark. Paris presents us with a history of insur-rection and bloodshed which makes Tokyo look like Eden, and the French have formed their views of the capital accordingly.[49] The capital was long viewed not simply as an economic and demographic threat, but as a politi-cal threat to both state and nation, to be kept under firm control, and we should not be surprised to find other aspects of the built city designed with social order in mind.

The Impassioned and the Impassive

Extremism seems characteristic of evaluations of Paris, as compared with Tokyo. Hyperbole is the order of the day: Paris's contributions to world culture are "second to none,"[50] or its threat to France is "apocalyptic." No one seems either uninterested or disinterested, and all are intense — even those who, like Balzac, cannot make up their minds. And both the lovers and the haters have influenced the form of the city.

Pity, by contrast, poor Tokyo, little hated but also little loved. Even those who are attached to the city portray it without passion; Tokyo's defenders often do little more than wrap themselves in an (often-vanished) city like a security blanket.[51] Tokyo *has* inspired literature and art, especially during the brief, bright 1920s.[52] But Nagai Kafū, mentioned above as one of the great Tokyo writers, is more typical: his work is described with words like "elegy," "melancholy," and "sadness for the past" — in sum, "love is an element rather wanting both in Kafū's life and in his work."[53] So, too, in literary visions of Tokyo, especially after the earthquake of 1923 destroyed the areas of which Kafū and others were most fond.[54] Thus one's literary impression is that Paris is both loved and hated, passionately (sometimes by the same people); in Edo and Tokyo, one can also see flashes of love and hate, and similar ambivalence, but what most strikes the reader is, by contrast, what is not there.

The Capital and the Country

At first glance, Tokyo appears to be on far better, and far less zero-sum, terms with the suburbs, the provinces, and the state than is Paris. Tokyo's suburbs, like all cities', are heterogeneous. Some are blue-collar, and many are full of regimented ranks of high-rise apartment projects, or *danchi,* which concede nothing to the sterility of French *grands ensembles.* Each has its stereotype: lower-class residential neighborhoods are typified by scruffy *kichin* apartments, and the danchi are thought of as socially isolated and atomized, soulless, and ugly. But neither Tokyo suburb has historically been seen as criminal, pauperized, radical, or threatening.

The dominant image of the Tokyo suburb, rather, is that of the single-family home on a tiny but private lot, with room for a little greenery. Such suburbs are not a terra incognita full of swarthy foreigners, to be traversed quickly or avoided altogether, but the shining goal of almost every young salary-earner or danchi-dwelling family. There is currently a small flow of upscale migration to central Tokyo by couples seeking more convenience and metropolitan amenities, but the suburban dream exerts overwhelming influence on the perceptions of Tokyoites today.

Tokyo's relationships to the provinces, while less rose-colored, are little less smooth. Regional groups occasionally decry the "overconcentration" of everything in Tokyo, but such critiques are never Malthusian, and remedies almost invariably emphasize self-help, not a French-style beggar-thy-capital strategy.[55] Nor has the Japanese state ever appeared to perceive the capital antagonistically. The early Tokugawa shoguns, of course, wanted it big and prosperous and splendid and intimidating. Once their power was secure, they ceased to pour resources into improving the capital (although *re*building, given the frequency of fires, was a constant expense), but they never really turned on it. Later in the era, the state repeatedly issued (invariably ineffective) decrees expelling unauthorized in-migrants. But the real concern of the regime was elite, not popular or urban, unrest. The major cause of metropolitan growth, the compulsory residence system for the lords, was not relaxed until the shogunate was simply incapable of enforcing it: keeping a close eye on the lords was more important than preventing the growth of the plebian population.

After the Restoration, Tokyo was the economic leader from the beginning, and this leadership has never been questioned by the state. The prewar state rarely tried to influence the spatial pattern of economic growth; after the war, successful efforts were made to expel factories from the capital, and a variety of decentralization plans (both intraregional and national) were advanced (see chap. 7), but none has revealed a serious anti-Tokyo bias.

One looks in vain for expressions of state hostility to the capital on the social or the political level. The agrarianists of the 1930s were sharply anti-urban, and Tokyo harbored many of the demons they sought to exorcise, but Tokyo itself was never the demon. None of the riots of the prewar period sought to change the form of the state, much less to secede from Japan in the manner of the Paris Commune. After the war, antistate movements did emerge in the form of the Japanese Red Army and other ultraleftist factions, but despite bombings and demonstrations, this movement was never identified with Tokyo.

In the case of Paris, by contrast, one's task is to winnow the literary and public statements of hostility from all these relationships. From the train, the suburbs do not appear so different from Tokyo's: some remnants of countryside, stark grands ensembles, a lot of single-family homes, some scruffy and decaying smaller apartments, and here and there a cluster of shiny new municipal buildings and facilities and stores.[56] And of course places like Neuilly are among the nation's elite addresses. But the stereotype? The margins have been suspect for centuries; as early as 1789, *Le Mercure de France* warned that "the Huns . . . are already among us." Inhabitants of the suburbs were characterized in the 1830s as "barbarians who threaten society" and, later, as "a cord which will strangle us one day."[57] The emergence of the Red Belt around the city—more recently superseded by ethnic ghettoes—simply meant that new realities were poured into old mental bottles. The margins were then and are now a place of esthetic disparagement and mythic mistrust.[58]

As for the city's regard of, and by, the rest of France, historically the dislike has been mutual. Parisians have traditionally looked down their noses at the provinces; in 1871, of course, they tried to withdraw altogether and were bloodily punished for their sins. The provinces, for their part, have long attempted to bring Paris down to their own level and/or use it to subsidize the rest of the country.[59] In recent decades, this view seems to have weakened, but as late as the 1970s, Paris was "unloved by the provinces," and DATAR, the state's regional development agency, viewed the capital as a "black hole."[60]

Given the power of local politicians in the French parliament, and given that many national leaders are simultaneously mayors of their hometowns, it is unsurprising that remarks denigrating Paris have been common from within the French state. Given the obtrusive state role in the shaping of Paris, it is not far-fetched to surmise that these views have played a role in the formation of the city as we see it today. Not all French leaders have been anti-Paris, of course, but a "love-hate relationship" has endured.[61] Even in the more peaceful interstices, the zero-sum attitudes noted above have led, right up until the latter part of the twentieth century, to management policies which have "consisted principally of enfeebling the Parisian region."[62] And Paris, for its part, does not like such intervention at all: when Socialist president François Mitterrand enhanced the powers of Paris's twenty ward, or *arrondissement,* governments, then-mayor Jacques Chirac protested that "Paris is menaced by a sociocommunist power which wishes to suppress Paris."[63] And his successor in Paris, Mayor Bertrand Delanoë, has not hesitated to take up the cudgel whenever he feels that the state is treading on Paris's prerogatives.

This cursory descriptive tour of the capitals has thus left us with some parallel visions of Paris and Tokyo, but many more divergent ones, some of nuance, some diametric. Some might be straw men, and some might be wholly inaccurate; the more detailed examination of each which follows will, I hope, indicate if this is so. In any case, the following chapters will take up each area of impression. For each, I shall first suggest possible explanations for the differences seen, and then marshal evidence for the accuracy (or inaccuracy) of these initial impressions and for the plausibility of each explanation. In the end, with luck, we shall not only perceive the different forms and functions of Paris and Tokyo, but also better understand how and why they came to be the way they are, and perhaps the way they may yet be.

2 | FORM AND PATTERN IN THE CITY

INFERENCE

Studies of the origins, developmental trajectories, and contemporary shapes of cities are legion. Politics, economics, and religion dominate the discussion, and they certainly play a role in any effort to understand the differences between Paris and Tokyo. But by themselves those three are unsatisfying, partly because each begs further questions of origin and evolution. Other, more diffuse forces have shaped these cities as well. However much any such factors have played a role in shaping either city, no single one will have dominated; some complex of influences has been at work. Even if *all* of these factors have played a role, they are not an exhaustive list of forces influencing the contemporary form of these cities.

Still, each of these can be linked, however hypothetically, to urban space and form. Thus each must then be examined in light of the actual history of the city to estimate the plausibility of its influence (or lack of influence), either directly or as mediated through social, political, and other institutions. Such historical evidence may at first seem oversimplified, as if essentializing Japanese and Westerners according to an outmoded Orientalism. But acknowledging some real differences — relative, to be sure — between Japan and France may prove useful in defining certain unarguable dissimilarities between Paris and Tokyo.

In one form or another, at least eight different forces may account for the differences we have already seen in the physical form of Tokyo and Paris:

Esthetics: Pieces and Wholes, Tangibles and Intangibles

Two aspects of esthetics are related to the forms of Tokyo and Paris today. The first is what might be described as a Japanese esthetic of parts (not necessarily integrated) versus a French, or perhaps Western, esthetic of integrated wholes. The second is a Japanese esthetic of intangibility and impermanence versus a French, or Western, esthetic of tangibility and permanence.

Augustin Berque has described the builders of European cities as being relatively preoccupied with the whole city and with "grandiose symmetries" among its parts.[1] Hellenistic and Roman cities were carefully and comprehensively planned,[2] and Paris grew from a Roman grid. This is not to say that disorder was absent, especially in the medieval city, or that the city did not have distinct sections. But they were never — as was the case with the commoner and aristocratic sectors of Edo — cut off from one another or internally composed of mutually isolated parts.[3]

Japanese city builders, by contrast, have traditionally been concerned more with parts, each growing incrementally with little relationship to the other parts or to the whole.[4] This is in keeping with the relatively reductionist, microcosmic focus of Japanese esthetics in general.[5] Such a focus is hardly absent in the West, but the esthetic has far more powerfully influenced a host of Japanese practices: beauty, perfection, and personal enlightenment may be achieved through the ever greater refinement of a smaller and smaller aspect of the physical or behavioral world.[6] The problem with such an esthetic, if applied to cities, is that it would result in agglomerations of mutually unrelated, unintegrated parts with no unifying principle — exactly what comes to mind when one thinks of Tokyo.[7] The notion that the city should constitute an esthetic whole came late to Japan and has not found an altogether hospitable home there.

Nor has the notion that the city should possess a relatively unchanging face over time. The contrasting tangibility and apparent permanence of Paris's urban form go beyond the simple difference between wood-based and stone-based architecture. Compared to Tokyo, Paris has historically resisted change in both its whole and its parts. Great importance has been placed in the permanence of material forms over time, and the identity of the city and its people derives at least in part from its "stable physical scene."[8]

Japanese esthetics — and, by hypothetical extension, Japanese urbanism — is far more characterized by implication, understatement, and ephemerality.[9] Artworks themselves are generally distinguished by an emphasis on suggestion, simplicity, and perishability: the Japanese value and are attracted by impermanence.[10] It could in fact be said that in Tokyo they have created the perishable city, and even fire and earthquake are inadequate explanations why. The Grand Shrine at Ise is demolished and rebuilt every twenty years with no notion that this disrespects the patrimony, and Japanese buildings and cities in general are simply not built to last, even now that modern technology permits.[11]

Nature and Artifice in the City

Perhaps consistent with an esthetic — and an urbanism — of flux, Tokyo is the hypothetical consequence of a culture based on the relative primacy of nature over human agency.[12] This is not to say that nature per se is more respected in Tokyo than in Paris, or that Edo was unplanned. And the indignities heaped upon Mother Nature during Tokyo's last century give the lie to any generalization that the Japanese are in essence inclined to harmonize with nature when it lies in the path of other goals.

Still, at the same time that nature is ruthlessly subordinated to human ends, concepts like impermanence, cycle, rebirth, and fatalism are relatively strong. Urban growth is "organic" and relatively unguided; cities and buildings are "provisional."[13] Not abstract concepts but concrete, pragmatic human goals have driven urban development, often without overarching regulation, or even the idea that regulation is possible. The idea of *nari-yuki,* the inevitable course of events, plays a powerful role in this ethos.[14] People are thus in harmony with nature not when they respect or preserve nature, but when they acquiesce in the intrinsically transitory character of reality and do not try to draw artificial distinctions between the natural and the man-made. And so they build their cities.

In sharp contrast to what might thus be described as the "inductive" development of Japanese cities is the apparently "deductive" development of Paris. Ever since Roman days, abstract principles have repeatedly been applied to the city to determine its form.[15] Although nature per se — in the form of ridges and valleys, river and swamp — has influenced the growth of Paris, and nature has been respected in many instances, it seems as if the city has been more superimposed on its setting than accommodative of it. It has in fact been said that "Paris is not a work of nature but a work of man."[16] As Le Corbusier put it: "The city . . . is a human operation directed against nature."[17]

But whereas the rationalist, deductive will of the early Tokugawa shoguns soon faded from the realities of Edo, never to be equaled, ever since the Renaissance that force of will has grown in Paris: space was increasingly manipulated to reflect mathematics, Cartesian philosophy, and Newtonian physics.[18] The baroque city raised this mechanistic impulse to a peak, granting plans and abstract concepts priority over life itself and imposing artificial order on the natural.[19] And although Haussmann and Paris's walls are gone, Haussmann's successors are alive and well and drawing further designs for the next phase of La Défense.

Unnatural Disaster

One manifestation of the emphasis on nature in Japanese culture, and especially Japanese urbanism, is the role of natural and "man-made" disasters, a factor almost totally lacking in the history of Paris. When it seems as if Mother Nature imposes her will on the city irrespective of human agency, it is perhaps unsurprising that a fatalistic acceptance of the impermanence of human achievements might follow.

Paris has of course been the scene over the centuries of countless destructive riots and insurrections. But in fact relatively few buildings were totally destroyed, and many — like the Louvre and the Hôtel de Ville — were rebuilt in the same hopefully eternal stone as before. Overall there has simply never grown up in Paris the feeling that everything the city has constructed could go up in smoke the next day.

Edo and Tokyo, at the other extreme, have long been evanescent cities. During the Edo era, there were hundreds of smaller fires and some eighty "large" ones; in the largest, the Meireki Fire in 1657, three-quarters of the city was reduced to ashes.[20] After the Restoration, new technology and better firefighting practices reduced the danger; still, between 1868 and 1891 there occurred 121 fires in which at least one hundred buildings were lost, plus 18 more in which more than one thousand buildings burned.[21]

Fire was, unsurprisingly, seen as inevitable as natural calamity. When the two combined it was especially horrific: in 1923, an earthquake was followed by fires in which two-thirds of Tokyo burned. And then, after the whole was rebuilt, World War II saw an area as large as all of Paris proper again reduced to a smoking moonscape.[22]

Two hypothetically helpful attitudes are consistent with this history of repeated assault by destructive forces seemingly beyond human control. One is the fatalistic idea that everything is impermanent, including the most robust physical, material things, such as the renewable Grand Shrine at Ise.[23]

Second, compared with Paris, in Tokyo far more value is placed on land than on buildings. Land in Tokyo is so expensive that any building upon it accounts for a relatively small part of the value of the total property and thus can be torn down and replaced with little compunction.[24]

Architecture and Technology

Certainly, disasters were exacerbated in Edo and Tokyo by the prevalence of wood in building; indeed, some have generalized sweepingly about the differences between this "culture of wood" and a European "culture of stone."[25] In any case, it is quite possible that the idea of transience — of both buildings and whole cities — is due at least as much to this simply technological difference as it is to any essentially Japanese religious idea of transience.

The question is, if fire and decay were such problems, why did the Japanese stick with wooden construction until the late nineteenth century? They certainly were capable of stonework, as the walls of any Japanese castle attest, and they could make tile and brick. But tall stone buildings? No. One reason might be that timber was abundant, easy to transport and work, and forgiving in an earthquake. There might have been an esthetic preference for wood, although of this we cannot be sure, as the paeans to warm, weathered wood were written long after it had become the building material of choice. It is possible that the absence of a drive to conquer nature robbed building technology of a major driving force.[26] And the well-ventilated, wood-and-paper Japanese house may be more attuned to the humid Japanese climate.

In any case, premodern Japanese architecture contrasts with the buildings and city walls of stone which have characterized the Middle East and Europe for millennia (including many equally earthquake-prone regions, and such originally forested areas as the Paris basin). And construction material may have combined with technology. Mechanics have historically been more advanced in the Middle East and the West than in Japan, perhaps because wood does not create the mechanical imperatives that stone does. The Japanese certainly did exhibit mechanical ingenuity in quarrying, transporting, and laying stones the size of boxcars in castle walls. But they had a default option — wood — which did not provide strong incentives to change. And so, while the Parisians were worshiping in spectacular Gothic cathedrals, the Japanese paid their respects to the statue of the Great Buddha in Nara — housed in the world's biggest wooden building, to be sure, but somehow not the same.

Soul Cities

Many urban historians cite religion as a, if not the, major factor in the genesis of the city.[27] Commerce, war, and the exercise of political authority played a role, in this argument, but "religion permeated all activities," and all were subordinate to the "moral norms of society."[28] Even in the Hellenistic West, where new, secular bases for urban organization became prominent, such urban plans as axial grids arguably reflect earlier images of the cosmos.[29]

Similar arguments can be made for the origin of Paris in particular.[30] The Lendit plain (today's St-Denis) has been described as a sacred spot for the Gauls and their ancestors. The Romans, of course, imposed their standard (cosmological?) urban grid on Lutetia, but Roman control remained "downtown," on the island and the left bank. Later development privileged the islands and both proximate banks of the Seine, and the bishop of Paris acquiesced in this evolution by locating on the Île de la Cité, which influenced its form critically. Aside from its institutional presence, Christianity also imported some ideas with urban implications.[31] One idea was an ambivalence toward the city which can be traced all the way back to Cain, who is said to have founded the first city after being exiled from his homeland by God. This ambivalence will be discussed in chapter 7 in the context of moral evaluations of the city. A second influence, more relevant to urban form, was Christianity's sharp division between man and nature, with the explicit dominion of man over nature.

Gothic Paris represents perhaps the acme of religious influence on the city. Architecture was but one realm in which God was to be glorified by man's works, with the soaring towers of Notre-Dame as the "visible cement of a Christian society." Indeed, the medieval city has been seen as basically "a stage for the ceremonies of the Church."[32] Thereafter secular forces gained strength, but religion never ceased to play a role in shaping the city either explicitly — Sacré-Coeur stands as a symbol of the dominion of Christian France over Paris — or implicitly, in the imposition of man-made plans upon everything the French state surveyed.

Such an imposition was a feature of early Japanese capitals also, specifically, their construction in accord with the "cosmomagical" Chinese axial pattern.[33] But the perishing and renewal characteristic of both the essentially transient Buddhist worldview *and* the cyclical, natural Shinto worldview soon took precedence over the static regularity of the Chinese imperial city plan.

Until the Tokugawa era, that is. The earliest Tokugawa shoguns wanted to create a seamless system which their successors would rule in perpetuity. They wanted no loose cannon and no loose ends, and they planned the polity, the economy, the society, and the capital as well on unprecedentedly secular lines. Nonetheless, one may infer religious factors from the siting of the castle: with mountains behind it, water before, roads to the left and rivers to the right (when viewed from the east), it is broadly congruent with Chinese geomantic principles.[34] Moreover, the approaches to the city were guarded (particular in the spiritually dangerous northeast quarter) by a set of Buddhist temples.

The internal structure of Edo was determined far more by military and sociopolitical factors, but religious considerations cannot be ignored completely. Throughout the Edo era, and up to today, a failure to differentiate sharply between man and nature, or between the city and nature, has been visible. A street layout designed to take advantage of distant mountains survives, as does the barely perceptible transition from city to country, both more noticeable in Tokyo than Paris. One longtime observer, noting the transience of all things Tokyo, simply calls it "a Buddhist capital."[35] And although one may be taken to task for attributing impermanence and lack of dualities to religious ideas several centuries removed, when a Japanese architect himself says that his "metabolist" emphasis on impermanence and "intermediate zones" derives from Buddhism, it is fair to take him at his word.[36]

Pragmatics and the Capital: Economics

Tokugawa Ieyasu built a political capital, and the Meiji leaders in the late nineteenth century did the same, but the market has triumphed, far more so than in Paris. We have already seen how the relative value of buildings and land in Tokyo has acted to transform the cityscape, and the government further obliges the market by considering old buildings an obstacle to urban modernization.[37] The Japanese state has spent more than a century explicitly pursuing Westernization, primarily economically, and has tended to view the city and its various parts in terms of the bottom line necessary to lure the foreign businesses and business people necessary to make Tokyo a truly global city.

This is not to say that the market matters little in Paris; rather, that in these two enthusiastically capitalist systems, bluntly economic considerations simply do not have the force in Paris that they have in Tokyo. In more than fifty years of visiting and living in Tokyo, I have never heard anyone use any word in the sense that the French use the term *patrimoine,* denoting public cultural heritage. For Paris, a host of considerations — from provincial jealousy to artistic integrity — have taken precedence on specific occasions over the city's immediate economic prospects. To those who consider La Défense a sellout to soulless capitalism and a blot on Paris's skyline, I would say, "Consider yourselves fortunate."[38]

Pragmatics and the Capital: Authority

Another realm in which pragmatics shapes the capital is politics or, more broadly, the role of authority in French and Japanese culture. The government has directly shaped the capital in both countries, but I suggest that there are two major differences in the nature of political authority in Japan and France (and perhaps, more broadly, the West) which are of particular relevance to the city. First, authority in Japan is "given," or hegemonic. Throughout Japanese history, political authority has rarely been challenged at its roots; its basic principles have enjoyed legitimacy in the eyes of the most important political actors.[39] Coups, bloodshed, and regime changes, yes; but revolution, religious wars, and radical upwelling of popular demands, no.[40] Government has tended to be seen as a natural organism, not something created artificially through either popular compact or Hobbesian necessity.[41] New regimes have worked hard to establish their operational legitimacy, but once secure, their exercise of authority in the capital has changed.

France, by contrast, has seen authority beset by both elite and popular enemies.[42] Romans and barbarians, Catholics and Protestants, monarchists and Jacobins, bourgeois and proletarians, communists and fascists — all have embraced rival visions of authority and have shed rivers of blood in their pursuit thereof.[43] Throughout the ancien régime, the state competed — especially in Paris — with rival power centers and concepts of authority — in sharp contrast to Edo, where the shogunate coexisted with numerous autonomous groups but never a rival.[44]

My second hypothesis about political authority in Japan and France is that in Japan its exercise was relatively "soft," relying relatively more on legitimacy and acceptance and, later, on rule by "myth" and "molding minds" than on "hard" applications of physical coercion.[45] From all this, two different types of urban authority may flow.[46] In a society characterized by contested authority and hard rule, one might expect a conflictual, intrusive and manipulative, and predatory state attitude toward the capital, and a built city which reminds (and convinces) people of (ideally permanent) political order. A society with given authority and soft rule, on the other hand, is consistent with a more symbiotic state-capital relationship, less conflict, less state intrusion into and manipulation of the capital, and less concern for creating a capital which embodies principles of order and permanence. Thus the hypothetical paradox of political and urban order: contested capitals will be more planned and orderly, reflecting (would-be) unquestioned power, while less contested ones may be laissez-faire and messy, because power does not feel the need to shape the built environment for purposes of psychic domination. And the un-paradox of rule: where the exercise of power is hard, so will be the form of the city; where it is soft, urban form will be fluid and nebulous.

The above certainly admits of exceptions, like the monumental attempts at legitimacy building in the contested early Heian, Edo, and Meiji periods and the relaxed way in which Louis XIV let Paris become an open city. But I suspect that the evidence will show that these were exceptions, and that a consistency between political antecedents and urban outcomes will be visible.

The Capital: The Sum of All Fears?

The corollary of the above is that in a society like France, marked by contested authority, hard rule, and an intrusive state, the form of the capital will be shaped more by fear — of foreign enemies, insurgent citizens, and crime — than in a society like Japan. Some argue that the role of fear is a constant, that the city is by nature the adversary of its hinterland, and that with rare exceptions cities must cope also with the threat of invasions targeted at themselves.[47] I disagree, and not simply because of Japan's insular safety: Japan has seen decades of civil wars, thousands of popular protests, and its full share of crime, all with a strong urban component. But with brief exceptions it has not designed or built cities to assuage its fears.

Granted, Europe — with many polities and few natural barriers — may be an extreme case. Between A.D. 500 and 1000 the continent was swept repeatedly by war and banditry.[48] Every advance in military technology brought changes in urban form: cannon-proof walls in particular were hugely expensive (requiring a more extractive state) and hard to modify, forcing cities to grow vertically within this carapace. Fields of fire outside the walls cut the city off from its context; inside the city, barracks, parade grounds, and broad avenues for troop movement consumed large chunks of urban space.[49] Where the primary threat was foreign, whole cities were walled; where it was rival lords or insurrectionary people, the ruler would have his own fortress inside the city. Some cities had both.

Paris's form was in great degree influenced by foreign threats. But it is clear from the government's obvious fears of (and not just for) the people that any fearful motivations in shaping the city — like Napoleon's construction of the rue de Rivoli and Haussmann's later program — had a strong antipopulist component. It would not be surprising to find that many of the physical features of Paris today were put in place not only to fend off foreign aggressors but to enhance intra-urban anticrime surveillance and reduce the danger of rebellion.

Japan, of course, is a lot harder to invade. But insularity alone does not explain why the impact of fear on urban form should be less in Edo and Tokyo than in Paris. First, there is the nature of warfare: Japan has a long history of civil war, but not of urban sieges and castle assaults: battles tended to take place in the field. Few fortifications were ever actually involved in warfare, and walled cities hardly existed. Edo was planned with defense in mind: narrow streets with lots of right-angle turns and T-shaped intersections, and massive walls and moats around the castle proper.[50] But within a few decades the danger of attack had faded, and broader streets and open spaces appeared — not for troop movement, but as firebreaks.

The second factor is the nature of Japanese weaponry, specifically, the general absence of guns in general and artillery in particular. Both were introduced, but neither ever really took root.[51] The largest early modern castles were easily the equal of the Vaubanesque fortress in robustness against artillery, but the fears which gave rise to them faded fast in the seventeenth century.[52]

The third factor is the general absence in Japan of governmental fear of the people. Concern, yes. Edo's design was intended to facilitate social control, with gated commoner quarters and restricted movement after dark. But there is simply no indication that the regime morbidly feared its people. Even in the later decades of the era, when food riots and political protests proliferated, the government never acted as if it feared overthrow by the people.[53]

EVIDENCE

All the suppositions raised above must be examined in light of more extensive evidence before we can reach any conclusions about the origins of the morphological differences between Paris and Tokyo. Here we take a closer look at our cities in regard to five of these apparent differences: permanence versus impermanence, planned versus unplanned, orderly versus disorderly, natural or organic versus artificial or mechanistic, and built with anxiety versus built with confidence.

Here Today, Gone Tomorrow — Or Not

Japanese cities in general and capitals in particular have been fluid in both time and space for millennia. Between A.D. 400 and 645, there were thirty-one different capitals; they burned over and over; and nothing that could really be called a city emerged until after 700.[54] "Tokyo" has also been hard to pin down.[55] In the fifth century A.D., imperial rule was extended coherently to the area, but the administrative seat of the region was west of today's central Tokyo. That area remained the center of the province for several centuries, although a number of lords occupied Edo Castle in the fifteenth and sixteenth centuries. But when Tokugawa Ieyasu occupied it in 1590, he set about giving his new fief a suitable capital. He built the biggest castle in the land, and distributed the nobles between and around the moats, with their villas on the highlands to the west of the castle and the commoner population to the east, on landfill that began the wholesale reclamation of the bay. The locus of power in Japan has remained here to this day.

Ieyasu hoped that Edo would change little. But it sprawled continuously, and the clear spatial demarcations between different status groups became blurred, and fire changed the cityscape frequently — not least, by destroying the castle itself. So the city struck its inhabitants as a shapeshifting amoeba, and no one would have described the city as static. And flux accelerated after the Restoration. Thousands of acres of aristocratic villas and estates were abandoned; in the west, much of this land was razed and reverted to farmland; downtown it became government buildings, barracks, and parade grounds, or was sold to private developers.[56] The area around the Imperial Palace became the political and economic heart of Tokyo; industry grew to the north, east, and south, while the population began to expand to the west. But in the downtown areas, the Edo cityscape survived.

Until, that is, 1923, when the earthquake destroyed almost all of it, and stimulated two trends which persist to this day: the depopulation of the city center, and the drift of Tokyo's demographic and political center back (after a thousand years) toward the west.[57] As the city revived, it increasingly took on its present-day dynamic, with the area inside the Yamanote rail loop line more and more devoted to tertiary economic activity, and ever more rail lines radiating outward from the station nodes of the Yamanote line, bringing ever greater number of suburban white-collar workers to the central business district.

Revival was more than complete by 1940. But the wartime devastation was even greater: 102 bombing raids, 768,000 homes destroyed, and 40,000 urban acres leveled.[58] Again, the basic outline of the city's street plan survived, and its place-names and natural landmarks, but over this substratum has flowed a continuous tide of apparently endless urban regeneration.

Clearly there is more to Tokyo's impermanence than simple destruction. Even before the earthquake, Tokyo was "in an agitated state of steady reformation . . . undergoing a sort of sustained moulting season."[59] In World War II, Germany's cities were also laid waste, but they were rebuilt far differently; and Kyoto, which was *not* bombed during the war, "generally resembles the chaotic cityscapes of other metropolises that *had* been devastated."[60] Among other factors, I shall suggest (see chap. 4), were economic imperatives, hands-off government, and a piecemeal approach to urban change. The most economically efficient land use — directly, by enhancing productivity, or indirectly, by accommodating the commuter population — has remained the rule, with little regard either to the metropolitan whole or to the esthetic compatibility of its contiguous parts.

Over the longer sweep of history, the impermanence of Tokyo seems irrefutable, and seems to have resulted most concretely from regime changes with urban implications — Ieyasu's takeover and the Restoration — disasters both man-made and natural, and a particularly economistic and iconoclastic view of physical construction. But impermanence is also fully consistent with a culture which accepts the limitations of reason and human agency, an esthetic which does not encompass wholes, and a society rarely threatened from below or from outside. The Japanese *can* preserve, and they *can* plan comprehensively, as I discuss in chapter 4, but they have not historically cared to do either very often.

Paris, by contrast, has stayed put, even though it did not become the capital once and for all until 1789. In Japan, often the ruler arrived at a spot and created his capital city; once such a capital was abandoned, it often vanished. Lutetia, on the other hand, was settled as early as the third century B.C. and never faded.[61] Under the Romans, it constituted a regional administrative center. At first the Pax Romana permitted an open city, but around A.D. 300, foreign threats led to the construction of a rampart on the Île de la Cité.[62] Subsequent centuries saw the decentering of Paris and the growth of a ring of great semi-autonomous (and often fortified) abbeys around the city.[63]

Such fortifications became a continuous enterprise during the seventh through the ninth centuries, as barbarian invasions of various kinds swept across France, culminating in "successive waves" of Viking attacks.[64] The king departed, and the city's population fell, recovering only in the tenth century.[65] After the reign of Louis VI (1108–37), the king spent increasing amounts of time in Paris; but he also had to share power with the ecclesiastical and municipal authorities as the city had in his absence developed a lively sense of its own autonomy.[66]

This identity was strikingly augmented, and given concrete form, under King Philippe Auguste. He took the throne in 1180 and paid much more attention to the organization and protection of Paris, his capital, giving it a formidable face to the outside world with its first real city wall.[67] Although the wall did not encompass the entire city, it gave Paris physical, fiscal, and administrative definition, created a hierarchy of inside and outside, and dramatically enhanced the attractive power of the city, which was in turn both "protected" and "mastered" by the fortress of the Louvre, incorporated into the wall. It ran through the lands of a number of abbeys, thus reducing their power, but by localizing and sheltering the urban economy it enhanced the power of the bourgeoisie and their municipal leader, the provost of merchants. ·

Thus while the history of Japan's capitals appears episodic, that of France's seems more cumulative. New dynasties and recurrent wars swept away parts of the city, and steady growth necessitated new walls, but the new often built onto, over, outside, and around the old. There was more radical political than urban transformation, the opposite of the Japanese situation.

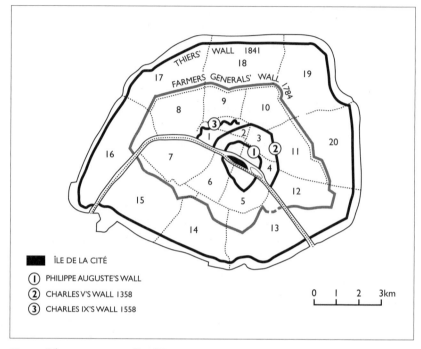

Fig. 10. The successive walls of Paris.

Political transformation was all too common after the long Gothic summer of Philippe and his successors, as wars, walls, and monarchs came and went.[68] The return of the king — Louis XII (1498–1515) — was followed by renewed emphasis on Paris, and by three trends.[69] The first was enhanced royal power, often in the face of both aristocratic and municipal opposition. The second was the embellishment of the city, sometimes from necessity (new fortifications in 1512, 1523, 1536, 1544, and 1634) and sometimes from a new sense of "grandeur" of the national capital, as Henry IV (1589–1610) and his minister Sully built public spaces and promenades. The third was increased regulation of the built environment: in 1548, a ban on further growth in sprawling suburban faubourgs was issued, and in 1554, an order to demolish nonconforming houses; building regulations were likewise issued, including height limits. In all, a fever of construction swept the city, but all this hardly represented a Japanese-style scrap-and-build mentality:

the assumption was that a good Parisian house would last several centuries. And some have.

The city's shape was nonetheless changing, in two ways. First, it was growing outward as the population grew, and the city limits were moved accordingly in 1638, 1672, 1724, and 1765.[70] Second, its center of gravity was moving to the west. From the Marais, the focus of elite attention was shifting toward the Louvre; when the Place Louis XV (now the Place de la Concorde) was completed in 1772, it soon became the heart of the city.[71] The Revolution shifted the public gaze back toward the east, but Napoleon I, although providing the city with a small number of impressive monuments, made surprisingly few structural changes aside from promoting — by locating his monuments to empire in western Paris — the increasing focus of national and monarchical symbolism there.

This is not to say that the impetus to morphological change was absent. By the mid-nineteenth century, Paris was approaching paralysis, stuck inside its medieval structure. Economic growth brought ever more people, and now it also brought factories and working-class neighborhoods, often housed in crowded, unhealthy tenements. Narrow, winding streets obstructed transportation, the city of stone defied easy access for the new railroads, and everything seemed to endanger further economic development. But the physical inertia of the city was formidable.

This Gordian knot was cut during the Second Empire (1852–70), when Napoleon III combined his own vision and dictatorial power with the administrative talents of Georges-Eugène Haussmann, prefect of the Seine. In 1859, he corrected the anomalous situation in which the city limits of Paris were well inside the 1840 city wall by annexing all the intramural territory, thus adding 13,000 acres to Paris's preexisting 8,500 and boosting the city's population by some 350,000 persons.[72] He also tore up the city center, running boulevards hither and yon in accord with baroque principles, simultaneously opening up the stifling tenement neighborhoods, facilitating the movement of troops, commerce, and public transport, and (with his successors, many of whom implemented the incomplete elements of his plans) creating the Paris we know today. Medieval Paris resisted change until he arrived, and his Paris has resisted change ever since.

We shall hear more of Haussmann; for now, he represents a cataclysmic transformation of the city. By 1875, the land inside the 1840 wall was full,[73] and the suburbs grew apace, ill-served by the public transit system, which focused on intracity and interregional travel, and was generally abhorred by the middle class. The new subway system, the Métro, offered a potential solution, but its lines stopped at the wall. The wall itself, having proved its uselessness in 1871 and 1914, was demolished after World War I. But instead of following the lead of other cities and creating a green belt,[74] Paris replaced it with a new wall of athletic facilities, public housing projects, and ultimately a moving wall: the Périphérique highway. Between the wars, rents were essentially frozen, and this plus the Depression effectively eliminated any incentive to build.

This logjam was broken after World War II, as the housing crisis was finally acknowledged and the imperative of economic recovery assumed new political importance. In 1948, rents were largely freed (and increased sixfold by 1954); factory construction was restricted in 1955, and office construction in 1958; building-height limits were relaxed in 1956.[75] This ushered in a wave of new construction, renovation, and gentrification in Paris; outside, it saw the building of the grands ensembles. The combination led to the final expulsion of the poor, who were not missed. Morphologically, what was noticed most was a brief fad of high-rise buildings — decisively rejected after the construction of the Maine-Montparnasse Tower in 1973 — and freeways, but President Giscard canceled the Left Bank Highway (in 1974) and in general brought a sane pause to the process.[76]

Since then change has not ceased, but it has been more regulated: high-rise buildings have been relegated to the periphery, many of the grands ensembles have been demolished, much of the Châtelet–Les Halles development is underground, and new towns in the suburbs have reduced the pressure on the city proper. The embellishment of the capital has not ceased: President Mitterrand in particular launched a number of grandiose projects in the 1980s which have transformed the city, for the most part beautifully. And its rebalancing has also occurred, particularly under Mitterrand, as new emphases on the eastern part of the city are intended to enhance the quality of life there. But the center of Paris remains largely unchanged, with the exception of the old area of Les Halles, now a park planned for redevelopment. The city is basically as Haussmann intended it to be.

This fact does not exactly imply permanence, but as cities go it is close to it, in dramatic contrast to Tokyo. Change in Paris has, like that in Tokyo, tended to be episodic, with two differences. In Paris, transformations are more supplementary or complementary than eradicatory, and in Paris, they are more the result of official will. Henry IV and Sully, Napoleon III and Haussmann, President de Gaulle and Paul Delouvrier, and Mitterrand all by himself, combined vision and authority in a way not seen in Tokyo. A vision of the permanence of human works and of the city beautiful as a whole, a linear and teleological sense of history, a sense of the efficacy of human agency and reason in general and public authority in particular — and the fear that the barbarians are at the gates — all are consistent with the minimal change that has characterized the form of Paris during the last two thousand years, compared to most of the world's cities.

The Visible Hand: Intentionality

The imposition of will on the capital has followed opposite trajectories in Paris and Tokyo. Premodern capitals in Japan were all purposefully chosen and extensively planned, but this voluntarism has progressively faded over the last four hundred years. This seems to have been less a single trend of declining intentions than a cyclical one, in which young and insecure regimes briefly attempted to use the form of the capital to boost their legitimacy, after which they relapsed into a more characteristic laissez-faire attitude toward the city.

In Paris, the process has gone the other way. Clovis was crowned in Reims; Charlemagne's capital was in Aix. During the Middle Ages, Paris's political primacy was questionable: at different times, Toulouse, Lyon, or Marseille might have become number one.[77] But gradually Paris became the focus of everyone's attention; when François I settled there in 1528, he was more ratifying reality than consciously selecting a new capital. The monarchization of Paris initiated by Henry IV and Sully really settled the issue once and for all, despite the removal of the court to Versailles under Louis XIV.[78]

In the same way that Paris became France's capital inertially, it grew inertially, without a model. The Romans, of course, had an urban plan. But this model was effectively killed off during the Dark Ages, and the labyrinthine medieval city was a new and essentially planless entity.[79] Paris-as-capital might be considered to have been "invented" during the thirteenth century by Philippe Auguste, his grandson Saint Louis, and his grandson Philippe IV.[80] But although the Capetian kings centralized power in Paris, they and their successors were all constrained by the form of medieval Paris, especially its walls. And after 1350, a century of calamity and depression commenced; it was not until the sixteenth century that urban development really began again.[81] But this time a new consciousness guided growth: science, technology, art, and royal intentions combined to produce increasingly rationalized, planned cities, absolutist capitals for absolute monarchs. The classical Roman grid model was superseded by a "radioconcentric" one featuring central palaces and dispersed — and usually embellished and monumental — public spaces connected by avenues and converging perspectives.[82]

But the overall form of the medieval city remained daunting, even to Louis XIV. He was the next monarch to really impose his will on the city's form, by tearing down the wall and creating the space occupied today by the grand boulevards.[83] But he had no coherent plan for the city, and for the most part realized his architectural intentions in Versailles. Napoleon I emulated Louis — an imperial capital for an imperial state — although his contribution to the city's form, too, was limited to a number of grandiose monuments. Then Napoleon III and Haussmann picked up the baton of political will, and it has never been relinquished, especially during the Fifth Republic. De Gaulle, Pompidou, and Giscard all had presidential ambitions for the city, and Mitterrand launched a program of *grands projets* which is only now fully realized. President Chirac had other preoccupations, but Mayor Bertrand Delanoë seems committed to both functional and esthetic transformations of the capital, having undertaken a peripheral tram line and redevelopment of the old Les Halles area. There is now little disposable land left in Paris proper, and the people of the city have rebelled against anything smacking of cold, market-oriented development (especially if it runs more than ten stories or so). But the legitimacy of voluntaristic, public determination of the city's form can still be seen in the Batignolles project, a joint public-private program of development for a former railroad yard.

The Japanese capital has traveled in the opposite direction: it has been purposive in selection, explicit in model, and decreasingly voluntarist in form. Paris was first an attractive city, and kings kept coming back to it. Japanese capitals were sited for a priori geomantic, political, and strategic reasons. Tokugawa Ieyasu valued Edo strategically, but after he became shogun, he stayed on as Edo's communications links, harbor, and position on a broad plain made it a better administrative center than more strategically positioned locations to the west and offered more elbow room for the great city he wished to build.[84]

When the Tokugawa regime fell in 1868, the question again arose of where to site the capital: Kyoto was still home to the emperor, but Edo had been the true capital for 268 years. It was nearer the center of the country than its rivals and still commanded excellent communications and trade routes (especially the ever more important maritime ones), and it still offered room to grow. The new government was run by former warriors, and Edo had always been a city of warriors, not dominated — in the national imagination — by grasping merchants (as Osaka) or effete courtiers (as Kyoto). And, finally, the overthrow of the Tokugawa freed up literally thousands of acres of noble lands, and hundreds of buildings in the capital immediately became available for use at no cost to a new, poor government.[85]

In addition to being consciously sited, Japan's capitals were from A.D. 645 onward modeled explicitly on the classical Chinese plan.[86] But they were not comprehensively Chinese cities in design and construction: most strikingly, the city walls called for in the original plans were never completed. These cities did not last as modeled: after the transition to feudal rule in the twelfth century, both Nara and Kyoto lost significance and "fell apart into a number of loosely clustered towns."[87] These were artificial cities, owing their stature to the royal presence, not intrinsically attractive cities which could survive its absence, like Paris.

So was Edo, and it was modeled also, albeit eclectically. The Tokugawa actually had three models in mind for Edo. The first was the Chinese directional orientation described above.[88] The second — visible in fig. 11 — was also Chinese: a grid pattern in the commoner quarters, built on landfill amid a network of canals for commercial convenience.[89] The third — also visible in fig. 11 — was the Japanese castle town typical of the era: a spiral pattern of moats and walls (integrated with the canals) which in this case amounted to three concentric rings. The result was an urban whole — administratively, cosmologically, strategically, and economically coherent.

Despite the fires of the Edo era, this model was still apparent in 1868, and was never really superseded. Despite its assiduous efforts to emulate and impress the West, Japan never adopted an overall model for the new capital of Tokyo. Piecemeal attempts there were — a building, an avenue, a streetfront, a station — and lots of unrealized plans were devised. That the Japanese could model whole cities is not in doubt: like Louis XIV taking his frustrations with Paris out on Versailles, Japanese planners vented their frustration with Tokyo upon the baroque capitals of Japan's colonies. But unlike Louis XIV, who prefigured Haussmann, the Japanese colonial planners seem to have been outside the mainstream. And so in Tokyo the Edo city plan was still visible even after the earthquake of 1923; indeed, it was not until the canals and rivers were covered with rail lines and highways after World War II (see fig. 12) that the feudal foundation of Tokyo became invisible.

Thus comprehensive modeling seems to have been not absent but evanescent in Japanese urbanism. The intentions of the early capital builders were clear. And the Tokugawa had not only a model but the will to carry out extensive public works, literally moving mountains and stemming the tide to shape Edo. But incentives to confront the inertial growth of the city became rare, and so "rational, planned, logical . . . Edo" became "unplanned, illogical Tokyo."[90]

Perhaps the hardest evidence for the inauthenticity of urban voluntarism in Japan began with the Meiji era. During this period, and for almost a century thereafter, the government directed itself obsessively — and mobilized the people energetically — toward catching up with the West. In area after area, this involved emulation, both because Japan felt that the West had invented a better mousetrap and because it felt that gaining Western respect required looking and acting familiar, that is, Western — and

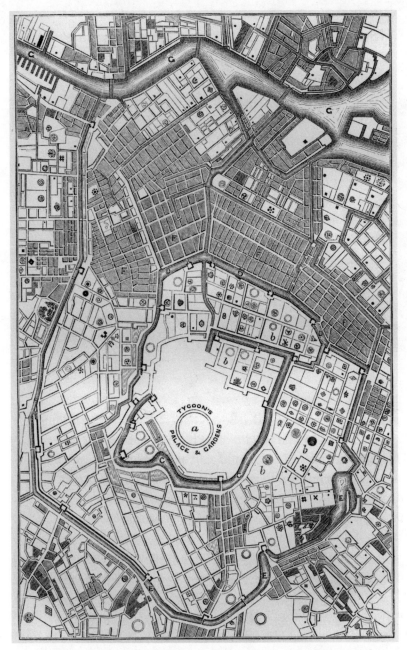

Fig. 11. Edo around 1850: (*a*) Shogun's ("Tycoon's") palace and gardens;
(*b*) residences of the daimyo, with circular marks representing the family crest
of each; (C) inner moat of Shogun's palace; (D) second moat; (E) outer moat;
(F) commercial quarter; (G) Todo River, to which moats and canals connect.

Fig. 12. Disorder? A Tokyo expressway, slashing and swerving its way through the city.

indeed, Tokyo soon featured a large number of Western-style buildings. But a backlash set in, and building after building burned, not to be rebuilt. What prevailed was what I would call "subcontractarian" urbanism, in which the government delegated development to the private sector and to individual landowners, provided infrastructure and incentives to private capital, and regarded subsequent urban evolution as something largely free of political agency.

Again: the sorts of voluntarism visible in Paris do exist in Japan, and not just in Kyoto and Edo. Planners like Gotō Shimpei guided the development of baroque cities in the colonies and also fought for planned reconstruction of Tokyo after the earthquake of 1923; and Suzuki Shunichi, governor between 1979 and 1995, mounted a series of "grand projects" rivaling those of Mitterrand. But Gotō failed in Tokyo, and Suzuki — whose handiwork required every bit of his forty-year career in city hall — is perhaps the exception who proves the rule.

The Invisible Hand: Nature and Nurture in the Capital

In fact, the handiwork that has shaped Tokyo — and shape there is, despite frequent descriptions of the city as "chaotic" — has been more often invisible than visible, in sharp contrast to Paris.[91] Chaos is a misperception, as the effectiveness of Tokyo's urbanism should suggest: "The curious thing about Tokyo to the foreigner is that despite a cityscape that appears confused, incremental, haphazard, and serendipitous, everything seems to function so efficiently."[92] There is pattern, even if there is no plan.

But there is, or was, a plan. In part, it escapes notice because outside observers focus on the material city, whereas the plan is largely social. As I have suggested, authority in Japan is "soft" and "given"; as a corollary, I suggest that the Japanese city is regulated, more than are Western cities, by social relationships, norms, and values. Political ritual plays a major role in all societies, but an exceptionally large one in Confucian societies like Japan's, and, "charmed throughout their history by the punctiliously correct performance of ritual," the Japanese "have made the whole city and its operation a fantastic diurnal ceremony," largely without the aid of a consciously shaped urban setting.[93]

Nonetheless, Tokyo has been clearly patterned over time. In its first centuries, Edo reflected three ordering principles: military/political, topographical, and sociopolitical.[94] In the first place, Ieyasu planned a formidable fortress, encircled by a spiral pattern of interlinked moats, rivers, and canals. This pattern was also, second, superimposed on the natural site, which "governed" the location of the castle on the eastern edge of the high ground.[95]

The third pattern imposed on Edo was in the lowland to the east and north of the castle. Here, in roughly 20 percent of the city, the Tokugawa pursued their sociopolitical goal of separating the classes and subdividing the commoners into discrete blocks. The checkerboard street pattern of eastern Tokyo is still based on this division. Yet as a modern map also shows, it was a pattern which faded across time and space. The grid pattern both unraveled at its edges, where it met other grid-patterned neighborhoods built on different axes, and failed to expand as the commoner population grew. Where rivers and canals were encountered the pattern was altered, as it also was in several instances in order to provide views of distant mountains.[96]

Thus Edo was established on a largely invisible pattern all its own. It was patterned by nodes — temples, junctions, bridges, commoner quarters, and villages — not centers or focal points, as was the case in Paris. The castle was the political center of Edo, but it was not the functional center of the city, and certainly not the center of a strongly concentric growth pattern; rather, growth took the form of filling in the gaps between the nodes. Urban sprawl in Edo did indeed assume a radial aspect, as population spread outward along the major roads; but highways, and especially rail lines, were a wholly new driving force after 1868. This new pattern did not supersede the older ones: the upland-lowland distinction continued, with the salaried middle class eventually replacing the aristocracy in the higher land, and the early subway lines curved around the spiral of moats, as did later elevated highways (as shown in fig. 13), only giving way to a more modern concentric pattern of highways and rail lines farther out.[97] But nodal growth continued: first a star pattern of rail lines poked out into the countryside and spurred linear development; then circular lines linked them and gave rise to concentrations of businesses at the junction stations, and the intervening areas between all these lines gradually filled in.

Thus the old patterns, though no longer clear, play a role in structuring Tokyo in ways different from Paris, but no less pervasively. The original Tokugawa allocation of land to the nobility, which gave the Meiji government the luxury of developing abandoned land rather than redeveloping urban land, meant that the sort of "surgery" performed by Haussmann was not needed to create a modern city.[98] And the nodal growth pattern which typified Edo meant that Tokyo was, from its inception, multinuclear in form. Every great city, in coping with its own size, has probably at least flirted with the idea of growth poles, new towns, or other forms of multipolar development.[99] Paris, for example, has at great effort and expense developed several.[100] Tokyo, while initiating a few, has for the most part preferred simply to promote existing nodes within the metropolis and then wait for the invisible hand of metropolitan expansion to determine which ones prosper.[101]

The implication here, that only visible hands have shaped Paris, is of

Fig. 13. Hidden order: a Tokyo expressway following the old moat, but also, in the interest of practicality, burying Nihonbashi, the most famous bridge in Japan.

course wrong. The tacit influence of topography on Paris's development has been less marked, but not absent. Paris sits in the middle of an ecologically and economically coherent great basin, agriculturally productive and well endowed with minerals, at a "natural convergence" of rivers and trade routes.[102] Other forces, more explicit, have become part of the substructure of Paris. The first is the old Roman grid, mirrored today in the intersection of the St-Michel–Sebastopol and St-Germain axes in particular and the repeated revival of axial development plans in general.[103] After the Roman era died away into the Dark Ages, and the medieval city revived,[104] the city was one of multiple autonomous jurisdictions: royal, academic, occupational, and clerical. The first were concentrated, through no conscious plan, on the Île de la Cité, the second on the Left Bank, the third on the Right Bank, and the last scattered throughout the city. But gradually the city of enclaves gave way, first, to the political power of the king, and second, to the socioeconomic power of the bourgeoisie. This last grew at first tacitly, as the center of urban life moved toward the bustling Place de Grève on the Right Bank, and then overtly, as a new Hôtel de Ville was built in the sixteenth century, symbolizing the independent identity of the city.

In general, visible hands played an ever greater role from that point onward in shaping Paris, with two striking exceptions: the suburbs and the natural environment. Paris grew concentrically, with each new urban ring marked by a new and larger wall, until it filled the wall erected by Thiers in the 1840s. But there the pattern stopped. Outside Paris proper, growth was "tentacular,"[105] following the rail lines as it did in Tokyo, and filling in between them. But in Tokyo, lack of a plan did not prevent the emergence of a tacit order, that is, the creation of a coherent metropolitan system through a network of circumferential lines. In Paris, those who built the railroads were focused on linking Paris with the rest of France, not the suburbs, and their trains served the provinces better than they did the banlieue. Parisian suburbanization, once it got under way in earnest, was dominated by the lower class. The result was utterly unregulated and woefully underserved subdivisions and squatter settlements, and growing "squalour" in contrast to the "magnificence" of Paris *intra muros*.[106] In recent decades this problem has finally been addressed, first by the elimination of the slums, then by public housing (however grimly monolithic) and the gradual extension of the Métro and the Regional Express System (RER) into the suburbs, and finally by the proposal of the A-86 and the Francilienne, major regional highways encircling Paris at a distance.

The final aspect of the tacit ordering of Paris involves nature. Edo was originally sited with mountains and water in mind, and internally structured both by views of distant mountains and by movement on and leisure alongside numerous rivers and canals. And much of Edo was occupied by aristocratic villas with broad grounds, forests, and gardens. It was, to one historian, "the greatest garden city in the world."[107] But this is not the same as saying that nature determined the form of the city; rather, the city determined the form of nature, which in Japan seems to be enjoyed most when it is privatized and subject to human control.

In Paris, like Tokyo, a verdant early modern city, with promenades, grand tree-lined avenues, parks, and gardens, was cut through with streets and rail lines, usurped by factories, and run over, around, and through by the automobile.[108] But in Paris there was a reaction. Admittedly, the salience of nature had to be ratified by visible hands: the creation of new parks, the preservation of the woods of Vincennes and Boulogne, and the role of the Seine in the city were all the work of the government. But there is a tacit element in Parisian culture which is less notable in Tokyo: the idea that Paris's natural environment is part of the heritage of the city, one of its treasures, not something to be bulldozed for the benefit of further growth.[109] So nature and nurture — the invisible and visible hands — combine, with a greater role for the latter in Paris, but with no less an ordered result in the former.

Authority and Anxiety

I have proposed that the nature of authority, and the apprehensions of that authority toward both external and internal threats, account for significant differences in the appearance of Paris and Tokyo. In Paris, the government's hand was relatively visible in the city partly because authority in general was more openly exercised there than in Japan, and partly because that hand, at many moments in time, was shaking with fear.

The impact of such fear fluctuated over time: under the Romans, under Louis XIV, and then in the twentieth century, it was minimal.[110] The succession of walls ringing the city expanded ever outward, but equally important were the fortifications such as the Louvre, the Châtelet, and later the Bastille *within* the city. Such buildings represented insecure and confrontational authority.[111] Walled cities, on the other hand, symbolized the independent identity and wealth of the city itself, and a city with both interior fortresses and external walls — like Paris until 1789 — suggested perhaps the height of opposition between monarch and people.[112]

This opposition waxed and waned; Louis XIV, although he never trusted Paris, removed its walls and preferred to protect the nation as a whole with a string of forts along France's borders.[113] The impact of this was dual: the creation of a ring of boulevards around the city, which grace it to this day, and the evolution of a more relaxed civilian architecture, begun with Henry IV's Place Dauphine and Place des Vosges. With the rise of absolutism, the city was becoming less warlike and more political.

Thiers' vast new city wall reversed this trend, but over time the impact of military considerations on the city was declining as it became more and more apparent that no wall could protect it, given modern weaponry. Ultimately France recognized this and removed the city wall once and for all. But, like the resulting Périphérique and the grand boulevards, residues of the rise and fall of war remain in Paris. Exercise grounds like the Champ-de-Mars are one; the Invalides hospital is another; and the rue de Rivoli — facilitating east-west troop movement in the city — is another. The Parisian skyline and cityscape, far taller than that of Tokyo until quite recently, is a fourth: walled cities were forced to grow upward.[114]

But aside from protecting the capital, the French state sought protection *from* it, and more so in the nineteenth century. Indeed, the troop movements for which the rue de Rivoli was envisioned were intended to quell insurrection in the Marais, not just to repel foreign enemies. Likewise, Thiers' wall was built in a way that does not make much sense unless one realizes that it was as useful against the city as for it.

But the most striking contrast in the form of Paris and Tokyo, as influenced by the government's attitude toward the people, comes not from official fears of the people, but from consideration for them. Ever since the Greek agora and the Roman forum, the citizenry has been a significant factor in Western polities, both national and urban, and consequently in the form of the city. Public plazas and squares for the people to gather in, council halls for their representatives to meet in, grand avenues and vistas and monuments to impress them proliferated in Western cities. And Paris is a city whose form is premised upon an active citizenry, a citizenry whose activism is recognized (if not always welcomed) by the state.

The contrast with Edo/Tokyo could hardly be more stark; indeed, they can historically be described as "cities without citizens."[115] I do not mean that the state excluded them because it distrusted them — although it did — but rather that Japanese authorities have historically simply not very often taken the people explicitly into account, either to mobilize, or impress, or repress, or accommodate them. And the city tells the story. From their beginnings, Japanese imperial capitals featured markets and avenues following the Chinese model, but "no public place where the citizens could gather."[116] Feudal cities were even less accommodating, built with narrow and winding streets which made attack difficult, and public gathering also. Indeed, the castle towns were expendable cities: the elites considered the town around the castle to be part of the battlefield.[117] If it burned, so be it. In contrast to Europe, where fortresses within the city were often designed to protect the lord from the people, in Japan castle towns demonstrated elite disregard for the people.

This is not to say that the government ignored the possibility of crime. As noted earlier, Edo was divided into mutually enclosed neighborhoods. All assemblages were suspect, and spaces for assembly were never provided.[118] Such spaces did emerge, especially at the ends of bridges, in temple and shrine grounds, and in the firebreak avenues cut through the city. But these spaces were all public by appropriation: the people occupied them despite the authorities' wishes. Still, crime was not insurrection, which the state did not fear. The most massive incidents of popular unrest — the food riots of the later Edo era — show this well: typically the government simply let such riots run their course unopposed, moving in after the violence subsided to provide relief and catch a few leaders.[119]

Over the course of the Edo era, the regime actually became more permissive, but never more inclusive of the people. A brief period of inclusion did occur during the Meiji era, when large public plazas, impressive public buildings, and even a few monuments and triumphal arches were constructed. But here again it looks as if these represented a brief interval during which the state was insecure about its legitimacy and eager to show the Western powers that it was just like them. Almost all of these attractions eventually fell to fire, earthquake, or developers, and few remain today. The people continued to appropriate public spaces, like Hibiya Park in central Tokyo. But even with the advent of democracy after World War II, the people have never really become a collective force in shaping the city, and Japan remains to this day noteworthy for the "virtual absence of civil society" in urban policy and planning.[120]

Not only has insurrection been a minor influence on the shape of Tokyo, but so has war, particularly foreign war — until 1945, Japan had been invaded only once, in 1281. Civil war has been a different matter, but historically Japanese warfare has tended to be between armies meeting on far-flung battlefields. This does not mean that the Japanese couldn't "do" fortifications. There is a long historical record of such construction,[121] and the late medieval period saw the appearance of several fortified cities under the control of municipalities themselves or religious sects. The castles of the late sixteenth and early seventeenth centuries were proof of Japanese skill: they were far larger than European or Crusader castles.[122] And the city of Hakodate was the site of a Vauban-style, star-shaped fortress.[123]

But all these feats seem to have been responses to short-term forces rather than reflective of any fundamental approach to social or political order or security, which was better achieved through social and legal arrangements. Ieyasu did build his castle town with guard towers on the castle walls, checkpoints, and a ring of temples guarding the major roads into the capital.[124] Inside the castle everything, from parapets to embrasures to massive gates, right down to the resplendent and awesome artwork, was designed to impress observers with the shogun's power.[125]

But in fact defense was not uppermost in the minds of the Tokugawa when they established their capital in Edo. Had it been, they might well have spurned Edo for a more strategic spot. Edo was sited more for administrative than military reasons: commanding a broad plain, its agricultural economy, and its communications routes, with plenty of room for a city to grow.[126] And in such a situation, security was better achieved by non-material arrangements, such as an extensive network of secret shogunal agents in the lords' domains and the system of alternate attendance, under which the lords were required to spend every other year in Edo, leaving their families there as hostages when they were back in their domains.

In any case, the Edo era was characterized by regulation of society without major restructuring of the capital with an eye to either elite or popular enemies. Initial structure, yes; but as time went on, many of the fortifications fell into disrepair, and commoners encroached upon aristocratic sections of the city. In perhaps the most symbolically important step — or nonstep — when the towering central keep of Edo Castle burned in 1657, it was never rebuilt. Finances were a factor, but it is clear that this was a regime which did not fear for its future.

Such fears did emerge in the mid-nineteenth century, including fears of foreign invasion. But, once again, they did not have much impact on the shape of the city, which sat open to the incoming Westerners. The fighting which accompanied the Restoration in 1868 included a few battles in Edo, but the castle itself was surrendered by the shogunal forces without a fight. And since that time the face of the city, although altered dramatically by the hand of war, has not been significantly altered by the hand of man in response to the exigencies of war, either domestic or foreign.

All of which is to say that the relationship between political authority and city building in Japan has been more passive than in France. Japan has had the luxury of relatively few wars and no real foreign invasions, hideously bloody religious wars, or sanguinary revolutions. Authority has seldom been challenged root and branch, and the rulers have consequently rarely felt the need to let such considerations shape their intentions for their cities. Indeed, they appear — with brief exceptions — to have concerned themselves only infrequently with their cities, and even less with their city-dwellers. But there is more here, I think, than simply the absence of fear. This history is consistent also with a Japanese conception of power as something to be exercised inertially, incrementally, and consensually rather than decisively, discontinuously, and individually. Napoleon III and Haussmann cut through the fabric of Paris in order to turn a medieval city into a modern one. Certainly Ieyasu planned a brand-new city, centered upon a stunning monument to military power. And yet, "where but in Japan could be found so deliberate and so successful an effort to convert the frowns of a fortress into the smiles of a garden, "with tree-shaded earthworks, sweeping lawns, and a flotilla of swans in the palace moat?[127]

CONCLUSION

Thus far I have posed three questions about the overall form of Paris and Tokyo: How different are they? In what ways? And why? In chapters to come, I shall consider the same questions in regard to specific aspects of the cities. A look at the history of the cities confirms my initial impression that Tokyo's form is relatively impermanent, changeable, and unplanned. But I have to back and fill a bit when it comes to order. Paris is obviously highly orderly in appearance and has become more so over time. Edo began life

Fig. 14. Fortress as garden: moat and walls of the Imperial Palace, Tokyo.

as a thoroughly ordered city, even more so than Roman Lutetia, but went straight downhill despite the best efforts of the shogun; modern leaders have hardly even contested the process. But at the same time, under the surface Tokyo is highly orderly socially and administratively, a paradox of invisible order to which we shall return. And by the same token Edo began as a verdant city, planned with external natural features and internal gardens, lakes, and rivers in mind, whereas Paris was in many ways more of a rabbit warren — and the Seine a sewer — until the modern era. But, again paradoxically, Paris has evolved into a tree-lined, Seine-blessed city, while Nature has been fighting a mostly losing battle in Tokyo for more than a century.

The final aspect of urban form of note to the casual observer is the defensive nature of Paris, manifest in closure (by wall or highway), intimidating buildings, and the oozing of authority out of every material pore. Tokyo, by contrast, is — and has been from day one — an open city, and it is clear that city hall and state alike have tended to let the people make of the city whatever they choose. The form of Tokyo today provides little evidence of concern for civil war, insurrection, or invasion. Paris is still ringed by forts, while Battery Six, a tiny wooded islet, sits all alone in Tokyo Bay. Granted, the remnant walls and moats of the Imperial Palace stir images of a mighty fortress, but they lost their military meaning more than three hundred years ago.

So, why? Among the factors we considered, Franco-Japanese differences in esthetics, frequency of natural disasters, architecture and technology, religion, and economics seem most consistent with the variability in permanence apparent in the two cities. As for planning, cultural views of nature and artifice and of both the nature and self-confidence of authority in the two societies are, again, consistent with what we see today.

The question of order is becoming a sticky one. We shall return to it, particularly the notion that French, or Western, culture emphasizes the ordering of the material world, whereas in Japan a disorderly material world — particularly its public space — is not cause for unease. Also, under the broad rubric of religion, we shall look further at the putative Japanese emphasis on social order, achieved by manipulating human relationships, not the relationship between humanity and its built environments. At this point, however, we can at least consider that the nature of authority, and the extent of anxiety among the ruling elites through history, are consistent with the differential foci on order manifest in the physical forms of Paris and Tokyo.

The same goes for explaining the defensive appearance of Paris and the blasé appearance of Tokyo: relative differences in conceptions of power, and how threatened it might be, and by whom, help our understanding. Frequency of disasters also contributes: much of the openness of Tokyo— what public spaces and avenues it does have — is designed for managing disaster, whereas seldom-burned Paris opened avenues in order to facilitate the movement of troops and impress the populace.

Finally, a word of caution. Almost nothing found in Paris or Tokyo is, or was, completely absent in the other. And relative absence is no indication of one culture's inability to achieve anything it sets its mind to. Can the Japanese build city walls? Of course. Can the French achieve social order? Of course. But over centuries these capitals have faced different incentives, established different priorities, and embraced different views of themselves, their societies, and the world which help us to understand why they have chosen the paths they have followed.

3 | FROM CENTER TO PERIPHERY

In addition to the overall impressions gained from a walking tour of Paris and Tokyo, different parts of the cities appear different in form and function, and in the minds of the citizens as well. Four aspects of the center-periphery continuum strike one most sharply: differences in the city centers; the differing clarity of the edges of both the city and the metropolitan region; the treatment and perception of these edges, or "margins"; and the extent of divisions within the city.

IMPRESSIONS

Empty at the Center?

Tokyo was famously described by Roland Barthes in *Empire of Signs* (1982) as having an "empty center," occupied by the great open expanse of the Imperial Palace Plaza and the palace itself, almost completely invisible behind walls and moats. In comparison to the center of Paris — packed with monuments political, religious, and commercial, with plazas, and with the natural treasure of the Seine — central Tokyo certainly does seem rather vacant. Indeed, some theorists are even more sweeping, arguing that Western cities in general are centripetal, and Japanese cities centrifugal or nodal, or that the whole idea of "center" and "periphery" is less helpful in understanding Japanese cities than Western ones.[1]

But aside from the sweeping generality of such views, there is a nagging problem here. If the centers of Japanese cities are more spiritual than concrete, perhaps these centers are just invisible, not empty.[2] The idea of a center which is physically empty but spiritually or symbolically full is not hard to embrace. Indeed, neither the Place de la Concorde nor the Place de la Bastille draws its significance from whatever might sit in its center today; both could be completely vacant but no less pregnant with a legacy of injustice and blood. Thus the nonexistence of anything tangible does not obviate the presence of something intangible. In any case, we must remain open to the possibility that Tokyo's "empty center" might be neither its center nor empty.

Clarity at the Edges

A second impression of Tokyo and Paris is that the latter is far more clearly differentiated from its context. There are a number of possible explanations of why this might be so. First, as suggested earlier, there is a general difference in the extent of holism in our two societies: Western culture has been described as more exclusivist, dualistic, and enamored of dichotomies and binomial oppositions than Japanese.[3] Sacred and secular, mind and matter, public and private, nature and artifice — all have been proposed as sharper categories in the West.

The city-country dichotomy exemplifies this proposition. Paris is starkly divided from its context, while Tokyo — if one can define it at all — merges imperceptibly with what is outside, as figures 15a-b and 16 imply. It has been argued that there is no "antithetical relationship" or "rural-urban opposition" in East Asia in general or Japan in particular, deriving both from a Buddhist avoidance of dichotomies and from the prevalence of organic, naturalistic Shinto beliefs or metaphors.[4] From early on the physical distinction was unclear, and while urban values reigned until the ascendance of the warrior class in the thirteenth century, subsequently they "coexisted" with agrarian ones.[5] Thus Edo, and then Tokyo, became amorphous messes, sprawling across more and more territory and resisting definition by either administrators or residents.

⌃ Fig. 15a. An ambiguous border (1): the house in the middle is in Saitama Prefecture; the one immediately to the right, and the one in the right foreground, are in Tokyo.

⌄ Fig. 15b. An ambiguous border (2): Saitama onions in the background, Tokyo eggplant in the foreground.

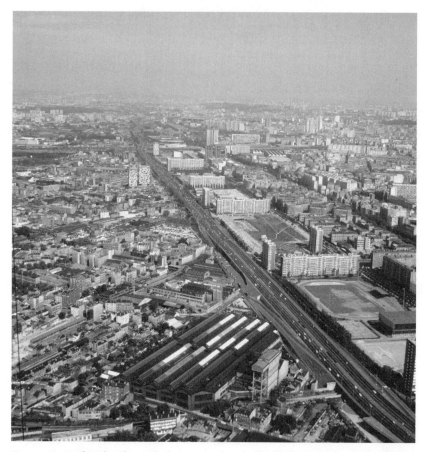

Fig. 16. An explicit border: orderly Paris within (*right*), disorderly suburbs without (*left*), and the new wall — Périphérique highway, green space, and public housing — making sure the twain never meet.

And then there is Paris. Its clarity is fully consistent with an urban-rural division which became visible three millennia ago in the Middle East.[6] The Romans expelled nature from the city, and (along with Judeo-Christian dualism, domination of nature by man, the Pauline implication of sinful nature, and not least the objective dangers of rural life during the Dark Ages) the West was bequeathed a sharply dichotomous image of city and country,[7] which imposed itself on urban form.

The Renaissance saw an increasing aristocratic taste for rural estates, and later a nostalgic rural romanticism. And in the modern age perceptions have come, if not full circle, at least a long way toward privileging the rural. The manifest pathologies of the early industrial Western city no doubt aided this shift. But the important point is the continuing distinction, and antithesis, between the countryside and the city.[8]

And so — for these religious, historical, esthetic, and philosophical reasons, perhaps, and for others to be considered in later chapters — we have Paris: distinguishable, with crystal clarity, from the outside world both physically and psychically. The "other reasons" mentioned by observers include most prominently the coherence of the city as an administrative, fiscal and economic, or military entity. Since at least Greco-Roman antiquity, politics in the West was associated with the city, as the words *polis, civis,* and *civitas* indicate, and cities were seen as administrative units.[9] By the Middle Ages, Western cities had also developed more or less autonomous administrative structures, with accompanying legal structures and an underpinning stratum of burghers.[10]

Where administrative identity was reinforced by walls — which were almost everywhere in Western Europe — the distinction between urban and exurban was accentuated. Walls were symbols of sovereign power, social markers, esthetic differentiators, clarifiers of legal jurisdiction, popular unifying structures, and mechanisms of social control over the urban populace itself.[11] And Paris, of course, fits this description to a T.

As a politico-administrative unit, Tokyo — like other Japanese cities — has been harder to grasp. The earliest Japanese words for politics derived from the religious term *matsurigoto,* and the word for capital (*miyako*) referred simply to wherever the ruler was; neither had any urban connotation.[12] And, conversely, the word for city (*shi* or *ichi*) implied a market or locus of religious observance, with no political implication.[13] The absence of walls or administrative clarity in general also challenged successive Japanese governments; the Tokugawa state, for its part, wrestled for more than two hundred years with the definition of Edo, drawing lines hither and yon.[14]

Economically, too, Edo and Tokyo stand in contrast to Paris. Paris's borders were until well into the twentieth century the limits of the detested *octroi,* or tax on goods entering the city. On the other hand, after the mid-1700s Parisians were exempted from the *taille,* the land tax.[15] The overall effect, we may surmise, was to emphasize the boundaries of the city. Indeed, one of Paris's walls was that of the Farmers-General (tax collectors), built in the 1780s; its function was purely fiscal, with tollhouses at every entrance.[16]

Such fiscal significance never attached to the edges of Edo or Tokyo. The dominant revenue source during the Tokugawa era was a land tax, from which urbanites were largely exempt. But such taxes often followed landownership, not city limits: an urbanite with rural property might well pay taxes on it.[17] And ever since, national standardization in matters fiscal has been the rule.

This leaves military considerations in our speculation about the clarity of city edges, and here the Western literature fueling our suspicions is abundant. Western historians often equate cities with walls, and walls with wars. The relationship between walls and wars may be reciprocal: war leads to walls, and fortified cities themselves were "incentives to aggression."[18]

It was not always thus. Greek cities were walled as an afterthought, as the need arose,[19] and Rome for long based its security on the well-guarded borders of its empire. The turning point came in A.D. 259, when the Germans broke into the empire and a wave of wall building began which — in France, at least — did not cease until the nineteenth century.[20] The elaboration of urban fortifications made them ever more costly; it is thus unsurprising that Paris, for example, let its walls decay or tore them down whenever foreign threats subsided.[21] But every time threat reappeared, the walls went up again.

Japan has no parallel, and not without reason: until the modern era, war was "unusual" in Japan; even the extended civil wars of the sixteenth century constituted a "departure from a more durable order."[22] And, until 1945, Japan was never successfully invaded. Certainly there was warfare, but against the Mongols in 1281 fortifications were built on the south coast at predicted invasion sites, and during the civil wars it was the castle, not the town, which was seen as worthy of protection.[23] Thus it is tempting to see

the Japanese as living in a less fearful state, and as not seeing fortified, visually defiant cities as the solution to whatever fears they might have felt.

Questions at the Margins

No society embraces all individuals, ideas, or activities with equal openness. All demonstrate some form of exclusiveness, whether based on gen-
der, ethnicity, socioeconomic position, morality, religion, or whatever. But
different societies include and exclude on different criteria, and because
societies build cities in their own self-images, it is possible that inclusion
and exclusion are inscribed on different cities in different ways as well.
These impressions of Tokyo and Paris in particular give rise to the suspicion that Paris is far more uncomfortable with the concept of "margins"
than is Tokyo.

This is consistent with my earlier suggestion that Westerners are more
enthusiastic dichotomizers than are the Japanese; in any case, the periphery
of Tokyo seems at first glance less problematic than that of Paris, in a variety
of ways. Paris has for centuries pushed questionable groups and activities
to its edges more concertedly than has Tokyo. And despite the premodern
vertical segregation of Parisian society, the persistence of poverty-stricken
îlots insalubres in the city center, and certain affluent suburbs, in general the
geographic margins of Paris have been its social margins also.[24] This tendency accelerated during the nineteenth century; Haussmann's downtown
projects resulted in higher rents which the working class could not afford,
leading to the emergence around the city of a peripheral mélange of helter-
skelter subdivisions, working-class neighborhoods, centers of debauchery,
and encroaching, illegal squatter shantytowns in the "Zone" outside the
wall. After World War II, the grands ensembles added to this mix huge
public housing projects occupied first by the working class and increasingly
by the immigrant poor.

Up to a point Edo was similar:[25] cemeteries, crematoria, execution
grounds, outcast ghettoes, and "pleasure quarters" were relegated to the
edges of the city. But once modernization began, the city exploded outward
and new rail lines enabled a commuter class to leapfrog the old margins and
create a solidly middle-class suburban world.[26] The best-known present-day

slum, Sanya, is in central Tokyo. As for the suburbs, they are architecturally and socioeconomically mainstream. Indeed, there is no such word in
common parlance in Japan as *banlieue*. There are words for "suburb," but
for the most part the suburbs are in matter and in mind simply extensions
of the city.

Divisions within the City

As this last implies, one might also expect fewer internal divisions in Tokyo
than in Paris, but in fact this does not initially appear to be the case. What
we see, rather, is a Tokyo which is internally differentiated but merges in
a blur with its context, and a Paris set sharply apart from the world *extra
muros* but increasingly homogeneous in socioeconomic structure and physical form.

If "form follows fear and vice versa" in the evolution of cities,[27] the city
walls of Paris clearly manifest such fears. But there have also stood within
the city fortresses like the Louvre and the Bastille, suggesting an equal
concern with popular threats. A more neutral functionalism also played
an earlier role, with clerical and governmental buildings in the Louvre–
Châtelet–Île de la Cité area, commerce spreading outward from the river-
bank Place de la Grève, and academia on the Left Bank.

Over time, both functional concentrations and internal fears faded, and
the trend toward ever higher land prices and rents thrown into high gear by
Haussmann has led to the ever more thorough *embourgeoisement* of Paris.
Those who do not fit this model have been marginalized in the northeast
quadrant of the city, the last step before being excluded altogether.

Tokugawa Japan in toto was created on a differentiated model, and
within Edo, warriors and commoners were segregated both mutually and
internally.[28] But my impression there differs from my impression of Paris:
these physical differences seem driven less by fear and more simply by an
ideal sociopolitical order.[29] The Tokugawa wanted stasis and thought this
best achieved by creating an unchanging society of orders and mirroring it
in urban space. But they do not seem to have feared the capital's populace
the way the French state did. It is clear that the Japanese are capable of
dichotomization, exclusion, and clear distinctions in city design. But their
hearts do not seem to be in it. Over time the clear segregation within Edo

blurred, as the commoner population sprawled in all directions, even into what were once the warrior quarters inside the moats. Once the modern urbanization of Tokyo began, intra-urban differences faded even more. The government did not necessarily want this; indeed, the Meiji state seriously considered expelling the urban poor by means of urban redevelopment, à la Haussmann.[30] But this plan fizzled, and it was the white-collar middle class that moved to the suburbs. Certain distinctive pockets — mostly slums of Koreans and outcasts — remained, but in general the edges of "social areas" of the city are as blurred as the edges of the city itself. Today the little slums are gone, and there appears to be more socioeconomic mixing in Greater Tokyo than in Paris.[31] In contrast to both the United States (suburban middle-class flight from inner-city fears) and Paris (suburban exile of the lower class), Tokyo's suburbanization reflects overwhelmingly the nonexclusive, nondefensive aspiration of a middle class for a better lifestyle.

EVIDENCE

The Meretricious Vacancy

So it appears, from our tour of the cities, that Tokyo may be more internally differentiated than Paris — with a possibly more vacant center — but less objectively *and* subjectively divided by inside and outside. The first of these impressions to be examined is the notion of Tokyo's empty center, made famous by Barthes. But the evidence suggests that Barthes was misled: although the concept of "center" may be problematic in Tokyo, the center to which he referred is anything but empty.

If what Barthes meant was that the whole concept of centrality ill fits Tokyo, the evidence backs him better. In the first place, the city was itself an agglomeration of villages and thus multinucleated from its beginning. Second, Edo always had two centers. Its physical center was the castle, the point of origin of the spiral pattern of moats and walls. Its "functional" center, on the other hand, was around Nihonbashi (Japan Bridge) in the commercial quarter to the east of the castle.[32]

But evidence such as the above does not directly address Barthes' comment. To do so, I would argue that the center of which he spoke — the Imperial Palace and its surroundings — is symbolically not empty but full and physically not empty but closed. Moreover, this center has not always been empty: the area became so in 1657. The real question is, Why was it not refilled?

The center of Tokyo "symbolizes the invisible power of the imperial system."[33] The Shinto religion, of which the emperor is the symbolic high priest, is "based on the worship of mana,"[34] and the palace grounds are full of it. A space is not empty when it is a "controlled, used, appreciated, enclosed space." The palace grounds are all of these, and a space so enclosed — by a structure, a perimeter, or a purpose — is "already full."[35] You can hardly see it; yet "to the perceptive and reasonably well informed visitor, the palace is very much *there*."[36] It "suggests the encompassing presence of mysterious divinity."[37]

The Tokugawa shoguns enhanced this, creating an image of rule based on absence, not revelation. They voluntarily rejected the "power of visual display" so popular among European rulers.[38] Accordingly, they created in Edo a "closed core" for the state,[39] disseminating as little information as possible and never feeling that the overt display of authority was essential to its exercise. After the Restoration, the emperor moved into the palace, and the tradition of imperial invisibility was superimposed on Tokugawa practice.

So, contrary to impressions, the palace is symbolically full and physically closed, but not empty. But this still begs the question, Why? The former quality derives simply from the emperor's coming in 1868; until then the mana quotient of Edo Castle was probably zero. The latter derives from the nature of power in Japan. It was only in their early years that the Tokugawa felt the need to advertise their power, and after the castle's main keep burned down in 1657, it was never rebuilt. A fancy new palace was built on the site for the emperor after the Restoration; it too burned, in 1944, and its replacement is so low-profile as to be essentially invisible.

Inside and Outside

My initial impression was that the physical identity of Paris is far clearer than is that of Tokyo, and I offered a number of reasons as to why this might in fact be so. Now we may look a little closer at some of the clearest reasons for clarity of the city's edges in the areas of (1) general (perhaps administrative or fiscal) preference or need for clear definition, (2) walls, and (3) the development of urban transportation.

A closer look at French history might suggest that my first impression was a bit overblown. Certainly there have been periods of ambiguity — most markedly under Louis XIV, when Paris was open. Many observers have noted how Parisian growth overran attempts to define it; by the seventeenth century, "centrifugal forces were breaking the old city apart," and the eighteenth-century writer Nicolas Restif de la Bretonne declared that "Paris devours its surroundings."[40] In the twentieth century, references and concerns increasingly focused on, first, the "small crown" of suburban departments, then the "large crown" of more distant ones, then a set of "cities within an hour" of Paris, and most recently the "greater Parisian basin."

But the state has fought such trends, both administratively and physically. During the seventeenth and eighteenth centuries, there were "constant" reissues of edicts setting and enforcing the city limits.[41] Even when Paris was unwalled, the limit of the octroi made it quite clear where the city ended. The elimination of the last wall in the early twentieth century could have ushered in a more open era, but instead it was replaced by a new "wall," discussed below. All this was certainly administrative, fiscal, and military in origin, but it is also at least consistent with a more general desire to distinguish Paris from the rest of the world.

The Japanese, for their part, are equally capable of drawing excruciatingly clear lines, including those between public and private spaces and different parts of communities.[42] But historically we do not see it — Edo was undefined from the very beginning. Part of the reason for this was military: Tokugawa Ieyasu chose to protect his castle not with a walled city but with an outer ring of vassals, each with his own castle at some remove from Edo. Additionally, he divided much of the region administratively, with multiple lords having responsibility for patchwork territories and pieces of single villages; this made administration confusing, but it also made alliances between potential enemies very difficult.[43]

A second way in which Edo was delimited — again, fuzzily — was religious: a ring of temples on the outskirts of the city which kept evil spirits at bay.[44] Some have also argued that these outlying temples in Edo served a secular defensive purpose as well, positioned as they were on all the main roads toward the city.[45] But if this is so, they were — standing in mutual isolation — hardly a definitive barrier.

Just as Edo was encircled spiritually but not physically, it was encircled legally but not physically. Commercial activities were banned in the countryside, and warrior residence was restricted to the cities.[46] But the combination of economic and demographic change broke the limits down: rustics flowed into the city, the suburbs sprawled, and commercial activities infiltrated the villages.[47] Ultimately, defining Edo became "almost impossible." The jurisdiction of the city magistrates was one Edo; the boundaries of authorized religious solicitations comprised another; the area forbidden to those banished from the city was a third. In 1818, the shogunate drew a "red line" around what it recognized as Edo, but this space was larger than the magistrates' and was under separate authority.[48] Throughout the era, neither military nor administrative, nor fiscal, nor esthetic considerations were apparently sufficient to lead the shogunate to resolve all these anomalies.

Drawing the Line: Ramparts and Railroads

The most definitive — and historically popular — way to resolve such ambiguities was to construct city walls.[49] Walls were not always militarily necessary, and could actually be militarily counterproductive, inspiring hostility and fear in both neighbors and citizens.[50] In most cases, however, even if military necessity cannot be seen, administrative and fiscal rationales are present. But the causality of city walls is sufficiently complex that one is, again, reluctant to dismiss the suspicion that for much of human history less tangible forces were at work.

We could trace Western city walls back to Sumer, I suppose, but Greece will do. Classical Greece and Rome represent a hiatus between earlier ages and later: for long periods, both Athens and Rome (and Roman Paris) were unwalled. But all were eventually walled in by force of circumstance, and walls became the rule.[51] For Paris, the transformation came in the third century A.D., when the Germans overran the empire and initiated a period of urbanization driven by fear, and "walled cities replaced an older image of rural tranquility and peace."[52]

But vestiges of the fourth-century Roman walls of Paris are almost totally gone, as are those of a wall built on the Right Bank by Louis VI in the early twelfth century. The "modern" history of the walls of Paris thus begins with Philippe Auguste, whose wall enclosed roughly 630 acres, with fourteen gates. It was the first to encompass both banks of the Seine, thus turning Paris from a collection of towns into a city, and the first to represent a complex of motives.[53] Defense was of course a consideration, but so was the subjugation of the church, a number of whose estates were cut off, or cut up, by the wall. And real estate valorization was also a goal: what was now inside the wall became more valuable, and encouraged urban development. And of course there was the octroi. Indeed, Philippe's wall was not militarily well sited: there are heights on both the Right Bank and the Left which, tactically, should have been enclosed but were not. And then there is the fortress of the Louvre, which completed the wall but could also be used, "if necessary," to control Paris itself.[54] In any case, Philippe's wall set a tone. In the late fourteenth century, Charles V built a new wall on the Right Bank, enhancing siege protection, and in the 1630s, Louis XIII extended the wall to fully incorporate the Louvre into the city.

By then the worst, militarily, was over, but the yen to enclose did not cease. This was partly because by then walls and urban development had produced a "powerful dialectic," and because of the octroi.[55] Louis XIV ordered the elimination of the walls in 1670, replacing them with circular boulevards and promenades with roundabouts and triumphal arches at the major junctions.[56] It looks as if, for a while, Paris might have begun to merge with its context. But the tax collectors continued their demands for limits on suburban growth and for controls on commerce. Finally, in the 1780s, the Farmers'-General wall was built. Purely fiscal in function, no more than a meter thick and 3 to 4 meters high, it was an "anachronism" in the free-trade eighteenth century and vanished from city maps "almost instantly"; its major function seems to have been to anger the people.[57] But it more than doubled the area of Paris proper — to about 8,200 acres — and although the city came nowhere near filling the space enclosed by the wall, the wall did fill the pockets of the Farmers-General.

For a while, at least. But further urban growth, combined with the wars of Napoleon, once again created incentives for walling in a bigger area, and in the 1840s, Paris's penultimate wall — Thiers' elaborate construction —

Fig. 17. The old fortifications of Paris, 1870s, with bastions, dry moat, free-fire zone, and a few leftover cannon.

was built. It was the biggest yet: 33 kilometers of wall enclosing almost 20,000 acres, with a 6-meter parapet, a 40-meter external ditch, a 250-meter glacis, and then a 500-meter belt of open land.[58] But it had two problems. First, it was militarily obsolete when built. Second, it enclosed a lot of nonurban land. The city limits did not move out to the new wall; thus there was now a major discrepancy between Paris and the area — again as large, with several hundred thousand inhabitants[59] — outside the city but inside the wall. This area soon became a morally, juridically, and economically problematic zone — and a frightening one as well. This problem was resolved in 1860 by Haussmann, who annexed everything inside the wall.

The military failure of Thiers' wall was clear to all, and its demolition began in the 1920s, but it was succeeded in midcentury by Paris's final wall: the Périphérique expressway and the belt of housing projects which filled the vacated space. The military imperative was gone, but technological, political, and socioeconomic considerations replaced it. And there is even more to Paris's last wall than this (see chap. 6).

In Japan, on the other hand, there was less. This is not to say that the

Japanese could not, if they chose, "do" walls or fortifications. Early settlements sometimes had wooden palisades, Kyoto was minimally walled, and a wall was built along Hakata Bay in the thirteenth century to defeat a predicted Mongol invasion.[60] During the sixteenth century, Japan did pass through a short-lived phase of walled cities, although considering the extent of civil warfare, it is curious that so little was done. These walled cities were the *jinaimachi,* or temple towns, quasi-autonomous communities centered upon Buddhist temples and designed to protect their inhabitants from the ongoing civil wars.[61] But the warring lords, who allowed such enclaves to exist while they focused their warfare on each other, eradicated them in the drive toward national unification at the end of the sixteenth century.

Their successors were the castle towns which, while formidably fortified, were unwalled. Edo Castle was the culmination of this tradition.[62] Such vast castles were essentially "cannon-proof," and "to all intents and purposes, impregnable until the age of aerial bombardment."[63] But, although the castle and its grounds were designed to reflect the sociopolitical structure, the incorporation of rivers and canals into the spiral structure of moats and walls meant that from very early on, the outer fortifications cut through the city such that there were commoners, warriors, and even lords both inside and outside the moat system.[64] As protection for the city the fortifications were meaningless,[65] and in the absence of military or insurrectionary threats, the fortifications were allowed to fall into disrepair.

So we see anomalous situations in which there was no apparent need for walls in Paris, but walls nonetheless, and an apparent need in Japan which did not lead to walls. When we turn to contemporary analogues of walls, again, the contrast is clear. I have in mind here modern transportation networks: roads and rail lines. Certainly such media can either link or separate parts of cities: it seems clear to me that in Paris they have tended to perform the latter function; in Tokyo, the former.

Japan's modern rail system, from its inauguration in 1872, was designed to bring at first foreigners (from the seaport of Yokohama) and then everyone else straight into the middle of Tokyo. In 1885, a loop line around the western edge of the city linked the line up from Yokohama to the main line to Tokyo from the north; after some intermediate steps, Tokyo Station opened in 1914, indirectly connecting the main lines to the north and south and completing a loop (the Yamanote line) entirely around the central part of Tokyo.[66] Thus Japan's leaders, in two respects, created a rail system which integrated rather than separated the metropolis. First, they built a main station in the middle of the city, with connections to everywhere. Second, they built a loop line, the nodes of which became termini for a host of suburban and long-haul lines heading outward. This loop line thus does not separate any part of Tokyo from any other, or Tokyo from its context; rather, it pulls the entire metropolitan area together.

In fact, Tokyo differed from Paris in a third way, which also integrated the capital region. From early on, trams supplemented railways, cutting across the inside of the Yamanote loop. These were gradually replaced, beginning in 1927, by subways which, unlike the Paris Métro, were linked into the railways so that, in more and more instances, one could board a downtown subway which would go straight onto the railway tracks farther out and continue well into the suburbs. Today there are more than 2,000 kilometers of suburban rail lines around Tokyo,[67] and the Yamanote line has been complemented by a number of circumferential rail lines which integrate the suburbs with one another.

The modern transportation system of Paris (divisible into rail and subway) has been far different in intents, explicit purposes, and implications for the city.[68] In the first half of the nineteenth century, the purpose of France's rail system was primarily to link Paris with everywhere else, and its form was radial. So was Japan's, but here the similarity stops, because in Paris a series of stations was built around the edges of the central area, making connections through Paris inconvenient, and the rail lines had few suburban stations, being designed to pull other regions to Paris, not to integrate the capital region. Omnibuses ran throughout the city proper, and Haussmann might have approximated the integrative function of Tokyo's Yamanote line with his Petite Ceinture rail line, which ran around the inside of Thiers' wall.[69] But this line (although complemented by another circle line outside the wall)[70] had no extensions beyond the city wall; in any case, it was eliminated in 1940, putting an end to any circumferential supplement to the basically radial system. By this time, suburban rail stations had proliferated, replacing (along with buses) the omnibus and later tram lines which had gradually penetrated the suburbs. But the major replacement for the omnibus and trams was the Métro, whose purpose was far from integrative.

The Métro, in fact, was a political football from its inception: for twenty years the state and Paris fought over it. The state wished it to integrate the rail system by linking Paris's stations, and to serve the suburbs; the city feared "encroachment" by the state-owned rail system and a population drain to now easily accessible suburbs: a wide-ranging Métro would "enrich [the suburbs] and ruin the heart of Paris," which would become "a city of work by day, deserted at night."[71] The state finally gave in, in 1895. The first line opened in 1900, and the city made sure that the state would not attempt to take over later: it built the tunnels too small for trains to pass,[72] thus preventing exactly the sort of interlinked rail system created in Tokyo. So the Métro became a vehicle of intracity integration only; it was not until 1928 that the decision was made to extend it into the suburbs.[73] Today the twenty-one Métro lines average only 2.5 stops outside the city.[74]

The appalling state of intraregional public transit was finally addressed after World War II, as a series of new public entities integrated the Métro, trams, and buses; the state systems and those of the eight departments of the Paris Region; and finally a unified intraregional ticket.[75] One can now go from Marne-la-Vallée to Cergy-Pontoise with only one change. Two new radial lines, the SNCF's Éole and the RATP's Météor, serve the suburbs ever better, and two outlying circumferential lines — the Orbitale — are in the works.[76] Within Paris a new tram loop line is planned for the inside of the Périphérique, reviving Haussmann's Petite Ceinture. But Paris's transit system is still largely engaged in overcoming its past.

Nowhere is this more visible than in the Périphérique, Paris's new wall. When Thiers' wall was demolished, 1,125 acres of military property and a 2,000-acre field of fire were liberated.[77] They were, however, filled in by buildings, creeping development, and, in the 1960s, by the Périphérique itself. Physically, the Périph' sharply demarcates the edge of the city.[78] Psychically, too, it is a powerful marker: a recent movie about discrimination against suburbanites, entitled *The Other Side of the Périph'*, was well translated into English as *The Other Side of the Tracks*.

One could explain the existence of the Périphérique simply in terms of amelioration of Paris's traffic problems and available space, much as Paris's housing problems were ameliorated by the mass of "social housing" projects sited there. And if traffic problems plus housing shortage plus vacant land were enough to explain the disposition of the spaces of the former wall, Ockham's Razor suggests we should stop there. But the green-belt option was seriously considered, and the creation of a new wall was foreseen and warned against; the simplest explanation may not be the fullest. In any case, the sharp demarcation of the edges of Paris remains overwhelming.

Distinctions at the Margins

"Margins" and "edges" are synonymous in many settings, but I have conceived them differently, in two ways. First, by margins I refer to transitional zones, not edges.[79] Second, "margins" has a strong normative aspect: edges are objective; margins (and marginal people) are subjectively — and usually negatively — perceived. To the extent that margins are objective, however, the evidence suggests that Tokyo, paradoxically, has far larger margins but a smaller marginal population than does Paris. The residents of Tokyo's margins are mainstream, whereas Paris has numerous marginals both (diminishingly) inside and (increasingly) outside the city. And Tokyo's margins have done nothing but grow, essentially since 1600, whereas Paris's margins grew until the time of Haussmann, and since then have shrunk, replaced more and more by clear edges.

As noted above, there was a correlation between margins and marginals in Edo: transgressive institutions were found along the city's edges. But over time such activities remained relatively fixed while the city's population progressively invaded the countryside. After modernization began in the late nineteenth century, the correlation between margins and marginals weakened, especially after suburban commuter rail lines began to extend outward.[80] The margins grew, seemingly without limit, and today the mix of residential, commercial/industrial, and agricultural land uses extends more than 100 miles in some directions. By 1910, the Tokyo transit system was carrying a half million people per day, in a city of 2 million; today Tokyo is perhaps the most transit-dependent city in the world, with plans for more than 200 additional kilometers of rail and subway lines by 2020.[81] And, significantly, planned extensions of the system are primarily intended to integrate the suburban margins further, both with each other and with downtown.

But these rail riders are the solid, hardly marginal, middle class. However, Tokyo is not without marginals, so where are they? Scattered all over the city, in small pockets. The closest thing to the old pleasure quarters might be Kabuki-chō, a wonderfully sleazy labyrinth of bars and nightspots near the Shinjuku city subcenter. One can see the homeless in train and subway stations, in the corners of parks, and under bridges and rail overpasses. A significant population lives in the relatively dilapidated wooden apartments along the western arc of the Yamanote line. But only the Sanya "slum" in northeastern Tokyo still retains its geographical identity, even though it would strike many Westerners, visually, as nothing more than an orderly working-class neighborhood.

Paris's margins, by contrast, have contracted dramatically over the last century and a half. Until then, despite walls and octroi, Paris was surrounded by a "limbo landscape" of cemeteries, abattoirs, garbage dumps, cheap taverns and inns, and so forth.[82] Thiers' wall, far from reducing this, expanded it by encompassing a large zone which remained, however, outside the city limits, and also by creating the 500-meter no-build zone outside the wall, which was too tempting to squatters to stay vacant for long. The result was a wide band of muddy alleys, jerry-built structures, and marginal enterprises, a "shapeless and dangerous magma."[83]

The first steps in eliminating the margins (but not the marginals) were taken by Haussmann, by annexing to Paris all land inside the wall. Urban redevelopment both physically eliminated central-city slums and enhanced the value of property to the point that many of the poor could no longer pay the elevated rents; both measures pushed many people out of the city. Thus Haussmann strengthened the correlation between physical margins and socioeconomic marginalism.

But this still left the "Zone" just outside the wall, a visually distinctive "great encampment of misery" at "the end of the world," between the city and the suburbs.[84] It reproduced, at a slightly greater remove, the zone inside the wall that Haussmann had expelled, and survived until after World War II. In the interim, periodic efforts were made to integrate both the suburbs and the margins with the city: new towns, metropolitan transpor-

Fig. 18. Barbarians at the gates (1): a suburban Paris slum just outside the wall, early twentieth century.

tation networks, and regional development projects were proposed. But Greater Paris continued as three worlds: the city itself, its suburbs, and a problematic — but visually distinctive — band in between.

After the war, Paris's margins gradually shrank in a wave of slum clearance and redevelopment, and Paris became perhaps the world's most clear-edged city.[85] This did not mean the integration of marginal people into the mainstream, but the French state is as opposed to marginalism as Paris seems opposed to margins, and incessant and sincere (and sometimes coercive) efforts have been made to integrate marginals — immigrants in particular — into mainstream French culture and society. To be sure, the French are more tolerant of ethnic and cultural diversity than are the Japanese. Nevertheless the hypothesis remains strong that clarity of edges — between both Paris and the outside, and between those who are part of French republican culture and those outside — is more attractive to the French than are imprecise zones at the margin. But margins are far easier to eliminate physically than socioeconomically or psychologically, and Paris has a long road ahead of it.

Distinctions within the City

Tokyo and Paris both have internal divisions. Tokyo's is epitomized by the lowland-upland-suburb continuum, Paris's by the east-west cleavage; in both cases, there are strong correlations between locale and land values, rents, incomes, demographics, and so forth. Both cities have distinguishable central business districts and government centers, although the diaspora of state ministries within Paris is reducing the concentration there. And Tokyo is also different in the clarity of places representing age-old villages swallowed by the city. But the major difference, it appears to me, is that Paris is a more homogeneous city, while Tokyo accepts more internal variety. In Paris, the differences and divisions seem to have a more physical aspect; in Tokyo, they are relatively social and cultural. Thus marginals are excluded physically from Paris but isolated socially within Tokyo.

Medieval Paris was highly differentiated internally: royal, ecclesiastical, and academic zones, and occupationally distinctive neighborhoods, were easily discernible, and the looming fortresses of the Bastille, Louvre, and Châtelet physically highlighted the divisions between elites and the people. But in succeeding centuries, despite a concentration of aristocratic residences in the east, the typical pattern was mixing, with rich and poor living side by side and even, later, on different floors of the same building.

By the mid-nineteenth century, however, all this had been transformed. The Revolution began, in a sense, at the Bastille in eastern Paris, and the east is still the center of revolutionary symbolism. Western Paris became the more prosperous sector, the home of the *haute bourgeoisie* and the focal point of imperial and national symbolism and monumentality. The lower classes were increasingly pushed to the east, and then out, and the old pattern of multiclass neighborhoods broke down,[86] reinforcing the east-west and inside-outside divisions.

In present-day Paris, three trends stand out in relation to the internal divisions of the city. The first — which does not distinguish Paris from Tokyo — is the depopulation of the central business district and the emergence, after dark, of a dual city of living and dead neighborhoods.[87] The second is the effort at socioeconomic enhancement of the city's east and reduction of the gap between east and west. A number of ministries, museums, cultural facilities, the new national library, and other state projects have been located in the east, to this end. The driving force here is political: the state's preoccupation with republican equality and social "solidarity." The third trend is Paris's response to globalization, which has also — in its most prominent manifestation — been excluded from the city and quarantined in La Défense. The causation here, one suspects, is largely esthetics mediated by politics: in a completely free real estate market, it is likely that central Paris would have become home to the headquarters of multinational corporations. True, the corporations have had more elbow room outside the central business district. But it is also true that the market has never been accorded supremacy in France. The heart, and the state, have their reasons.

Tokyo, on the other hand, not only was built from the outset upon internal divisions but has preserved these divisions more than has Paris, including the division between the global and the local. These divisions, however — unlike those of Paris — have been more social in nature and less reflected in the built form of the city. Tokyo's internal divisions today are similar to those of prerevolutionary Paris, when different classes mixed physically but maintained their disparate identities socially.

These divisions began with clear physical distinctions between internally homogeneous neighborhoods of commoners and warriors.[88] In time the commoner population spread into the area inside the moats,[89] but this apparently did not concern the regime, because class distinctions — in dress, manner, speech, residential design, and a host of sumptuary regulations — remained clear even when not reinforced by the form of the built environment. And when the feudal system collapsed in 1868, so did the political rationale for physical divisions within the city. The result was a huge degree of physical mixing within the city, which did not, however, overwhelm the exquisite differentiations of the social hierarchy.

That mixing has continued to this day. The identity of the old downtown and uptown, though less distinct than before, is still reflected in a continuum of the city's wards.[90] Mini–central business districts have sprung up in Ikebukuro, Shinjuku, Shibuya, and, more recently, farther out in Kichijōji. The slums and ghettoes of outcasts and ethnic Koreans have vanished or merged with their surroundings. Distinctive cityscapes remain, among them the amusement districts of Harajuku, Roppongi, and Kabuki-chō; the upscale residential neighborhoods of Denen Chōfu and Seijō; the suburban danchi; and the centers of long-swallowed villages. But the real distinctions in Tokyo are reflected not in architecture or urban form but in attitudes and behavior: the social hierarchy is still elaborate, and the former outcasts and Korean-Japanese are still discriminated against. And foreigners are still outside the tribe. The Meiji government tried to restrict them to the seaports, and then (after they pushed their way in) to the Tsukiji section of Tokyo. In 1945, the Japanese government at first hoped to keep the American occupation limited to neighboring Kanagawa Prefecture.[91] And some suggested in the 1990s that the new Waterfront City Subcenter might become a ghetto for foreigners and their businesses.

But overall, despite the physical differences within the city, it is the social and cultural dimensions of difference which really set Tokyo apart. Insofar as the cityscape is any measure, market-driven globalization has been given free rein in Tokyo, but the result is the growth of several centers of global economic activity within the city rather than their concentration beyond the city's edge. The evidence still seems to support the impression that internal differentiation is greater, and inside-outside differentiation less, in Tokyo than Paris.

CONCLUSION

As one walks outward from the center of Paris, one passes from a center full of monuments, congested plazas, architectural wonders, and riverine promenades and vistas, through an — again — architecturally wondrous and monumentally well-endowed, but relatively consistent cityscape. And then one comes up against the Périphérique, and, unless one is willing to hunt around, that is where the tour ends. Suddenly Paris ends, with almost no ambiguous transitional margin; what is outside is unquestionably not Paris — neither to the eye, nor to the Parisian mind. The transition is abrupt, has been for many, many years, and is not going away. The interior is undergoing a campaign of east-west equalization, or rebalancing, and the region is being better knit together. Some of those still in the city are marginal to its society. But the edges of Paris are as clear as they have ever been.

A similar trip out from the center of Tokyo (best not attempted on foot) begins in a space of intangible fullness: the Palace Plaza is wide open, with gravel walks, lawns, and small pines, but you know that somewhere behind the walls lies the linchpin of Japan's historical political, cultural, and spiritual identity. You are denied access; better to turn around and head outward, through a teeming and endlessly variegated city, with enclaves of all sorts filled in between with low-rise urban residential development. And somewhere along the way the density of buildings begins to decline and the frequency of cabbage patches increases, and only thus do you realize that you are on the margins of the city. But really to get outside, you have to keep going, on and on, like the salarymen who commute from 100 miles away on the Bullet Train. And even when you realize that you are no longer in Tokyo, unless you have gone east or south across a river, you have no idea when you crossed from inside to outside.

So these cities continue to diverge before our eyes. But why? The evidence suggests that in their centers there are deep, basic cultural differences — in conceptions of authority, of centrality, and of religion — behind what we see. Moving outward, Tokyo's topography, its Edo-era administration, and its social differentiation created a legacy of variation; France's unitary state and a different concept of how to control society (by expelling undesirables rather than controlling them socially in situ) are consistent with its internal form, a form elaborated and intensified by Haussmann's policies. But also, the form of the city suggests that esthetics has played a greater role in Paris, and an untrammeled economy in Tokyo.

Finally, toward the edges, again, conceptions of and anxiety about social control, how to deal with the Other (defined socioeconomically, and now ethnically), and tolerance of ambiguity versus a desire for clarity are all consistent with the existence of a broad, fuzzy margin in Tokyo and a smaller and smaller margin in Paris. Add to this a state authority for centuries fearful of either foreign invasion or rural or urban insurrection or both, and a city dependent on the octroi for its fiscal health, and it is not difficult to understand why Paris might have chosen to close itself off behind its ever more imposing walls, and to shelter itself inside a transit system not shared with the outside. By contrast, a middle class with suburban aspirations and a metropolitan transit system which has grown irrepressibly for more than a century, combined with political and social unconcern for Others at the margins, might help to explain why Tokyo is so open, with edges which are both subjectively and objectively ambiguous to this day. Ever since the Tokugawa regime lost its defensive imperative, secure in the sociopolitical system it had created, Edo and Tokyo have been relatively free to grow, independent of the state. Paris, by contrast, is a city which has been more directly manipulated by political authorities for centuries, and it is to this subject that I now turn.

4 | THE MANIPULATED CITY

Paris, far more than Tokyo, has been the plaything of its rulers, a canvas upon which national goals and personal egos have been brushed with broad strokes. But why might this be so? Both Japan and France have often had regimes which have guided, regulated, and shaped society and economy. Why might the city — the capital, even — have escaped the manipulative inclinations of successive Japanese governments? Or has it? Japan has certainly seen splurges of city planning. Has the backsliding after every burst reflected lack of sustained official interest, or have there been countervailing forces which have defeated regimes intent on shaping the city? If no interest, why? If frustrated interest, why? And of course the extraordinary cultivation of Paris is equally needful of explanation.

STATE INVOLVEMENT

Our initial questioning presents us with three propositions about the shaping of the city. First, the guided growth of Paris reflects both official interest and public power, whereas the unguided growth of Tokyo (and even of Edo and Kyoto after their initial realization) seems to reflect more of a lack of interest than a lack of power. Early French monarchs embellished the capital with walls, fortresses, bridges, and self-promoting statues, arches, and plazas, albeit with little overall plan. Napoleon I, however, set out explicitly to make Paris "the most beautiful city ever . . . the beacon of Europe and the capital of the world,"[1] and his successors have never let up. But they have not simply tried to embalm Paris and create Williamsburg-sur-Seine; they have tried — and are constantly trying — to "superimpose a smoothly running, modern metropolis" on the City of Light.[2] And the state — sometimes in concert with the Hôtel de Ville, sometimes in conflict with it — still holds the trump cards when it comes to urban planning.[3]

In Tokyo, lack of interest seems to have played the key role, especially over the last hundred years. The early shoguns built Edo to their plan, but then largely relinquished control to commoner administrators. After a burst of planning, the Meiji and successor regimes basically turned Tokyo over to the private sector and to economic forces, seeing the quality of the urban environment as predominantly the responsibility of individuals, neighborhoods, and private enterprise.[4] The state has been passive toward the capital, preferring to play an organizing, enabling, and mediating role; planning has been aimed at creating infrastructure, a "pragmatic instrument for the organization of city-space" with a "relative absence of architectural and planning visions."[5]

Urban Form and Public Authority

But this arrangement is anomalous, and begs further questions. Hence a second proposition: that the Japanese have never felt, as strongly as the French, that architecture in particular and urban form in general are essential to the exercise of political power. In Japan, with an ineffably legitimate emperor in whose name all regimes have governed for 1,500 years, a populace basically of no concern to the elites, and a historically strong and hegemonic social hierarchy, the manipulation of civic space might not be necessary.[6]

Thus we may begin with the provisional assumption that the Japanese, historically, have bothered to manipulate the urban environment only during brief periods when it was expedient: to consolidate new regimes and assert social control, to facilitate *private* economic dynamics, or to impress foreigners, either Westerners or colonial subjects. In fact, the Western-style, baroque capitals Japan built in its colonies strengthen the suspicion that intrinsically Japanese architecture and urban forms may be simply inappropriate as instruments of political authority.

In the West, it has simply been a given that architecture is the handmaiden of authority and social engineering. No further justification need be offered for my initial proposition that state involvement in the formation of Paris can be at least in part explained by a broader cultural conviction that authority can fruitfully manipulate the city toward a variety of goals.

Form and Fatalism, Descartes and Design

Having stuck one foot into the swamp of intangible cultural explanation, let me go one step further, with a third proposition: there is in Japanese culture[7] a predisposition less toward voluntarism than toward fatalism, which is consistent with the differences we see in Paris and Tokyo. Overt human agency, let us imagine, plays a greater role in Western culture, whether it is seen in gardens, cities, or political leadership. The reason that Tokyo is more organic than Cartesian in form may be because Cartesian ideas do not resonate in Japan, and the human role is not as inherently manipulative toward nature as in the West.

This is not to say that the Japanese do not value control. Few things are as rigidly controlled as a pine tree in a Japanese garden, and (as noted) the absence of surface order in Tokyo does not denote absence of pattern or of social control. But dirigiste concern for control coexists with laissez-faire urban and horticultural principles of "design without designers."[8] Exactly how they interrelate I do not know at this point; nor do I know how — or if — either relates to urban form. But there is a deep and wide difference between Tokyo and Paris in the extent to which they have been manipulated by public forces, and it should be addressed, even with such diaphanous tools as this.

SHAPING THE CITY: COMPREHENSIVE PLANNING

The Visible Hand: Paris

The Romans initiated Paris's history as a systematically planned city. This city plan waxed and waned expediently, particularly under the exigencies of defense, and the city's first real "city planner" — an individual with an idea of the whole city and an "urban policy" designed explicitly for Paris — was Philippe Auguste.[9] He did not just build a wall; he developed markets, port facilities, and cemeteries, subdivided land, and paved streets on the premise that a more efficient city, and a city more clearly under the command of the king, were legitimate state goals.

For the next two or three centuries, Paris grew under its own inertia; the state added "triumphal entrances" and "symbolic edifices," but overall development was in the hands of entrepreneurs, speculators, and builders.[10] Kings like Henry IV identified the fortunes of the city with their own,[11] and Henry was responsible for some magnificent projects like the Place des Vosges and Place Dauphine. But he competed with other power holders in the city, his urban works had to be pursued in concert with them, and he never tried to plan for the city as a whole.[12]

This age of state deference came to an end with Louis XIV, although his most famous achievement, Versailles, was not in Paris at all. His actions fed straight into the Enlightenment, with its concern for "open spaces and long vistas, well-ordered streets and 'natural' spaces," based on the assumption that reason and science — and architecture — could "effect and reform social behavior."[13] But it was not until the advent of Napoleon I that Enlightenment principles really took shape, overlaid with his own imperial ambitions. Napoleon's legacy in the area of comprehensive city planning is debatable: John Russell credits him with "the center of Paris as we know it."[14] To Pierre Pinon, on the other hand, Napoleon contributed "grandeur" but "no vision, no plan of the whole": he may have added two splendid arches, one column, two beautiful streets, and quays, plazas, and bridges, but "monument does not mean city."[15]

Taking on the city was the role, rather, of his nephew, Napoleon III, and his agent Haussmann, under whom for the first time "the state implicated itself directly in the shaping of the capital."[16] Napoleon wanted a grand capital, Haussmann wanted an efficiently functioning capital, and the private sector wanted to make money — it was a perfect ménage à trois.[17]

Haussmann's vision was comprehensive: he wanted to improve Paris's hygiene, public safety, transportation and traffic flow, aeration, water supply, and quality of life.[18] Accordingly, he planned water treatment and sewage facilities, demolished the old slums where insurgents thrived, broad-

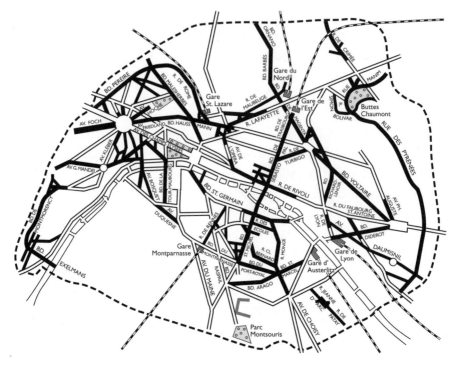

Fig. 19. Napoleon III and Haussmann's plans for the redevelopment of Paris.

ened and straightened streets (for traffic and troop movement), increased tram and omnibus lines and linked the railway stations, pushed buildings back from the street, and increased the number of parks and gardens. But three of his strategies stand out. First, the "openings" (*percements* or *percées*) seen in figure 19: the demolition of buildings, or of whole blocks, in order to create broader, straighter, or brand-new streets according to Napoleon's vision of the city, and/or to eliminate slum neighborhoods. Second was the annexation in 1859 of the suburban areas inside the wall.

Third was Haussmann's technique of paying for this stunningly grand-scale operation: the mobilization of capitalism's instincts behind state goals.[19] He expropriated land and paid for it with money borrowed by the state; sometimes he redeveloped it and sold the much-appreciated land back to private interests in order to repay the loan, and sometimes he let private enterprise buy it, pay for redevelopment, and then keep it to run or sell.[20]

Early on, this simple strategy worked beautifully, but it had two problems: the Council of Paris, enlisted by landholders who opposed expropriation, frustrated him at several turns; and his projects drove up property prices all over the city, which meant that his expropriations became more and more expensive. Gradually his debts ballooned amid speculation, fraud, and profiteering; finally in 1870 the emperor fired him, although his designs continued to determine urban redevelopment in Paris for another half century.

But even in his own day Haussmann's achievement was grand: a city doubled in size, dozens of grand boulevards, "twenty churches, five mayories, six barracks, la Villette, la Santé, Sainte-Anne, Tenon, seventy schools, seven markets, a new world."[21] Still, it had its limits. One of these was spatial: Haussmann's plans paid almost no attention to either the new areas just inside the wall or the suburbs outside and left them to the tender mercies of slumlords and developers.[22] The second was social, and followed from the first: Haussmann tried to eliminate poverty by demolishing slums and expelling the poor to the cheaper suburbs.[23] In doing so, he created a belt of discontent around the city, and some dangerously seething pockets just within, in places like Belleville. The two factors would come home to roost in 1871.

After Haussmann's departure came a hiatus in the planning of Paris. This was clearly related to the exercise of political authority: monarchist French regimes have tended to see great symbolic significance in Paris and have wanted to remake it to reflect their power, but more democratic regimes — certainly including the Third Republic — have typically been dominated by the provinces, which were at best indifferent and at worst hostile to the fate, and form, of the capital.[24]

Indeed, Paris's evolution all the way up until the end of World War II was largely unplanned. The wall came down, gradually, and the Métro was installed; social housing was initiated and gradually came to fill in the zone where the wall had been.[25] The only comprehensive planning effort was the Prost Plan of 1934, a management plan for a 35-kilometer region around the capital. Its goal was to weaken and limit the growth and redevelopment of the capital, and perhaps to let conditions there become so bad as to reverse the population inflow.[26] But the urge was no different from that of Louis XIV or of either Napoleon: calculatedly using the state to shape the city.

After World War II, this urge survived, and even grew, although its premises gradually changed.[27] Initially limits were put on industrial, and then office, construction, and factory elimination was subsidized.[28] Decentralization was the policy du jour, and the government called for national land use planning in order to "stem the current which carries all the country's vital forces to the big centers [and] to recreate sources of life in the regions...which...tend to become deserted."[29] Such a plan was forthcoming for Paris in 1960: PADOG,[30] which aimed to limit the growth of the "congested capital," promote cities in the "disorganized suburbs," and build growth poles in the "deprived" provinces.[31]

But the Fourth Republic was not as anti-Paris as the Third. New efforts focused on making the provinces more attractive, not Paris less so, and although Paris was considered too large, it was allowed after the mid-1950s to begin to rebuild itself with new infrastructure, slum clearance, and development of unused public land. The state did broaden participation in development projects, providing in 1961 for the creation of mixed public-private corporations (*sociétés d'économie mixte,* or SEMs),[32] but it did not relinquish ultimate control, and it did not stem the trend toward gentrification begun by Haussmann.

Indeed, the 1960s to some constituted the second coming of the baron, in the person of Paul Delouvrier. Charles de Gaulle — never one to think small — became president in 1959, and he appointed Delouvrier to prepare a master plan for the Paris region — the first in one hundred years. Delouvrier rejected PADOG: French vitality required Parisian vitality; thus Paris could not and should not be artificially constrained, but rather its growth should be planned.[33] The decks were cleared administratively with the creation in 1963 of DATAR,[34] an agency intended to promote provincial growth with a variety of tax breaks and subsidies, and in 1964 of a new Department of the Seine.[35] Paris was now a department unto itself, no longer sharing a department with a number of left-dominated municipalities. And in 1965, the Master Plan for the Paris Region was published.[36]

The 1965 master plan had three central foci: to promote new towns (eventually five) in the outer suburbs, in order to absorb population growth and attract economic activity from downtown; to facilitate commuting with new rail lines and the Périphérique; and to concentrate high-rise business development at La Défense, with secondary business-based "employment poles" near the major stations. All this, it was hoped, would enhance quality of life and occupational, recreational, and residential freedom of choice; improve citizen access to both urban amenities and natural resources; guide the pattern of (now polycentric) metropolitan growth; and increase the economic efficiency of the region. And so it did, or so it appears forty years later.

But de Gaulle, whatever his ambitions, was not Napoleon. De Gaulle appreciated Paris's problems, but he had no comprehensive vision; he "knew he had to do something, but he didn't know what."[37] Delouvrier came up with concrete solutions, but he too had a problem: political opposition and a general drift away from dirigisme. Marxists saw the plan as the tool of capitalism, liberals saw it as an unfair constraint on free enterprise, and urbanists in city hall saw it as "economic rationalism with irrational urban effects."[38] Objections mounted, ministers did end runs around Delouvrier, President Pompidou evinced a preference for the market, and Delouvrier resigned in 1969.

With him went comprehensive planning — although some of the components of the master plan, such as the new towns and the RER rail system, continue to make progress. The 1970s were a period of discrete projects, not overall plans, as seemingly every public agency on every level of government got into the act: several state ministries, the region, the city, the capital market development agency (Caisse des Dépôts), the public housing bureau, the national railroads, the Port of Paris, the subway authority, and a variety of SEMs all came up with their own urban development plans.[39] An alphabet soup of state regulations and land use categories — ZACs, ZADs, ZUPs, etc.[40] — and restrictions governed development. But city hall in particular outpaced the state, redeveloping whole quarters while President Giscard (1974–81) proclaimed that "the age of gigantic cities . . . is over" and used the state to slow the pace of redevelopment and the scale of operations.[41]

Thus the state reduced its ambitions for Paris. With the decentralization of power in present-day France (see chap. 7) the president, prime minister, prefects, regional and departmental councils and presidents, and mayors all have a say in the affairs of the Île-de-France region, and the "public interest" becomes ever harder to articulate. Yet the French retain their affection for planning, and for state primacy, as one can see in the most recent master plan, introduced in 1994.[42] Overall, planning for and by the capital reflects three consistent themes and one tactical change.[43] The themes are, first, the increasing acceptance of Paris as a great city, partly because of a new "rising tide lifts all boats" view of regional growth, and partly because the success of France in competition with the rest of Europe demands it. Second, Paris is being redefined in a larger and larger sense geographically and demographically: transportation planning, for example, includes ever more distant cities and links among the suburbs, not simply channels to the center. Third, planning aims at a rebalancing of the region, with promotion of the new towns and other growth poles around the periphery and of socioeconomic equalization and "solidarity" throughout, especially by providing more low-cost housing.

The tactical change is necessitated by the process of political decentralization which France has undergone since the 1970s: the state is more modest, speaking of "concertation" and "partnerships" with, instead of "control" and "tutelage" of, local governments.[44] It is struggling to make national goals compatible with decentralization — but has not yet found the key, as the 1994 master plan for the region makes clear.[45] The plan establishes a regional population goal of 11.8 million by 2015. Given a regional population of 11.1 million in 2002,[46] this will take both serious carrots in the provinces and serious sticks in Île-de-France, primarily the strategic state siting of infrastructure, environmental protections, and limits on land development and office construction.

Thus behind tactical change lies strategic continuity: state primacy in the shaping of the region. The 1994 master plan "responds in its grand principles both to the concerns of the state in regard to land use management and to the demands of localities" but reflects the state's "fundamental responsibility" to plan "an urbanism which is stable and most responsive to the concerns of the State, the elected officials of the region, and the whole of the people." Unsurprisingly, the plan has engendered much opposition. It also must compete with the city's own effort, the Local Urbanization

Plan, published in 2006.[47] How it will relate to the will of the state one cannot say — even a new law of 1995 authorizing the Île-de-France region to prepare its own master plan stipulates that this will be done "in association with the state"[48] — but it certainly carries forward the traditionally voluntaristic, calculated shaping of the capital by, and for, political authority.

Tokyo: The Sound of Hands Not Clapping

The history of Japanese cities is, with a few brief exceptions, a story of minimal and singularly ineffective state manipulation. We have already noted the early Japanese capitals modeled on China, the semi-autonomous temple towns of the sixteenth century, and the castle towns; if any question remained whether the Japanese *can* plan cities, the Tokugawa capital of Edo laid them to rest. Tokugawa Ieyasu's initial goal was to "build an impregnable military stronghold" and, secondarily, to "pour society into a new physical mould."[49] He manipulated not only the physical form of Edo but also its demographics, and if Edo had unplanned aspects, that was clearly due to absence of will, not of capability.

But this laying on of hands lasted only until the great Meireki Fire of 1657. The city was broadly transformed after the fire, again by shogunal fiat, but now neither politics nor defense nor social hierarchy reigned. The major imperatives were, rather, fire prevention and fiscal solvency.[50] Many lordly households and temple communities were moved to the outskirts of the city, and limits were set on the scale of mansions. Many of the spaces thus vacated were left empty as firebreaks, and many streets widened for the same reason. New bridges spanned the rivers to facilitate escape from disasters. And all these operations required the forced relocation of warriors, commoners, and clerics. Unquestioned authority was required, but it was not exercised in order to reflect or enhance itself. Indeed, the fire marked a turning point in state willfulness toward the city.[51] Comprehensive planning went out the window, and land use came increasingly to be determined from below. The space of Edo became more and more the plaything of the people, in a process that I describe below as "insurgent land use." The political was in retreat.

A resurgence of politics, and an activist state, came in 1868, but with nothing resembling Tokugawa molding of the city. The potential was there: vast swaths of land were confiscated from the nobility and shogun-ate, and wherever the state chose to plan, its prerogative was absolute.[52] But for the most part it declined to plan the city, restricting its efforts to partial projects, infrastructural improvements which would facilitate the private-sector economic development it favored and deferred to, and plans in response to foreign impetus. French- and English-style urbanism offered the Champs-Élysées, Regent Street, and the rue Rivoli as inspiration, and the resulting brick façades along the Ginza symbolized the modern, cos-mopolitan (and fireproof) capital.[53] But foreignism was not enough: the new buildings were too expensive and ill-suited to Tokyo's humid climate, and the plan was downsized and then terminated in 1877. The governor still wanted to make Tokyo an international city and the state wanted in-ternational acceptance, and in the 1880s the German architectural firm of Ende and Bockmann was brought in to transform the central part of the city into a suitably grandiose, baroque governmental-corporate complex. But agreement on what to put where, who was going to pay, and what the balance was to be between commercial and imperial Tokyo was impossible to achieve, and almost none of the Ende-Bockmann plan was realized.[54]

Other plans, however, were proposed subsequently. The most success-ful ones focused simply on streets and bridges, water and sewer, sanitation, slum clearance, and fire prevention, while a comprehensive plan which also included rail lines, markets, slaughterhouses, and crematoria was — as ever — opposed by the Finance Ministry and private landowners and was scaled far back.[55] Most of these plans emanated from the state (the gover-nor of Tokyo was a Home Ministry bureaucrat), but the state's real position was that "city planning... was not a responsibility of government at all"; it wanted a "livable" city, but a "visually well-ordered utopia" was not a goal.[56] With the referee uninterested in the game, urban development became a free-for-all involving developers, city hall, the city assembly, party politi-cians, and different ministries.[57] A unified national city planning law — Japan's first — was hammered out in 1920,[58] but before it could have an effect on Tokyo, the earthquake did.

The 1923 earthquake turned almost half of Tokyo into vacant land, but again the state dithered while the private sector mobilized. Governor Gotō Shimpei devised a comprehensive rebuilding plan, but while Parliament

Fig. 20. Japanese architect, neo-baroque style: the headquarters of the Japanese governor-general of Taiwan, 1919.

debated it, landowners raced to rebuild where they had been before. And then Parliament cut the budget by 90 percent.[59] Gotō persevered, and did manage to widen and extend Tokyo's streets from 14 percent of its surface to 26 percent, to increase its park area by 16 percent, and to add some four hundred bridges. The overall shape of the city was unchanged.[60]

But why? It is almost as if there is something un-Japanese about concerted, willful state intervention in urban design. The last — and again brief — exception to this pattern underscores it: city planning in Japan's colonies. In Taiwan, Korea, and Manchuria, Japanese planners, encouraged by Gotō Shimpei (president of the South Manchurian Railway before he went to the Home Ministry), designed "avant-garde and utopian" baroque capitals whose "broad, straight streets, generous parks and plazas, and impressive symbolic government buildings demonstrated political control."[61]

So there were visionary, grandiose, comprehensive Japanese planners. But they failed at home. Partly this was due to political constraints,[62] but it makes one wonder if they were not simply outside the mainstream of Japanese conceptions of space and city, if Japan was forced to adopt a foreign vocabulary in order to repeat the foreign lessons it had learned in imperialism. In any case, the prewar years show few instances in which state will and capability fused in the shaping of Tokyo. Urban planning was primarily the prerogative of the Home Ministry, which was also responsible for public order and deeply concerned with the political attitudes of the people.[63] The ministry went to great lengths to cultivate politically correct popular attitudes but never seized upon urban form as a useful tool.

This perspective continued after the war, as did governmental ineffectuality regarding the capital. Once again the regime had open land at its disposal — almost 200 square kilometers had been laid waste by American bombing — and once again the response was weak and unrealistic. Initial reconstruction plans set a population limit of 3.5 million for the capital; this was exceeded within a year.[64] Refugees and returning soldiers streamed back into the city, private landowners objected, local governments (now free of central command) were opposed or impecunious, and state funds were unavailable. And the absence of an overarching plan opened the door for personalization and politicization of land use decisions, and for all the gifts, bribes, and other largesse which this entailed.[65] Coherent planning, especially for the capital, was impossible.

In time, however, planning did reemerge, although it was not always completely realistic and did not really confront the continuing growth of Tokyo. The Capital Region Development Law of 1958 called for London-style growth: a "purified" central city with industry expelled, a green belt 10 kilometers wide, and an outer ring of satellite cities.[66] But industrial development and suburban sprawl, and suburban cities which did not fancy a pastoral future, all outran the planners; the plan was an "instant and spectacular failure."[67] National development plans were already focusing on the entire Pacific coast, concentrating on large-scale industrial concentrations and a connecting transportation network. Limits were imposed on industrial construction in Tokyo itself;[68] but beyond that, its form was a peripheral concern.

Tokyo came to the fore in the 1960s with the inception of the Zensō (Comprehensive National Development Plan)[69] process, and even more with the growth of an independent planning capability within the Tokyo metropolitan government itself. The first Zensō, in 1962, was a growth-pole policy, aiming at interregional balance in economic growth by specifying specific cities for promotion, primarily through public spending; the capital was not a major focus.[70] The hope was that both metropolitan densification and rural depopulation would thus be alleviated; but although regional disparities did decline, industrial and demographic concentration along the Pacific coast actually increased.[71] The response, in 1969, was a New Zensō,[72] which still put emphasis on giant projects and concentration of core administrative functions in the major cities, along with an emerging technophiliac bent: ever better transportation and communications networks would overcome spatial imbalance. "Overconcentration" in Tokyo, Nagoya, and Osaka was noted, but people continued to move, and the cities continued to grow.[73]

Tokyo's internal form also became the focus of planning in the 1960s. City hall had already designated (in the 1950s) three outlying areas as "city subcenters," and in the 1960s height and infill limits on buildings were relaxed and the state for the first time delegated major city-planning prerogatives to municipalities, opening the way for major change in both the horizontal and vertical dimensions of the capital.[74] A large area in the western suburbs, cutting across several municipalities, was slated for promotion as Tama New Town; this and the subcenters (the number of which grew with time) have come to symbolize Tokyo's own nodal approach to its form: "decentralization" and "deconcentration" *within* the capital region, not away from it. Tokyo would contribute in its own way to reducing congestion, but not at a cost to its own primacy. State and capital seem to have decided on a division of labor in which the former focused on the nation as a whole, and the latter (with a lot of state funding) planned its own future.

So Tokyo's primacy grew under the Zensō plans. The Third Zensō (1977) recognized that the metropolitan areas were getting too big but again approached the problem from a win-win perspective, as one of enhancing urban amenities — employment opportunities, education, health care, etc. — in the provinces in order to keep their populations at home, to intercept those who might otherwise migrate all the way to metropolitan areas, and to attract the "overflow" from metropolitan areas.[75] But metropolitan To-kyo's population continued to grow. For one thing, its population tended to "overflow" only as far as its outermost suburban ring; for another, Gover-nor Suzuki Shunichi (1979–95) continued to promote growth poles inside the capital and launched a campaign to make Tokyo more convenient and livable.[76]

Indeed, Tokyo's role grew apace in the 1980s, largely as a correlate of the globalization of Japan's economy. Japanese corporations and capital inter-nationalized, multinationals flocked in, and Tokyo's boosters (both local and national) began to speak of World City Tokyo.[77] Suzuki accommo-dated them with grandiose plans to create a corporate-residential-cultural-recreational Waterfront City Subcenter complex on landfill in Tokyo Bay, which I discuss below. But others began to speak of a "Tokyo Problem" and of a problematic "unipolar concentration." In 1987, the state responded with a Fourth Zensō.[78] This plan explicitly acknowledged excessive demo-graphic and economic concentration in Tokyo, but also Tokyo's crucial global role. To reconcile the two, the plan's themes were "multipolarity" and "interchange": once again, certain urban functions were to be dis-persed to designated provincial cities, and transportation and communi-cation technology promoted.

Given free rein, the capital — by itself and in concert with its neighboring prefectures — began to plan apace,[79] arguing that Tokyo's own internal tax and subsidy policies could push service and administrative functions away from the center of the city. And the city's horizons expanded: its multi-polar self-concept now included nodal growth in contiguous prefectural cities.[80] But it was becoming clear that laissez-faire urbanism had its limits.[81] Population kept on growing, infrastructure never kept pace, and high-rise development lagged: by the 1990s, Manhattan — roughly the same size as Tokyo's central business district — had almost twice as many residents and almost three times as many workers as Tokyo's.

Parliament grasped the Tokyo nettle in 1992, establishing the Investiga-tion Committee for Relocation of the Capital, which reported in 1995 that a new capital should be realized between 38 and 185 miles from the center of Tokyo and become home to some six hundred thousand people. May-ors and governors all over the Tokyo region screamed and mobilized their

MPs, but planning and site investigation got under way. Relocation played a significant role in the Fifth Zensō (1998): Tokyo's primacy was again lamented — if trends continued, its future was "grim" — but promotion of multipolar provincial regions and capital relocation were going to alleviate the problem.[82] But the nettle's sting was too much. Tokyo mobilized its political allies; a decade of economic stagnation straitened the government's circumstances; and site selection turned into an intense political contest among candidate regions. In 2003, Parliament declared itself unable to agree on a site, "effectively shelving" the project. By 2005, the enabling legislation behind the whole grand-scale Zensō process was in question.[83]

Thus we have seen in Japan a city-planning process which has historically been episodic, politically or economically focused, state-centered (in authority and financial support) and state-regulated, but realized by local and private interests in the absence of a directly manipulative state.[84] Japan does not seem to be a felicitous setting for those who fancy comprehensive city designs, nor an arena for leaders who feel that their power needs reflection in an urban mirror. When one shrinks one's focus to projects within the city instead of the city in toto, the impression changes, but — at least compared to Paris — the public hand still lies more lightly upon Tokyo.

SHAPING THE CITY: PIECE BY PIECE

Taking Care of Business

Promotion of commercial areas is nothing new in Tokyo, or in Japan. The Chinese model for Kyoto called for public markets in specific places, and the Tokugawa shoguns laid out separate quarters for different commercial activities. But since the Meiji Restoration such promotions have taken an overwhelmingly private form, albeit with government encouragement and facilitation. Ginza Brick Street and the whole Ginza-Marunouchi-Otemachi business district were and are — with the exception of Tokyo Station at the core — the bountiful fruit of private efforts. The state's own Ende-Bockmann plan, by contrast, has left little trace.

Since World War II, private proposals for downtown Tokyo have proliferated. In the 1960s, city hall turned a huge tract of land in Shinjuku over to the private sector and unleashed a "perfect frenzy of development" there.[85]

As the economy — and downtown rents — continued to climb, other areas were redeveloped, either on public landfill in the bay or on sold-off public land.[86] All were intended to accommodate ever more business; bigger was better, and limits on or redirection of growth (except within the capital) were never proposed. The business community's response was unabashed: in 1988, Mitsubishi Real Estate put forth its Manhattan Plan for sixty skyscrapers, which would double Tokyo's total downtown office space.[87]

But the Manhattan Plan ran afoul of a public plan to alleviate the office shortage and enhance Tokyo's international stature: Governor Suzuki's Waterfront City Subcenter project.[88] City hall had set up a study group in the early 1980s to plan the use of roughly 1,000 acres of landfill in the bay, and a few years later the group proposed an office-residential-retail-recreational-cultural complex. Opposition came from many quarters — the state feared loss of control, the ruling party feared loss of patronage, business worried about adequate profit, and the citizens worried about housing costs — but Governor Suzuki persevered, offered something to all, won the support of a couple of strategic ruling-party factional chiefs, and managed to set up a "third sector" public-private partnership development corporation, in which city hall retained ultimate control.

Waterfront City Subcenter Development, Inc., combined prefectural capital (52 percent) with private (from more than fifty corporations); the governor chaired the corporation, and Tokyo retained ownership of all the land. It was intended to be profit-making, but both the corporations and taxpayers no doubt suffered grievously from the impact of the economic stagnation which plagued Japan during the 1990s. The Waterfront City Subcenter area grew slowly, with grand but almost empty hotels and vacant office buildings in the late 1990s. New rail and highway access helped, however, and by 2008 the area appeared bustling, if not crowded or entirely built up. It has, after all, been only twenty years — La Défense did not bloom overnight, either — and I suspect that in time the subcenter will be regarded as a success by most.

However, what is most significant about the Waterfront City Subcenter is not its financial success, but rather that it came about at all. The keys to its realization, I think, were the individual leadership of Suzuki Shunichi, whose twenty-five years in Tokyo administration followed by sixteen years as governor gave him a reach unparalleled by any aspiring urbanist in Japanese history; Suzuki's longtime links to a small number of ruling-party leaders; the limited nature of the project; and Tokyo's manifestly accepted importance to Japan's globalizing economy combined with the city's own unprecedented wealth in the midst of the 1980s boom. The Japanese state's role was as ever: it did not take advantage of the boom to make an autonomous imprint on the capital. But Suzuki saw and seized his chance, here and in instances we shall see below.

By contrast, the Hôtel de Ville has never been able to exercise such independence. Markets have long been regulated in Paris, but a coherently planned business district was not envisioned until the twentieth century. When it was, it came (fortunately) to a bad end. To Le Corbusier—"a good architect but a catastrophic urbanist"—organically grown cities were anathema; his (stillborn) Plan Voisin of 1925 was to raze the center of Paris and reorganize it with a grid of streets and eighteen geometrically regimented skyscrapers "in the middle of vast green spaces."[89]

The next attempt to plan a business center for Paris went better, although it too has its scathing critics. By the 1950s, Paris had a serious shortage of office space; it also had a long-standing esthetic yen to extend the Grand Axis which began at the Louvre (or, arguably, even at the Place de la Bastille) and stretched westward to the Arc de Triomphe and the Porte Maillot.[90] In 1954, DATAR had designated the area around La Défense as an area for priority development, and in 1956 it created EPAD, the Public Corporation for the Management of La Défense, and allocated to it roughly 1,800 acres in the loop of the Seine beyond the western edge of the city.[91] Unlike Tokyo's Waterfront Development, Inc., EPAD was state-dominated. It did, on the other hand, share an intimate liaison with the private sector. And, like Haussmann's Paris, it was premised on the need to protect the heart of the city while promoting its economic fortunes.[92] Waterfront Development, Inc., by contrast, had no protectionist motivations; the virtue of its plan was that landfill had neither purchase price nor prior landlords, nor obstreperous local officials.

The vision for La Défense was grand: a great pedestrian esplanade built atop a station-parking-highway complex, flanked by France's tallest skyscrapers, a convention center, art galleries, theaters and performance spaces, restaurants, public art, and shops, with housing and schools just behind. It was self-financing: EPAD bought land with money borrowed with the state's guarantee, sold the building rights, and with the proceeds built infrastructure and repaid the loans as well. But it was also slow. Partly this was the result of policy: EPAD sold each part of the project before going on to the next.[93] Partly it was the result of infighting among different cabinet ministers, between state and municipal members of the corporation, and among the biggest private developers involved. A major blow was the Oil Shock of 1973 — not a single square meter of space was sold between 1974 and 1978.[94]

In the 1980s, however, the French economy and La Défense both recovered.[95] State contributions increased, the transportation network was knit together, and in 1989 the bicentennial of the Revolution was celebrated with the opening of the Grand Arch at the west end of the esplanade, looking eastward toward classical Paris — spared from capitalist inundation — and westward toward its destined goal (or next victim, depending on one's point of view), the far side of the city of Nanterre. Today La Défense is a hub of activity, not only during the day but also in the evening. The fears that it would be an after-hours desert have not been borne out. It has fully occupied housing — both upscale private and down-at-the-heels public — parks and noisy playgrounds, schools and grocery stores, rock concerts and demonstrations, and more. Granted, La Défense has had twenty-five more years to grow than Tokyo's Waterfront City Subcenter. Given another decade or so, and some general economic recovery, Waterfront City Subcenter will probably also be successful, particularly since its original goals have been scaled down — from a working population of 110,000 and a residential population of 60,000, to 70,000 and 40,000 respectively — and because it too is becoming a tourist attraction beyond predictions.[96] But it will never be the same as La Défense because its motives are more purely economic. This may sound odd to anyone who has seen the global-capitalist monumentalism of La Défense, but "social solidarity" is a pillar of all French urban planning, and La Défense has a full component of public housing and plebian recreational facilities. Waterfront

City Subcenter is residentially and recreationally for more favored social elements, at least until windsurfing spreads to the Japanese working class.

New Towns

The same is true of Tokyo's sole new town, Tama New Town. Including parts of three suburban cities, Tama looks to the strolling visitor not unlike the new towns of Paris. The fact that Tokyo, with a far larger population than Paris, has undertaken only one really coherent, large-scale new town may reflect, again, a less manipulative view of the city. It is also more homogeneously middle class than the Paris new towns. But the major way in which Tama differs is in its orientation toward and integration with the capital.

The "new town" idea entered Japan before World War II, and the result was a small number of privately developed, upscale residential suburbs like Seijō and Denen-Chōfu. They are, however, neighborhoods, not towns. It was in the 1960s that the idea came into its own, when city hall launched a study group to locate a site for a new suburb where some three hundred thousand to four hundred thousand people could escape the housing shortage and suburban sprawl which characterized much of the region. Tama was so designated in 1964; construction began in 1969, and in 1971, people began to move in. But it had its critics from the outset, primarily those who saw it as simply another suburban "bed town" with little or no local employment. At the beginning, it did not even have the rail links to make it a convenient bed town, and growth was slow.[97]

In subsequent years, (private) rail links, plus highways, have multiplied. So have infrastructural amenities of all sorts — two universities, shopping malls, plazas, stores large and small, and office buildings. But growth overall has been disappointing — the population peaked at 145,000 in 1994 — as has been local employment. Indeed, the new town's own promotional motto is "Close to business, far from crowds," and the "business" scene shown on its website is central Tokyo.[98] The website also highlights the short travel times to Tokyo and elsewhere, and Tama is not much of a place to go to look for a job. It does fit in with Tokyo's efforts to promote a multicentric metropolis, but it is hardly a center of independent growth.

Such independence is more in evidence in Paris, although here too the new towns were intended to be part of the metropolis, not freestanding cities. The idea of new towns arrived early in the twentieth century, and in the 1920s as many as twenty "garden cities" were planned.[99] But until the 1960s, the generally Malthusian opinion of Paris dominated, forestalling any intentional promotion of the suburbs, with the exception of the grands ensembles after the war. This all changed with Delouvrier, however, whose 1965 master plan called for a series of new towns (nine, later reduced to five) around Paris.[100] Like Tama, these towns were to be integrated with the capital; unlike it, their scale was far larger in total, they were more purposively planned, and — again in total — they have served better to reduce the congestion of the capital region.[101]

The device used for developing the new towns was, as in the case of La Défense, the public management corporation (EPA), which brought state, regional, and municipal officials together.[102] The state sketched the outlines of each new town and designated the land inside as a special zone in which that town's EPA had rights of purchase or expropriation; money for land purchase or compensation came from loans or the state; and infrastructural development was funded by state, region, and municipalities in combination and by the EPAs themselves, with the proceeds of land resale.[103] As the new towns developed, different administrative umbrellas evolved, some municipalities dropped out of the projects, and the cities were — like Tama — scaled down, from envisioned populations of up to 1 million each, to 300,000 to 700,000, then to 100,000 to 200,000.[104] But in this more modest incarnation, and with the completion of additional (public) rail links to Paris, the new towns succeeded: between 1975 and 1995, they absorbed some 40 percent of the region's population growth and became home not only to 850,000 residents but to 400,000 jobs.[105] Indeed, they have not even fulfilled their potential: according to DATAR, the towns could easily increase their populations, although many of the municipalities whose territories are partly in the new towns are opposed to further growth.[106]

Paris's new towns, like Tama, are endowed with walkable town centers, commercial quarters, promenades, universities, and recreational facilities; visually, no one of them appears superior to Tama in this respect.[107] And Tama is clearly attracting residents and enterprises. But taken together they represent a far greater investment of state effort and (therefore?) a more effective example of rational land use, guided regional growth, reduced distance between home and work, and urbanism with a social conscience.

Bells and Whistles: Embellishing the Capital

We shall look in chapter 5 at the differences between Tokyo and Paris in their inclinations to monumentalize the cityscape. Here, in addressing more broadly the tendency to manipulate the city per se, there is one last type of activity to note: small but stand-out projects of a noncommemorative nature. In Paris we can see three types: presidential and otherwise public projects, and public-private partnerships; in Tokyo, there are really only two: municipal and private.

The ruler's grand projects have a long history in Paris, although the sole purpose of most of the kings and emperors was to commemorate themselves. Since World War II, successive presidents have chosen to do so more indirectly, under the pretext of enhancing the grandeur of Paris with multifunctional projects. Georges Pompidou initiated the museum, built in the 1970s, which bears his name, but no one surpassed François Mitterrand, who sprinkled *grands projets du président* all over the city: the pyramid at the Louvre, the Arab Institute, the La Villette museum, and so forth. In a less individualistic vein, successive governments have also built urban redevelopment plans around key state undertakings, the biggest of which has been the Bercy-Tolbiac area in southeastern Paris. Here, on more than 100 otherwise unattractive acres of rail yards and ratty housing, the relocated Finance Ministry and new National Library and Omnisports Palace were proposed in the 1970s to form the core of an area embracing the Gare de Lyon, 900,000 square meters of office space, and 5,200 partially subsidized housing units.[108] Suddenly the desirability of the neighborhood to private developers rose, and gentrification has followed.

A second project of this type is in the northwest Batignolles quarter, where Paris pitched its bid for the 2012 Olympics.[109] The proposed Olympic Village was to be built on about 150 acres of — again — rail yards and related warehouses and commercial buildings on an unprepossessing site, overseen by a combined state-region-city committee (the overall coordinating group for the bid, Paris 2012, was chaired by the city's mayor, Bertrand

Delanoë). Paris is in the process of buying much of the property at the site; most of the rest belongs to the national railway, which was to contribute it to the Olympic movement until after the games. But the Olympics were simply the public driving force behind a desire to redevelop the area for the long term — a park, public housing, office space, and presumably a host of ancillary enterprises will fill in the space — and the failure of the Olympic bid will not derail it.

Moving further from public direction is the third type of project, the public-private partnership without a core state enterprise. Here, too, Paris is distinctive in that it is clear that the public sector has the upper hand, although it would perhaps be more accurate to say that the public and private hands are scratching each other's backs. One of the first major projects of this type involved the removal of the market at Les Halles. The de Gaulle government decided in 1959 to move the market out of Paris. The project became a political football kicked around by the state, the city, and the popular lovers of the market as it was, and after the old market was demolished in 1971 the area was for several years nothing but a hole in the ground. In 1977, the state withdrew from the fray (Mayor Jacques Chirac essentially traded for the site, giving up the old municipal abattoir at La Villette) and a public-private SEM,[110] with majority city hall ownership, was set up. Today the site is a pleasant park, sitting over an underground (and private) shopping mall and the world's largest (and public) subway station, and the city is finally about to act on its prerogatives, announcing in 2005 plans for an elaborate redevelopment of the park.

Other SEM-directed projects have been initiated on a smaller scale since the 1960s, the Maine-Montparnasse Tower, Front-de-Seine, and Place d'Italie redevelopments among them.[111] All were primarily commercial or commercial-residential mixes, all were private in primary funding and profit, but in none did private capital have a free hand. And since the late 1970s, as Paris has privatized many services, SEMs have become "the veritable private arm" of city hall.[112]

One may debate whether French SEMs constitute public cooptation of the private sector or a capitalist takeover of the government. But in any case, the blurring of the line sets Paris apart from Tokyo — where it is easier to tell who is really running the redevelopment show — as does the consistent reluctance of the Japanese state to play a major role. There is one exception to this pattern: Tokyo's bid for the 1964 Olympics, a state-controlled initiative which resulted in broad transformation of one part of the capital with stadiums, boulevards, and subways. Beyond a couple of stadiums, the Olympic project followed in the Meiji tradition of urbanism limited to infrastructure; rather than use Tokyo as a canvas upon which to paint a picture, the organizers used it as a roadbed, building elevated highways which frequently followed old rivers and canals, turning them "into dank, shaded and noisy bits of water."[113] In other words, the Japanese state has most often simply improved the capital's infrastructure so that others, if so inclined, might embellish it. Perhaps fortunately, both city hall and private developers have been so inclined.

Only a few projects need be noted to illustrate the municipal and private manipulation of the capital. On the municipal side are the Tokyo International Forum, the Edo-Tokyo Museum, and the New City Hall. The Forum, built on the old site of city hall near Tokyo Station, is an architectural tour de force. The museum, too, is both engaging within and striking without; a little massive, perhaps, but also a worthy embellishment of the skyline. But the real dazzler is the New City Hall in Shinjuku. This forty-eight-story twin-tower wonder, with its colonnaded plaza and facing metropolitan assembly building, is a stunningly graphic, completely un-Japanese symbol of a wealthy, imaginative, dynamic regime. There is no national government building anything like it, and I am sure that it was designed that way.

But perhaps Tokyo's burst of embellishment is an exception, too, requiring the fortuitous coincidence of Suzuki's skills and longevity with the unprecedented prosperity of Tokyo in the late 1980s. Certainly it will be a long time before Tokyo will be able to afford anything like it.

In the meantime, however, there is the private sector. Despite Japan's fifteen-year period of economic stagnation, certain sectors of the economy have thrived, and construction never seems to cease in Tokyo. Two examples of private-sector vigor, governmentally unleashed, are Ark Hills and the 2016 Olympics project.[114] The former, in central Tokyo, is a wholly private undertaking by the Mori real estate corporation, with a hotel, office tower, three high-rise apartment buildings, concert hall, restaurants,

» Fig. 21. Into the future:
   the New Tokyo City Hall,
   1991.

⌄ Fig. 22. Out of the past:
   the Hôtel de Ville, Paris;
   sixteenth century, recon-
   structed 1892.

and television studio — and, in the center, Herbert von Karajan Platz. The name is a bit jarring, but a plaza named for a Japanese would be jarring too. There is something emblematic going on here, like the utilization of a Western model for Japan's colonial cities and the partial inspiration of the New City Hall by Notre-Dame. There is nothing unique about openness to the world — Paris, after all, has streets named for Lincoln, Eisenhower, and Franklin Roosevelt — but it is as if there are some things that the Japanese want to do to cities — at least some of the time — which they simply cannot accomplish within their own architectural or urban traditions.

The development proposed as part of Tokyo's bid for the 2016 Olympics stands in sharp contrast both to Paris's Batignolles project and to Japan's own 1964 Olympics bid. It was more municipally driven than either of the others, and predominantly funded by the private sector. It included a 100,000-seat stadium, an Olympic village for 18,000, and numerous other facilities. The bid itself was three-quarters privately funded, and operating costs were to be covered by ticket sales, private money, and International Olympic Committee subsidies. Built on landfill in the bay, the new facilities would not require the acquisition of any land, and one's impression was that the taxpayers of Tokyo were getting something for nothing. Reality is apt to be different, since Tokyo's Olympic bid was unsuccessful, but the real significance of the project lies in its typically joint municipal-private nature.

CONCLUSION

Although the French have never done anything in or to Paris that the Japanese have not done to manipulate Tokyo, there is a great difference in the extent to which they want to, the reasons why, and the ways they try to do so. In the realm of comprehensive planning, Edo led the way. Shogunal power surpassed that of the French kings to shape Paris, but their manipulative impulse soon faded, and the public authorities have been in the background ever since,[115] content to set up Tokyo as an easel upon which others are allowed to work. By contrast, Paris was the canvas on which Philippe Auguste, Henry IV, and Napoleon I sketched and Napoleon III and de Gaulle (with Haussmann and Delouvrier respectively) did a veritable Jackson Pollock job. Certainly, Paris's history has been one not of continuous planning but of "a succession of sporadic impulses" driven by the combination of a willful leader with a good design, an imaginative agent, and sufficient financial resources to see them through.[116] But such impulses have come repeatedly and cumulatively, whereas in Tokyo they seem to have come only at the onset of new regimes, and then fizzled out.

Paris thus caught up with and passed Edo/Tokyo as the object of authoritative manipulation. This is not going to change: Paris's most recent regional master plan was a state creation; its next one will be drawn up by the region in association with the state; and the Local Urbanism Plan of 2006, compiled by the city, accords with a set of goals and procedures prescribed by the state in order to sustain the "republican compact" in France's cities.[117] And by 2009, the city and the state were in competition to see who could remake Paris most dramatically: the mayor's office announced plans for six high-rise projects to be located around the edges of the city, beginning with a 700-foot pyramidal building at the Porte de Versailles; and President Sarkozy proclaimed a new master plan for the city featuring an elevated rail line above the Périphérique.[118] Many elements of both initiatives are still hypothetical, if not fanciful, but the duel between the two visions will be interesting to watch. The absence of any such vision in Tokyo has led, on the one hand, to the total failure of an attempt to set up a new capital à la Ieyasu and, on the other, to governmental default, which leaves the city increasingly in the economically driven hands of the private sector.

This difference is visible also in the piecemeal redevelopment of our cities. In Paris, such projects tend to be either statist (or, more accurately, presidential) or state-implicated (and ultimately state-controlled); in Tokyo, state participation has for a century been minimal, with city hall and private developers dividing up the action between them.[119] But neither the public nor the private sector has succeeded in defining the city's identity as has been done in Paris, whose spatial and physical identity derives largely from manipulation. Tokyo today has, in one view,[120] perhaps the most impressive concentration of contemporary architecture of any city in the world, but its projects are swallowed by the "overwhelming power of the city" and its "infinite sea of buildings."

Overall, my initial impressions have been reinforced. First, the role of the public sector in the shaping of cities is significantly greater in Paris than in Tokyo. Where the Japanese public sector does participate, it is more likely to be the city than the state. Second, urbanism and architecture have been much more rarely the tool of political authority in Japan, perhaps due to cultural conceptions of power discussed above. Third, a laissez-faire, or subcontractarian, attitude toward Tokyo contrasts with the systematic, rationalistic, calculated pursuit of a desired future in Paris.[121]

Additionally, two expectations to be pursued in later chapters have emerged from this examination. In the first place, insofar as conscious motives have driven the evolution of Tokyo's form, they have been strikingly pragmatic and predominantly economic. I need, by contrast, add nothing here about the extent to which esthetics and the sociopolitical "republican compact" have not only supplemented but sometimes superseded economic objectives in the shaping of Paris. It is not that esthetics are unimportant in Japan. But beyond the architecture of individual structures, esthetics seems to have been divorced from the city in a way not seen in Paris.

Finally, the shaping of Tokyo has been simultaneously more globalized and less cosmopolitan than that of Paris. In terms of foreign direct investment, receptivity to foreign people and capital, and truly open intercourse with foreign ideas and influences, Tokyo is still a fairly parochial place, and its form does not make it a particularly easy venue for foreigners. Foreign influences on the form of the city, rather, have been mostly of two types: foreign architectural idioms which seem necessary to demonstrate Japan's modernity and international savoir faire, and urban redevelopment designed to accommodate "the needs of global capital accumulation by *Japanese* corporations."[122] If "cosmopolitan" is defined as "belonging to all the world," then Paris, on the other hand, may be without peer. The form of Paris exudes self-confidence; Tokyo's has been described — unfairly, in my view — as that of "a 'wanna-be' city" with an "urban inferiority complex."[123] But it is a description that cannot be rejected out of hand, especially after one has taken a long look at one particular form of manipulation of the city: its role as monument.

5 | MONUMENTS AND COMMEMORATIONS

Strolling along the wide plazas of Paris, one can admire the arches, statues, and souvenirs of conquest and read the city's history in the commemorative structures in which it is so rich. And, reading Western literature on monuments, one feels that, of course, this is how a capital city should be: "A city is not transformed simply because one modifies its streets and squares. It is transformed when great monuments are built in its bosom. These radiate in successive waves across the city — like a pebble which, falling into a lake, provokes concentric ripples — to modify its appearance and its functioning. . . . To build a monument is first and foremost to compose the city about it. . . . The monument . . . crystallizes the urban form around itself."[1]

Monuments are portrayed in this literature as the result of a universal human desire to overcome death and evanescence, to perpetuate the self, be it individual or institutional.[2] Monuments display the past, instruct the living, and shape the future.[3] Paris epitomizes the monumentalist impulse: indeed, today the whole city has been described as a giant monument in and of itself.[4]

And then there is Tokyo. The Japanese obviously value the past and are as desirous to commemorate as any, as the innumerable cemeteries of Tokyo attest. But one can walk far and wide without seeing anything that a Westerner would call a monument. In the 1860s, Robert Fortune, who

found Edo a "wonderful place," said nonetheless that it "cannot be compared with London, Paris," that it had "no Champs-Élysées or Versailles,"
and that its castle "did not seem a very imposing structure."[5] Its landscape
has been flatly called "anti-monumental," revealing a "lack of physical statement about urban power, prestige, and metropolitan and national ambi-
tion."[6] Disaster, be it earthquake or war, is not the explanation — anything
once built can be rebuilt. Whatever muse it is that keeps the Japanese connected to their past simply does not often command them, or their leaders,
to make the connection with physical structures.

COMMEMORATION WITHOUT MONUMENTS?

Muses, however, are not the most satisfying explanation for two differences
we can see in Paris and Tokyo. First, there is less explicitly monumental
construction in Tokyo. The Japanese certainly can "do" monuments: the
Great Hall of Buddha in Nara, another Buddha in Kamakura, and the
Grand Shrine in Nikko are only three from the past; and Tokyo Tower
and the New City Hall monumentalize different aspects of postwar Japan.
But the capital is not highlighted hither and yon with monuments, and
the periods of monumental effort seem to have come in short-lived waves.
Why this should be so — presuming that it actually is — is consistent with,
although not necessarily caused by, certain aspects of Japanese religion,
national identity, political authority in general, and the relationship of
people to authority in particular.

Second, what monumentalism there is in Tokyo seems to be of a different kind than what we find in Paris, a sort of commemoration without
monuments. Again, the Japanese are just as immersed in their past as are
the French and can recall it quite well. But their own sites of memory appear to be more social and less physical, less "national," less driven by partisan or populist political conflicts, and indeed less political or public and
more economic and private than the lieux de mémoire of Paris.

Less Is Less

Religion can, at least hypothetically, influence the form of a city in two
ways: as beliefs about man, the divine, the cosmos, and eternity; and in the

institutional impact of religious architecture. In Paris, until roughly the time of the Revolution, both were arguably at work: church architecture — particularly its Gothic variant — followed an explicit pursuit of timeless immortality, with cathedrals which soared toward the heavens, toward "something more than human."[7] Even after 1789, and the later subjugation of Paris to the secular, scientific ministrations of Haussmann, religious monuments survived: the Panthéon, Notre-Dame, and Sacré-Coeur might be more touristic than spiritual in function today, but their origins remain apparent. Our ability to interpret Parisian monumentality in religious terms declines with time, but it persists.

Japanese religion contrasts sharply with the common Christian ideas that presentation reflects piety and that architectural magnificence reflects a "Will [which] can overcome death."[8] Japan has had grand religious buildings and vast temple complexes, but Buddhism preaches the evanescence and illusory nature of all things; Shinto subsumes human existence under the pantheistic wings of nature; in both, death is a part of life, to be accepted, not conquered. Monuments are an attempt to change reality: if reality is not real, why bother?

As in France, however, we would expect to find a diminishing religious influence, over time, on whatever monumentalist impulses have existed in Japan. Specifically, in the late sixteenth century, Japanese politics was thoroughly and brutally secularized, as the state builders eliminated the clergy once and for all as active participants in the polity. In the process, they destroyed thousands of religious buildings. Ever since, religion has been more the handmaiden of government than an independent influence, certainly in the area of urban space and form.[9] The greatest surviving Tokugawa-era religious construction is Nikko, built to the greater glory of the deified founder of the regime; the political origins of the impressive Meiji and Yasukuni shrines in modern Tokyo are equally transparent. Without explicitly political stimulus, Japanese religion does not seem a likely vehicle for the erection of monuments.

But here lies another suggestion of a nonmonumental Japanese approach to the city. Pierre Nora has suggested that "sites of memory" which help generate identity are most likely located at points in time and space where there is a "break with the past."[10] Might one assume as corollary that the fewer the breaks, the less fragile the identity, the fewer the monuments? Japan has notionally been ruled by a single dynasty for 1,500 years; even the shoguns were de jure vassals of the emperor. The resumption of imperial rule in 1868, therefore, was not a break but a "restoration," and it has been argued that the events of 1945 were less of a break than they appeared.[11]

One cannot argue that Japan's national identity goes back for millennia. The Meiji rulers made explicit attempts — some architectural — to promote patriotism and national identity. But although they and their successors continued assiduously to "mold Japanese minds" through schools, media, etc.,[12] they did not keep up their monumentalist efforts for very long. So is it a secure national identity which sets the Japanese apart from the French — who have been divided on the subject of Frenchness ever since 1789 and who had to be transformed from "peasants into Frenchmen" as late as the twentieth century[13] — and which freed the Japanese from littering their cities with pretentious statuary? Or is it simply the different ways in which political authority in Japan and France has chosen to commemorate history and promote identity? I have argued that political authority in Japan has historically been more secure than in France in its hold over the nation, and thus that "no further elaboration of the principle by 'art' has ever been deemed necessary."[14]

Japan certainly had monumental models at hand when its urban age began. China's cities were endowed with huge walls and gates and ceremonial plazas, all designed to represent the cosmic order and the power of the empire. And Japan briefly borrowed, but soon discarded, Chinese monumentalism, as it did Chinese city planning. Truly monumental architecture did appear in Japan, particularly in the castles of the late sixteenth and early seventeenth centuries. But the need for "public display" of power faded.[15] And relatively few place-names in Edo then or Tokyo now commemorate individuals or military exploits, in contrast to the hundreds of such instances in Paris.[16] Bursts of monumentalism have been brief, and their landmarks have burned or fallen down. Perhaps they were not replaced because they had not worked in the first place; alternatively, perhaps state goals changed, rendering them unnecessary. But I suspect rather the influence of a ruling ethos or basis of legitimacy which rendered popular support moot.

Indeed, a quick look at Japanese and French history suggests that the position — or lack of same — of the people in the eyes of the regime has played a role. From very early on, the urban populace was a consideration in the design of Western cities. The center of the Greek city was the agora; that of the Roman, the forum. Their successor cities were built around open markets and plazas in front of civic buildings and churches.[17] Paris, of course, fit this pattern from the day the Romans laid out Lutetia.

Japanese leaders, by contrast, not only did not want the people to see them but did not seem to care what the people believed. In any case, at hardly any time in Japanese history until the late nineteenth century — and not truly until 1945 — did the exercise of political authority depend on the mobilization or intimidation of the people, much less on their meaningful participation in political life. Unsurprisingly, monuments were rarely a vehicle of political authority.

A Different Monumentalism

This does not mean that the Japanese are any less connected to their past. The past is very much with them, but they seem to remember it in different ways than do the French. And I can imagine several reasons why this should be so.

In the first place, I would suggest that the Japanese commemorate relatively more with ritual, the French with physical monuments, and that the Japanese — as already argued in regard to the Imperial Palace — do not need commemorative devices as material and explicit as those of Paris.[18] Of course, rituals take place in settings, and the two may merge,[19] but it is my impression that the ritual is relatively important in Tokyo, and the setting in Paris, and that whereas the setting is an intrinsic part of the exercise of power in Paris, in Tokyo it is only a setting. In particular, statues are rare in Tokyo, and the best known is that of a little dog, Hachikō, in Shibuya. Temples have statues of Buddhas, bodhisattvas, and guardian demons. But in public spaces statues are rare.

Moreover — and this is my second suggestion of monumentalist differences — it seems that a disproportionate number of statues are of foreigners, such as the nineteenth-century English expatriate architect Josiah Conder.[20] Monuments in general, like baroque cities in the colonies, seem

Fig. 23. Commemoration Japanese style: the Loyal Dog Hachikō.

often to be foreign in derivation, as if indigenous forms of commemoration are not sufficiently monumental to provide foreigners with the impressions they deserve. Herbert von Karajan Platz has already been mentioned; the Statue of Liberty replica in the Waterfront Subcenter also comes to mind. I am not quite sure what is at work here, as Paris is unquestionably filled with monuments of international repute and meaning. But Parisian monuments do not ape foreign ones, and seem to be the product of a more self-confident national culture.

Third, in addition to a disproportionate attentiveness to foreign audiences in its monuments, Tokyo (like Edo before it) seems more concerned with elite perceptions than does Paris. Certainly Versailles was designed to awe the French nobility, but in Paris I think a popular audience was a relatively stronger consideration. In Japan, by contrast, the greatest architectural monuments of all—the feudal castles—were intended overwhelmingly to convince elite rivals of the uselessness of any challenge to Tokugawa power. The great art of the era, while also "designed to display authority," was also "specifically by and for" the elite.[21] The Meiji regime did build monuments for public consumption, but very little of them remains; ritual and education appear to have been more significant ways to "mold Japanese minds."

Perhaps because Japanese monuments are less populist in function, they do not appear to have become embroiled in partisan politics to the extent that Parisian monuments have. In Paris, the Right and Left cannot even agree on where to celebrate Bastille Day, and contestation has been unending as partisan and popular forces lay claim to commemorative symbols of one kind and another. Nothing remotely resembling this can be found in Tokyo — to the relief of the riot police — with the occasional exception of Kudan and Hibiya, where the Left holds its rallies, and the House of Parliament, which everyone uses opportunistically for demonstrations. But contested monuments are rare: even the Yasukuni Shrine, in domestic politics, is a minor issue.

This is not to say the Japanese people do not matter. Indeed, in a society which does not officially monumentalize much, it is the people who by default play a major, if informal, role in commemoration. My surmise is that this commemoration, relative to its Parisian equivalent, takes two forms. First, it is more often private than public. Public spaces in particular and exteriors in general tend to be an "anarchic mess";[22] interiors and private spaces, on the other hand, are intensively managed by those to whom they belong, and commemorations — including memorial religious services — take place largely inside the home.

Second, commemoration among the Japanese is relatively often informal or, as I have termed it, "insurgent." Informally, villagers have placed humble religious images and commemorative markers all about the countryside, and Japan's cities are largely organized around popular place-names, especially those of "famous places" (*meisho*). Such places, named for historical significance or natural beauty, people or gods or events, conjure up thoughts with a linguistic, not physical, stimulus; they constitute an "immaterial monumentality" which is "radically different" from that of the West.[23] This creates a "narrative urbanism," giving Japanese cities "stories where other cities have monuments."[24] In other cases, popular determination of the symbolic meaning of places and spaces was not tacit but actively

Fig. 24. A Tokyo entertainment district at night.

counter to official policy. In Edo, for example, the regime intentionally did not create large public spaces and, with the exception of officially sponsored festivals, tried to prevent large assemblages.[25] But, in the same way that the Parisian Left expropriated the Place de la Bastille, the people of Edo repeatedly expropriated spaces like bridge approaches, temple and shrine precincts, and streets.[26] The people of Tokyo have done the same with Hibiya Park, Yoyogi Street, and Harajuku, turning them unbidden into performance spaces. The greatest of these, the *sakariba,* or entertainment districts, around the train stations, are truly monuments to popular consumption and license, a riot of neon, commerce, food, drink, and flesh.

Which brings me to the final reason that I think there is a difference between monuments in Paris and Tokyo: in the same way that the people of Tokyo, by default, have staged their own commemorations, so has private enterprise. And when private enterprise builds a monument, it is more likely to be commercially pragmatic rather than, as one sees in Paris, either an instrument of public power or an intended esthetic embellishment of the city. These private monuments are usually not dedicated to the historical past but rather to the splendors of contemporary capitalism; as such, perhaps they would be better termed "statements" than "monuments."[27] It may be fitting that the name most memorialized in the architecture of Tokyo is that of the developer Mori, found all over the buildings and projects put up by that family's huge company.

THE MONUMENTAL RECORD

Paris: The Capital as Monument

Lutetia had all the architectural embellishments of a typical provincial Roman city, but for most of its first millennium Paris was preoccupied with self-defense. Certainly defense and display were not incompatible, but it was not until the sixteenth century that French kings began concertedly to put a monumental face on Paris, to make it — as François I wished — a "New Rome," with magnificent entry gates and later a proliferation of statues.[28]

The consolidation of Paris's position as capital during the sixteenth and seventeenth centuries went hand in hand with its royal appearance, which peaked under Louis XIV.[29] Louis wanted a capital as "theatrical representation of the king's greatness," with "royal, sovereign" urban architecture, a ceremonial avenue from the Louvre to the Bastille, and monuments like those he initiated at Invalides, Place des Victoires, and Place Vendôme.[30] But Paris was a frustration, and in 1682 Louis decamped for Versailles.

But although Louis was forced to realize his monumentalist ambitions on the road, as it were, the mainstream swept back through Paris soon enough. The Revolution was one of those historical breaking points which, I have suggested above, enhances the monumentalist impulse, especially once the Jacobins set out to create a "unitary republic" out of "many regions and diverse populations."[31] They emphasized language and ritual more than construction, but Napoleon I compensated for that: "Paris doesn't

Fig. 25. Commemoration French style: Henry IV.

have enough buildings; we must provide them."[32] And it was, especially in the west, toward the Champs-Élysées and Arc de Triomphe, creating a new "geography of symbolic monuments."[33]

Napoleon built his monuments to the west because that was where the vacant land lay;[34] where symbols and commemorative rituals went, structure followed, and the Napoleonic quarters became the *beaux quartiers*. What began as a symbolic political division became, under Napoleon III and Haussmann, a socioeconomic one: Napoleon I had satisfied himself with monumental embellishments, but his nephew followed up by rebuilding the city in toto. But in doing so he also superimposed symbolic and socioeconomic division in yet another way, for his monumentalist impulse ended at the city wall.[35] In general, however, the late nineteenth century may have marked the acme of public monumentalism in Paris. The Third Republic followed a historical break almost as cataclysmic as the Revolution and coped in part with a "system of institutionalized democratic pageantry," especially in Paris, which rose to the level of "statuomania," so many were the images erected.[36] And Sacré-Coeur was an intrinsic part of this traditionalistic strategy for the "symbolic domination of Paris" by "explicitly counter-revolutionary" monuments.[37] The emergence of a spirit of preservationism added to this atmosphere: in 1887, the first historic preservation law was passed, and in 1913, it was strengthened to protect everything within 500 meters of two thousand places officially listed.[38]

But history was still up for grabs, in a way never witnessed in Japan, and the people were active participants — as subject and object — in the struggle to control commemoration. After World War I, the location of a new tomb for an unknown soldier was contested, with the Left demanding that it be in the Panthéon, and the Right (successfully) calling for the Arc de Triomphe.[39] And if large monuments stimulated conflict, so did little ones: place-names in Paris have been viewed since Napoleonic times as pedagogical, and they are driven by ideology, especially in the Red Belt, where the names of revolutionary heroes proliferated in the early twentieth century.[40]

The political tide turned under Vichy, and nearly one hundred politically incorrect "public political monuments" of various kinds were destroyed under German occupation.[41] After World War II, the taste for public political monuments never completely recovered, and the monumentalist impulse changed in three ways. First, public monuments became less overtly partisan, with museums, concert halls, and residential/commercial complexes seen as distinctly safer.[42] Second, governmental efforts were made toward "unification by monument." François Mitterrand made his first official visit as president to the Panthéon, and in particular tried to launch more projects in the disadvantaged eastern side of Paris, a drive which has not waned since. The bicentennial celebration of the Revolution was studiously evenhanded, with festivities and commemorations nationwide and at the Bastille, Place de le République, La Défense, the Panthéon, the Eiffel Tower, the Champs-Élysées — and even Versailles.[43] Third, as is the case in Tokyo, the relative number of private-sector monuments has grown. La Défense must rank first in this genre, although like Ark Hills in Tokyo it might be better described as a statement rather than a monument, and neither it nor Montparnasse (the nearest rival) will ever equal the pure effervescence of a Tokyo sakariba.

In any case, La Défense encapsulates almost all of my suspicions regarding the distinctive Parisian way of commemoration. It consciously conveys an image not only of a cosmopolitan, futuristic Paris but also a national Paris, embodied in the rhetorically symbolic name of the area and the heroic statue of the defenders of Paris against the Germans in 1871. The power of the state is clear, from its dominant role in EPAD, to the mixture of housing, to the siting of public transit under the plaza. The role of the people is also clear: the aim of La Défense was to lure not only the offices of multinational corporations but the public as well, to create a cultural and consumer mecca, and thus the people had to be accommodated — as they are, by a kilometer-long esplanade. Capitalism is a thus a constant in (actually, just outside) Paris, as it is in Tokyo, but the private provision of public space in the two differs dramatically.

Tokyo: Capital without Monuments

If Japan had a monumental age, it came and went early on. Between A.D. 300 and 600 grand imperial tombs were raised; they were superseded in the next few centuries by palaces, Buddhist temples, and Chinese-style city plans.[44] In the eighth and ninth centuries, the Heian capital's ceremonial Suzaku Boulevard was 84 meters wide and almost 4 kilometers long, and the city overall was "grandiose, monumental, and geometrical."[45] The Tōdai Temple in Nara housed a statue of the Buddha 16 meters high, in the largest wooden building in the world.[46] But neither a Tiananmen-style grand plaza nor any other popular gathering space was created, with the exception of two public markets which never really thrived. The result, already, was a "city without a citizenry."[47] And its physical monumentalism was incomplete too, and the gates and walls were allowed to fall into disrepair.

But it may be more accurate to describe public monumentalism as a series of waves, rather than a single one which ebbed a thousand years ago. In 1579, the hegemon Oda Nobunaga built a castle which, to the Jesuit Luis Frois, "as regards architecture, strength, wealth and grandeur may well be compared with the greatest buildings of Europe."[48] He was succeeded by Toyotomi Hideyoshi, "the most prolific builder in Japanese history," who built even vaster castles in Osaka and Kyoto in a "massive, untrammeled,

Fig. 26. A Japanese castle:
Osaka Castle, similar in
style to Edo Castle but a
bit smaller (about 170 feet
high versus about 190).

even vulgar" display of power.[49] But his power was demonstrated as much
ritually as physically, in parties, parades, plays, and war with Korea, and
the physical did not endure—his palace in Kyoto lasted only from 1587
until 1594.

But Japan's Louis XIV moment was not over yet. The early Tokugawa
era was one of material monuments-as-power, and of displacement of the
people. Ieyasu built the largest castle in Japan, and his successors built huge
palaces, mausoleums, and temples in Edo and elsewhere and encouraged
the lords to erect elegant urban residences whose every architectural detail
reflected their rank.[50] But Edo Castle was the last material gesture of the
palatial age, and the Japanese did not just stop building, they did not even
rebuild, at least on anything remotely approaching a monumental scale.
Partly this was a matter of finances, and partly it was because the regime's

power was now secure. But it is also consistent with a distinctive sort of monumentalist thought.

What the later Tokugawa era suggests, that is, is a "less is more" vision of material power. Reminders of state power became low-key, and the ruling elites did their best to make politics "invisible"; they "forfeited the opportunity to bind the ruler with his subjects through public and/or visual displays, as monarchs did in early modern Europe."[51] And so Edo did not become a city "loaded with royal icons . . . which force rulers perpetually upon the public gaze."[52] The fortification of European cities was deemed "culturally inferior": "only tyrants live in castles."[53] Authority was based on the imposition not of images but of rules, which dictated the behavior of both elites and masses in exquisite detail.[54]

Edo-era monumentalism thus began in a material way but ended up social and cultural. Its early emphasis on monuments as the manifestation of power also focused more on rival elites than on popular threats. The third shogun, Iemitsu, did build a shrine complex in Nikko, to commemorate Ieyasu and to manifest the "divine authority" of the shogunate, showing that "the gods approved of Tokugawa rule."[55] And a number of shogunal palaces were built in Kyoto, where the imperial court could not miss these "reminders" of the Tokugawa presence.[56] But to the extent that Japanese capitals became monumental, they did so largely oblivious to the people. The government did not want the people gathering, and constant popular encroachment led to bans on construction, recreation, and even entry.[57]

Such bans reflected the growing inability of the regime to exclude the people from public spaces; the predecessors of today's sakariba grew up in the streets and, as mentioned, at the approaches to the city's bridges.[58] And when the people decided to commemorate something, again, the government in the long run tended to cave in, as it did in the case of the Forty-seven Rōnin, a famous epic of vendetta whose protagonists, forced to commit ritual suicide for their illegal act, became the heroes of a highly popular kabuki play and were entombed at the Sengaku Temple, which promptly became a scene of popular pilgrimage. The last thing the regime wanted was the romanticization of this crime, but authorities were powerless to prevent it. Later Japanese governments relented; today there is a statue of the leader of the rōnin at the temple, and — perhaps inevitably — a highly commercialized annual festival commemorating their loyalty and sacrifice. But one guidebook of 1920 asserts that a visit of fifteen minutes suffices.[59]

The Meiji era saw another wave of more Western-style monumentalism, but this too reverted in time to a less materialist, more elite-directed, less populist pattern, albeit with two new characteristics: monuments now often had either foreign models or foreign audiences; and private corporate interests became involved in the business of memorialization and symbolic communication. The wave rose slowly: much of Edo Castle burned in a series of fires in the 1850s and 1860s, most of the remaining gates and walls were unceremoniously destroyed at the beginning of the era,[60] and the emperor lived in an auxiliary palace for sixteen years. But gradually a capital-as-symbol view grew: in the 1880s, the Ginza-Marunouchi central business district took shape on land sold off by the state, and a new imperial palace was built.[61] Paralleling the trend in Europe, statues, parade grounds, triumphal arches and Shinto gates, museums, pageants, and ceremonies proliferated; the capital was to become "a massive state theater" and an "official sign of Japan's progress."[62] But, like Edo's Louis XIV moment around 1600, this "baroque moment" did not last. For one thing, "the monarchy in Japan was nonvisual," in contrast to that of France.[63] Moreover, the effort did not serve its international purpose, as we shall see, and after the 1923 earthquake demolished many of the arches, they were not rebuilt. The whole episode lasted only from roughly 1890 until 1923 and, even at its height, was "unpretentious" relative to what occurred in Europe.[64]

The capital was, however, designed to "to serve the ends of power," even if they did not require monumental representation or popular mobilization.[65] The business district was one such end, and city planning which focused on infrastructure and completely ignored the practical needs of Tokyoites was another: the Meiji city builders were initially no more concerned with the people than their predecessors had been.[66] Gradually this attitude changed, in two ways. First, mobilizing the people became a state goal, albeit to be achieved more through the schools and army reserve associations than through physical symbols.[67] Second, the image of the people as potential troublemakers grew. Once again the people had appropriated open spaces, especially in the new commercial districts where amusements concentrated, and in the 1890s the police began to tighten up on popular behavior in the station plazas and amusement districts.[68] From the day it opened in 1903, Hibiya Park attracted crowds bent on demonstrating, protesting, or commemorating as they wished, and insurgent memorialization became a continuing problem for the state.[69] But once again the people were upstaged in the eyes of society's symbol manipulators, this time not by domestic elites but by the outside world. Having no indigenous models of modern architecture, the Japanese turned to London and to Paris, whose "grand, permanent, and monumental" style seemed the epitome of modernity.[70] When a new imperial palace was finally built in the 1880s, the exterior was Japanese in style, but the interiors were largely Louis XIV.[71] The adoption of Western models was not due solely to the lack of native models, however. The West was also the audience for monumental Tokyo. Japan was subject at the time to a series of unequal treaties which gave foreigners exceptional privileges there, and the state hoped to speed treaty revision by impressing the foreigners with Japan's modernity, cosmopolitanism, and power. Architecture was one ingredient in the plan: Tokyo's form would be manipulated in order to manipulate foreign perceptions.[72] The 1880s were the high point of the intended foreign seduction, with the "truly monumental," baroque Ende-Bockmann city plan the centerpiece. But the foreigners were unmoved, and the treaties remained unrevised.[73] The domestic audience had never really mattered, the foreign audience sat on its hands, and the "half-hearted attempt" at a monumental capital passed once more,[74] leaving little more than one flamboyant exception: the 1896 equestrian statue of the warrior hero Kusunoki Masashige. But he, too, represents a Paris-Tokyo difference: the statue was a private gift from the wealthy Sumitomo family to the emperor, not a public project.

The American Occupation of Japan, of course, encouraged historical amnesia, and the Americans helped by destroying a large number of statues deemed militaristic;[75] curiously, Masashige escaped. The entire nation focused on recovery, and, when prosperity provided both the resources and the will to put on a show, the desire to impress the foreigners with Japan's innocence and modernity again meant that the past would receive short shrift. In 1958, the Eiffelesque Tokyo Tower opened, fulfilling "an important patriotic goal"; as in the Meiji era, "this particular message abroad about the onset of a new era for Japan was delivered in the language of

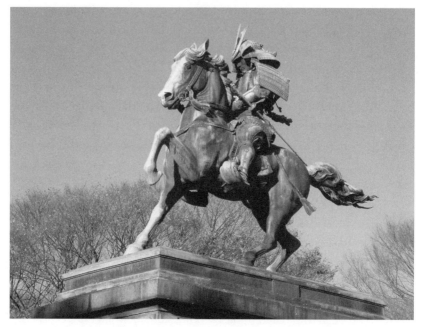

Fig. 27. Japanese commemoration with Western flamboyance: Kusunoki Masa-shige. For every Japanese who knows about it, tens of thousands know about Hachikō.

architecture."[76] But it wasn't *Japanese* architecture. A more successful monument — again, to Japan's contemporary achievements — was the 1964 Olympics, which included some gracefully widened avenues and park space, and some clearly Japanese-inspired buildings by Tange Kenzō.[77]

But most of postwar Tokyo's monumental projects have tended to be more municipal or private than state-sponsored. Tokyo had Governor Suzuki Shunichi — its Robert Moses, if not its Haussmann — not François Mitterrand. And he was most definitely a monumentalist by inclination. His magnum opus, the New City Hall, is the biggest building complex built in twentieth-century Japan and "a fortress of governmental authority and administrative power."[78] Eclectically inspired — by a feudal Japanese castle, a wood-frame Edo-era house, a computer circuit board, and Notre-Dame — the New City Hall is a "bold assertion" of Tokyo's own "identity and authority" vis-à-vis the state.[79]

The success of public monumentalism, however, may be questioned. the New City Hall is, of course, fully utilized; the International Forum, on the other hand, is not, and is a financial albatross around the city's neck.[80] As statements, of course, they succeed by their very existence; functionally, however, both private and "insurgent" monumentalism may be more successful. The former includes everything from the splendidly outlandish branches of the Yodobashi Camera discount-store chain to the megacomplexes of Ark Hills and Tokyo Midtown: architecturally they aim to attract attention, and thereby to "sell something more effectively."[81] It also includes private commemorations, such as the ceremonies which take place within the Imperial Palace.

The latter, insurgent, monumentalism includes both the political — demonstrations on both the Right and Left which take over public spaces in the central city — and the apolitical: neighborhood shrine festivals and historical markers, street players, and the "public theater" of dancers in Harajuku of a Sunday afternoon. The authorities still have not been inclined to admit the citizenry fully into the urban-planning process,[82] but this has not stopped the people from deciding for themselves what will be commemorated, when, or where. This is not so say that the same does not happen in Paris, but that the gap between what the government allows or encourages and what the people usurp is wider in Tokyo. Still, the people's ability to usurp Japanese public space is only by default: in the immediate postwar period, the outer palace grounds were the focal point of demonstrations, until the authorities used the device of parade and assembly permits to expel them to Hibiya Park — evidently the proximity of the grounds to the symbolically not-so-empty center was more than conservative elites could stomach.[83] But as this last suggests, monumentalism in Tokyo inheres more in behavior than in bricks and mortar, and more in sites than in edifices. The ultimate expression of this is perhaps the designation of individuals as Intangible National Treasures. As noted, commodified monumentalism by economic interests, and foreign-inspired and -oriented monuments, are relatively prominent. Over and over again, in everything from Chinese city design to the "Parthenon" in Tama New Town, we see a reliance on the foreign in attempts at monumentalism. And public monumentalism is present to an absolutely lesser degree in Tokyo than in Paris. The validity of a religious source of this disinclination is impossible to evaluate here, but it seems clear that political authorities have not felt — and still do not feel — that their grip on power, or the people's identification with the nation, depends on impressing the people through architectural media to anything remotely approaching the extent seen in Paris.

Are there exceptions in Paris? Certainly, from the old regime's "orchestrated public rejoicing" on the Champ de Mars, the quays, and the royal plazas to the July 14 parade along the Champs Élysées.[84] And are there exceptions in Tokyo? Certainly. But the great castles did not endure and the statues which we do find in Tokyo are upstaged by little Hachikō. The Grand Shrine of Nikko perhaps proves the rule by being both magnificently monumental and almost universally trashed by art critics for its garish arriviste pretensions.[85] Finally, there is the commemorative, monumental Yasukuni Shrine, whose true purpose, I would argue, is not "to remind" so much as it is to mobilize votes for today's politicians, while Tokyo's truly commemorative space, the Chidorigafuchi National Cemetery, is distinctly modest and almost completely ignored by the state.[86]

6 | THE CAPITAL ENVISIONED

This tour of Paris and Tokyo has been thus far literally an ego trip: I have recounted, and tried to interpret, some of the visual characteristics of the two cities as a visitor might see them. But how these cities have grown has been determined by how others see them. There is more to form than topography, technology, war, disaster, and diplomacy; more to center-periphery contrasts than walls, religion, and authority; more to manipulation than culture, resources, and power; and more to monuments than legitimacy, elitism or populism, or cultural conceptions of space. When one stops walking and sits down to read, the histories of Paris and Tokyo reveal many similarities in the way natives and outsiders, rulers and ruled, politicians and poets have perceived the capital. But they also reveal deep differences in "objective" perceptions, value judgments, and likes and dislikes, all of which — mediated through centuries of public- and private-sector decisions — have arguably influenced the visual, physical differences the foreign flâneur can see.

Specifically, three things have struck me in a comparative historical reading of Tokyo and Paris. First, normative evaluations of Paris — and Western cities in general[1] — have tended to be much more ambivalent, and far more often negative, than those of Tokyo. Second, there is a relatively strong element of fear in views of Paris, but not of Tokyo. Third is the question of intensity: Paris inspires passion, both negative and positive, whereas both Edo's and (even more) Tokyo's admirers and detractors are decidedly more tepid. This is not a matter of Oriental Inscrutability versus Gallic Effusiveness; neither stereotype survives close examination. But the differences must be accounted for.

EVALUATIONS OF THE CAPITAL: ROOTS

But how? A fairly diligent reading of Tokyo and Paris history reveals two types of possible bases for evaluations of the capital. In the first place, I suggest, are deep cultural predispositions toward cities in general, based in religion and morality, and in conceptions of nature and artifice. Then, second, there appear to be overlays: historically subsequent perceptions of the capital as a possible parasite, as a threat of some sort to the country, and as the locus of modernity, industry, and capitalism.

The encomiums heaped on Paris over the centuries need no recapping; what has struck me in a comparative vein, however, is the — at best — deeply ambivalent perceptions that Paris shares with cities in general in the Judeo-Christian tradition. Greek and Roman civilization, of course, viewed cities positively, as centers of freedom, citizenship, and political life,[2] and during the Dark Ages the church, too, assumed a more positive stance, as the relative safety of cities was contrasted with the barbarism outside. But ambivalence continued: medieval cities were places of safety *and* sin, and Paris did not escape this dichotomy, as an arena for free speech and thought but also for pleasure, temptation, and perdition.[3]

In Japan, such schizophrenia never developed. The Chinese tradition noted the virtues of rural life and on occasion decried the "vice and corruption" of the city.[4] But overall there was no notion that the city was distinct from or superior to the country or vice versa, such distinctions being more "a cliché of our Western cultural traditions."[5] Nor did Japan generate its own anti-urban tradition. Indeed, during Tokugawa rule Edo became the center of a vibrant, vigorous, and self-confident urban popular culture. Pro-agrarian and antimercantile ideas did arise, but I will suggest below that the foci of such ideologies were then and later luxury, mammonism, and poverty wherever found, and that the city never became an intrinsically morally problematic place.[6] Just as Confucianism, Buddhism, and Shinto took no firm moral stand on the city, neither does Japanese culture distinguish invidiously between the world of nature and that of human artifice. Rather than seeing the hand of man in the city as opposed to — and either superior or inferior to — the workings of nature, it sees the city as mediating between man and the gods, man and nature.[7]

In the West, by contrast, ambivalence is once again apparent, as nature has been at some times seen as peaceful, innocent Arcady and at others as "brutish and ignorant."[8] The Greeks and Romans tended to conflate city and hinterland: citizenship appertained equally to urbanites and country folk. But with the fall of the Roman Empire, an age descended where nature was abhorred as the fearsome abode of evil, and urban artifice was embraced for its safety and at least the prospect of minimally civilized life. The medieval city also carries many favorable images. In any case, a realistic pro-urbanism endured for several centuries; it was not until the eighteenth century that European urban life was so much improved and so rapidly changing that people entertained the alternative luxury of romanticizing the countryside and posing a pure, virtuous Nature against urban "seats of malignancy."[9] Over many centuries, the cultural raw material for normative evaluations of cities in general and the capital in particular has been overlaid with manifestations specific to different periods. In both Tokyo and Paris, such overlays have included perceptions of the capital as a threat. Objectively, cities were dangerous places in sixteenth-century Japan. During the civil wars, lords offered all sorts of privileges to merchants in order to lure them to the city, followed by the Tokugawa edicts limiting commercial activities to the city.[10] These carrots — including the vast consumer demand generated by the urban warrior class — and sticks combined to contribute to a sweeping wave of urban growth during the seventeenth century.

But what affected perceptions of the city was not size but commerce. The feudal political economy was warrior-dominated and agriculturally based, but state policies forcing the samurai to live in the cities threw this system out of kilter by exposing the warriors, it was believed, to debasing commercial behavior and lascivious pleasures, thus debilitating and impoverishing the ruling class and robbing the villages of talent and an elite presence which would help integrate rulers and ruled. The response was Nativist political thought, or *kokugaku,* which advocated enhancing city planning and urban social control, and limiting conspicuous consumption.[11]

But kokugaku was not intrinsically anti-urban. It advocated removal of the samurai from the cities, especially Edo, but once the samurai were back on the land, the cities would not be a problem. If the villages could be revived under samurai guidance, then the social hierarchy would be righted, the economy would be appropriately agrocentric, and the cities could go their way unhindered. In fact, few of the Nativists' ideas became policy, particularly those calling for rustication of the samurai. The only really effective limiting factor on city growth was the expanding economy of the countryside, which meant that the occupational benefits of city life could be obtained increasingly without going there. Such expansion did not occur in preindustrial France, and perhaps as a result Paris has long been perceived as a vampire, a parasite whose growth drains the rest of the country of its economic and human resources. Feudal Japan had not one but three major cities with populations in the hundreds of thousands and their own economic and cultural identities, plus some three hundred castle towns sustained by the presence of the ruling class. France, by contrast, was dominated — and threatened — by Paris to a greater degree. The biggest difference, however — and this is simply my own impression — is that, in the case of Edo and Tokyo, the city was the indirect target of criticism for the presence there of undesirable things, whereas Paris was seen as intrinsically threatening, not for what it had but for what it was. This difference becomes even clearer when one listens to those who observed a second overlay, as Paris and Tokyo began to modernize under capitalism. Factories, commerce, mechanization and commodification of an increasing share of life, fetid slums, dazzling wealth and grinding poverty, rapid and dislocating social change, huge inequalities, disease, filth, environmental blight, crime, alienation, financial booms and busts, exploitation — all this became the stuff of daily urban life. Paris, for example, became simultaneously a world capital and focus of awe and admiration, and everyone's whipping boy: wicked, artificial, brutal, chaotic, corrosive, dehumanizing.[12] As industrialization progressed, the negative — of the city as both a social and a physical danger — grew relatively stronger. In some cases — Balzac,

Baudelaire, Benjamin, and Marx, among others — the poles mingled in a love-hate relationship.[13] But, as we shall see, the negative views were the ones that found a receptive audience in the halls of the French state.

But not in Japan. The potential was there: industrialization swept Japan in the late nineteenth century at a breathtaking pace. And although Japanese tradition did not provide much of a vehicle for anti-urbanism,[14] the Japanese learned quickly: in opposition to the virtuous, communal village was posed the avaricious, alienating, exploitative, criminal city, with Tokyo the "hotbed of evils."[15] This ideological current, although still present today, crested between the world wars, as radical agrarian thought decried the moral corruption, hedonism, and mammonism of the city in particular and the entire concept of modernity in general, and the impoverishment of the countryside.[16] Yet it was not the same as with France. Perhaps this was because anti-urbanism in Japan had no indigenous roots.[17] Or perhaps it was because the pathologies of the city — industry, capitalism, and modernity — were non-native, whereas cities were homegrown. Some criticized "urban" lifestyles and "urbanized" young people, even if found in the village.[18] Others implied that cities had become corrupted by capitalism.[19] The ethnologist Yanagita Kunio, even as he argued that urbanization and industrialization had "caused the ruination" of the countryside, dissolved the dichotomy by arguing that there was no intrinsic opposition between city and country, that *every* Japanese has a hometown *furusato,* and that this hometown could be a city, or even the nation as a whole.[20] Thus Japanese anti-urbanism was ill-designed to support anti-urban policy, and it rarely did. The same elites that extolled agrarian values before World War II promoted a full-speed, industrializing war effort. And since the last war even Tokyo's harshest critics have acknowledged its economic efficiency.[21] In other words, Tokyo has been treated as an issue or a problem (and sometimes even as a victim) rather than as an adversary.[22] There is a consensus that contemporary Tokyo excessively concentrates economic, political, and cultural functions and institutions, and population. But the remedy is almost never zero-sum. In fact, the state's most recent response is to preserve the central city milieu with a law severely restricting large-scale suburban construction by commercial, educational, and medical establishments which might otherwise want to move out from downtown.[23] In other words, it seems as if the solution envisioned is not to change a problematic Tokyo but rather to protect it, to create mini-Tokyos throughout the country, or even to allow Tokyo to absorb the entire nation.

EVALUATIONS OF THE CAPITAL: EVIDENCE

Thus, although Paris has its lovers and Tokyo its detractors, what strikes one about views of these capitals, when juxtaposed and viewed in light of their physical forms, is the opposite. And the diaphanous nature of cultural traditions may play a role here. Edo and Tokyo have shown manifestly negative characteristics — vulnerability to warfare, fire, earthquake, and disease then; overcrowding, overcentralization, and environmental degradation now — and yet a wholesale critique has never been articulated, much less determined governmental action. Parisian dynamism, on the other hand, has arguably sustained the French economy for almost two centuries in the face of provincial stagnation, and yet it has been hammered by its critics and by successive French governments for much of that time.[24] Evidence for this argument will also be adduced in chapter 7 and the conclusion, which focus on fears of the capital and on its relationships. Here I instead consider some evidence for the origins, suggested above, of views of the capital.

In the case of Paris, most of the evidence consists of a body of literature in praise of the city so vast and familiar as to need no recounting. But it is supplemented by two other distinctive genres: one attacking Paris, and another defending the capital against what it sees as a concerted attack. What sets the latter genres apart, however, is the idea that Paris is bad just because it is Paris, and the early emergence of these ideas.[25] One imagines only with difficulty Japanese equivalents to *Paris and the French Desert, Fear of the Suburbs,* or *The Scandal of Paris;* nor have Tokyo's defenders had to take up their cudgels in works like *The Assassination of Paris, The Conquest of Paris, The State against Paris,* or *The War against Paris.*[26]

In Japan, urban thought was less ambivalent — albeit less passionate — for many centuries.[27] A critique of the capital did develop during the Edo period, and reforms were adopted from time to time, but they tended to aim at cleaning up Edo — attacking luxury, waste, gambling, and sloth;

eliminating slums and unauthorized migrants and prostitutes; and improving fire protection.[28] Nor does more recent evidence suggest any long-standing current. The official agrarianism of the prewar period was largely the cynical tool of a centralizing state;[29] indeed, ever since the Restoration, the state has simply evinced minimal and episodic interest in the cities.

Industry and commerce, capitalism, and modernity and Westernization all had their critics, and Tokyo was an easy lightning rod for them. But Marx — always ambivalent about cities — was an uncertain guide for the Left, and both the Left and the radical agrarianists on the Right were split.[30] The critics had limited objective material to work with: they were essentially creating an agrarian "tradition" from scratch; much industry was not urban at all; and capitalism was (and still is) subject to state regulation and unable to run pathologically free. And, despite the images of urban proletarians and masses, there were relatively low levels of social atomization, deviance, and extreme deprivation.[31]

After the war, initial consensus was built around reconstruction, with Tokyo playing a major role, but by the 1960s, the downside of geographically concentrated industrialization was becoming visible in the demographic crowding and environmental pollution along the Pacific coast and in the emptying out of Japan's villages. More regionally decentralized economic growth was attempted, but the only potentially anti-Tokyo aspect of such policies was the expulsion of heavy industry from the capital, which in fact enhanced the city's attractiveness to both people and corporations.[32] The idea that a city could actually be too big grew during the 1970s; as metropolitan Tokyo rapidly eclipsed Osaka and Kyoto and approached one-third of the national population in the 1980s, the concept of a "Tokyo Problem" entered popular discourse. But those who saw Tokyo as the key to Japan's economic growth and international competitiveness and stature remained dominant. Ever more efficient transportation and communication systems overcame time and space in ways that Paris is only presently attempting to approximate, and the Parisian factor of the capital as home to a growing, and problematic, foreign population was missing in Tokyo. Such factors as these seem to have pulled the rug out from under those who might otherwise have launched an effective anticapital narrative.

Such a narrative has been a leitmotif in Paris, however, and anyone wish-

ing to attack capitalism, industry, or urbanism has a fertile French tradition to cultivate. Industrialization easily melded "old moral, esthetic, or
hygienic condemnations of the capital" with a new social and economic
critique.[33] Haussmann's aim was to create a glorious city, and his works
have elicited praise from legions of Parisians and visitors ever since. But his
motives were not all positive. Haussmann's social control considerations
derived from a centuries-old problem, as did concerns for sanitation and
public health, though all had become more acute during economic modernization. The threat of Paris as a whole was ended once and for all by the
Commune, but "fear of the suburbs" soon replaced it, and negative images
of the capital characterized the Third Republic throughout its lifetime.
Whereas in Tokyo the overlay of modernity did not lead to a widely popular critique of the capital, in Paris it did.

In any case, the critique survived the war, although it appears to be
fading today. During the 1950s, anti-Parisian forces were still strident,[34]
but the ascendance of Delouvrier and his master plan marked a turning
point in both policy and image. In the 1970s, a national consensus began
to emerge that put a vibrant, economically flourishing Paris at the center of
French aspirations; although negative perceptions of the city persist with
considerable frequency and strength, they no longer presuppose sacrifice
of the capital to larger national goals. Still, French cities in general and
Paris in particular are viewed more problematically. In recent years, the
French cabinet has included ministers with responsibility for such issues
as "social cohesion," "social exclusion," "integration and equal opportunity," "solidarity," and "the fight against poverty" — all references to urban
problems — and urban affairs in general, all foci strikingly absent from the
Japanese cabinet. And, of course, the police of Paris are still commanded
by a state prefect. That is, Paris is not only a Problem, with distasteful and
unhealthy qualities — it is a threat.

FEAR OF THE CITY: SOME SPECULATIONS

This subject is a crucial one, which seems to me one of the really major
differences between Paris and Tokyo. As such, it deserves detailed examination, and in this light I would suggest three different aspects of possible

fears of the capital. The first is *political:* fear of Paris by the state and the nation, and of some of Paris's parts by the city itself, is far greater than what one finds in Tokyo. Paris's first uprising came in 1358, and although the Revolution began in Paris, it was just one battle in "the metropolitan civil war that has wracked Paris in one form or another for hundreds of years."[35] In Japan, by contrast, the capital has never symbolized political conflict or violence. Edo was stereotypically a city of "fights" (*kenka*), but that was how the state chose to define much collective disorder, and accordingly ignored it. Food riots were a problem, but the state usually let them run their course before mopping up some of the leaders.[36] Outbursts of metropolitan violence have occurred in Tokyo, especially in a series of extremist bombings in the 1960s and 1970s, but the police eliminated the radicals, who left little residue.

The second possible form of fear, closely linked to the first, is *socioeconomic,* and here, too, we find Paris is more feared, and fearful, than Edo or Tokyo. Class analyses of the Revolution are complex, but it is clear that bourgeois fear of the lower classes crystallized during the first half of the nineteenth century. By midcentury, Paris was a city of "profound divisions and class hatreds," and a "Manichaean" perception of the capital emerged,[37] with Parisians fearful of a ravening horde of proletarians in the east and the suburbs, and the rest of France scared of the whole incendiary metropolis.

Class hostility can be shrugged off as a determining feature of perceptions of Tokyo. There was a great deal of dire poverty in Edo, but social conflict was actually greater in the counties around Edo, not in the center.[38] Any fears thus generated, while quickly politicized in Paris, remained largely apolitical in Tokyo. Edo and Tokyo both had infamous slums, but these were feared more as sources of fire, disease, and common crime than of insurrection.[39] During the Meiji era, an unhealthy pauper class was seen as a threat to national goals of economic and military strength, and slums as eyesores, sinks of disease, and firetraps. But, in fact, the rapid redevelopment which followed the 1923 earthquake, plus Japan's equally rapid economic growth, led to the relatively effective amelioration of slum conditions and poverty in the capital.[40] This does not mean, of course, that sociopolitical critiques of Tokyo have disappeared. But the inferred receptivity of the poor to left-wing appeals — found also in Paris — while present, is overshadowed by a relatively heavy emphasis on the putative attenuation of social attachments and decay of community in the city.[41]

The final way in which the capital may be seen as fearsome is as the abode of Others, as the site of somehow alien social groups. And here, too, one sees some parallel fears in Japan and France, but with a correlation of Other and place in Paris which one does not see in Tokyo. The Japanese are insular in more ways than one, but no image of Tokyo or any of its parts as an ominously alien redoubt has emerged.

Paris, on the other hand, has seemingly long been associated with cultural Otherness. In the last two centuries, the Other became defined by class, and most recently by ethnicity — black and/or Muslim — and associated with the suburbs rather than with Paris as a whole, but the negative evaluation has survived this transition quite well. What was once feared as the Red Belt is now feared as foreign territory, the potential breeding ground of terrorists and, in 2005 and 2006, rioters. The French are by any measure more tolerant and inclusive of cultural Others than are the Japanese, but here again we see the politicization of fear in Paris in a way not seen in Tokyo.

URBAN FEAR AND URBAN FORM

Political Fear: Aux barricades!

The putative tendency of Paris to insurrection is "one of the permanent preoccupations of political power in France."[42] And not without reason: fully a thousand years ago, King Robert the Pious initiated a "dangerous collusion" between the king and the people of Paris against his bourgeois rivals.[43] Once admitted, the people were loath to renounce their role, and when Philippe Auguste built his fortress in Paris two centuries later, he had his own people, "already known for unruliness," in mind.[44] Sometimes foreign wars drew the people in: in the 1350s, Étienne Marcel, provost of merchants, leapt into a simultaneous English invasion and succession struggle to enlist the people of the Paris Commune on the side of the dauphin; he failed, but this rupture between king and capital was to be repeated.[45] And sometimes the wars were religious, as in the late sixteenth century, when Paris, under the Catholic League, rose against the king.[46]

Between the thirteenth and fifteenth centuries, tension between king and people hardened, as Parisians realized that taxation was a growing tool of the state, and the kings grew to recognize that their power depended on control of Paris, which they had to fortify against outsiders and "hold ... without being the prisoner of the Parisians."[47] The split came to a head in the rebellion of the Fronde (1648–53), which was "largely concentrated in and around Paris" and whose suppression by Louis XIV subjected the city to violence, pillage, and privation.[48] Such conflict was primarily between crown and capital, but in 1789 this balance changed dramatically. Throughout the eighteenth century, Paris had been changing: the gap between the rich and poor grew, and state power encroached on municipal autonomy. Given the simultaneous emergence of the idea of a social contract legitimizing royal rule, it is unsurprising that class envy and perceptions of the state as despotic also deepened.[49] Thus the political culture of Paris drew further away from that of the rest of the nation, and the horrors of the Revolution confirmed all the provinces' worst fears.[50]

The wave of revolution receded, and Paris was quiescent until 1830, but polarization within the city and between the city and the provinces grew,[51] and fear began to influence the form of the capital. Institutionally, Napoleon stripped the city of mayor and assembly and made himself its "sole master" by putting the capital under two state prefects.[52] Physically, he added the Place de l'Étoile, a triumphal monument which was also an "admirable emplacement for artillery ... and was so intended."[53] And his successors went beyond, encircling Paris with a wall and forts the placement of which "defied military logic except when seen from the Paris side."[54]

The year 1848 solidified the revolutionary role of Paris and the cleavage between capital and country: for the first time, a revolutionary outburst in Paris was not followed by one in the provinces.[55] It was followed by the Second Empire, and by Haussmann's further efforts to shape a counter-revolutionary city. He "encircled" the obstreperous Faubourg St. Antoine with open boulevards (read: gunnery ranges) and cut a boulevard right through it as well; the improved rue de Rivoli facilitated troop movement from the barracks in Courbevoie, and wider, straighter streets all about made it harder for insurgents to hide and easier for the police to move about.[56] Haussmann's programs overall only heightened hatreds in and of the capital: nearly ten attempts were made on the life of Napoleon III, and the capital took its revenge in the Commune of 1871, "the century's greatest paroxysm of violence."[57] But ultimately Paris lost terribly.

This did not signify, however, the end of Parisian violence. While the Right took over Paris proper by the turn of the century, the Left took over the suburbs, and a new opposition was born.[58] Moreover, the state's presence made Paris a magnet for dissidents from all over, and from the 1890s straight on into the interwar period, anarchist bombings, bloody riots, and strikes wracked the city. In 1932, President Paul Doumer was assassinated there, and in 1936, some half million people rallied to commemorate the Commune. The Right and Left fought it out in the streets in the 1930s, the dead and injured were counted in the hundreds, and many feared civil war.[59]

After the war, fears refocused, from Paris versus France to Paris versus its suburbs, and over time they became significantly less political. Reorganization of Île-de-France into more departments broke up the Red Belt; the communists were domesticated; and by 1977, the state no longer feared municipal autonomy enough to deny the capital a mayor. Many of the cities in the banlieue are still communist-ruled, especially in Seine-St-Denis. But such regimes are no longer a threat; nor is Paris as a whole — the greatest postwar outbreak of insurgency, in 1968, no longer represented Paris against France.[60] This does not mean that all fears have faded — an attempt on the mayor's life was made in 2002. But the role of fear in the way the capital is shaped and run has changed significantly.

Such a record of objective turbulence and subjective recoil is not to be found in Tokyo. The raw material for fear was by no means absent, but it was thin: for most of the Edo era, whatever fears the regime may have entertained were based on elite disloyalty, particularly in the provinces.[61] The Edoites, as noted, were a turbulent crew, and there were scores of small protests (many legal) and a few major food riots, but deaths were infrequent, and the state was satisfied to look upon most disturbances as common crime. And although administrative responsibility for Edo was in the hands of state magistrates, everyday administration was in the hands of commoner elders, and neighborhood-level controls were exercised by residents themselves. The institutional form of the capital does not seem to have been shaped by state fear of its people.

After the Restoration, social control was a major concern, and the state — wary of "antisystem movements" — preemptively forbade Tokyo any municipal autonomy, making both the governor and mayor state officials.[62] But most of the political unrest of the Meiji period was provincial.[63] Indeed, one standard punishment for illegal political activism in the capital was banishment, which suggests that the state did not fear adding to the sum total of radicals just outside the capital.

In the twentieth century, Tokyo became more politically restive; after almost forty quiescent years, nine riots occurred between 1905 and 1918, and as industry began to concentrate in and around the cities, labor conflict urbanized also.[64] But (with the sole, and preemptively crushed, exception of the regicidal conspiracy of Kōtoku Shūsui in 1910) one looks in vain for signs of fear of the Revolutionary Capital, on the order of Paris, in either the halls of state or the provinces. In the immediate postwar period, Japan saw an unprecedented wave of labor strife and (often communist-led) political protest, but neither the largest (in 1960) nor the most violent (around 1970) of all the postwar civil disorders brought into being an image of political danger in the capital, much less a set of political assumptions with implications for the shape of the city.[65] No barricades here.

Lower Classes and Middle Masses

One very plausible explanation for the low degree of political fear of the Japanese capital is the weak sense of socioeconomic class in Japan. I shall not pursue the origins of this, but it is a simple fact, at least relative to western Europe. The Tokugawa common people protested incessantly, but they never demonstrated any significant hostility to the social order.[66] After the Restoration, industrialization brought a modern working class into existence, but at no point did real class hostility ever grow strong. Tokyo has seen its share of riots, most notably in 1905, 1918, and 1960, but the first were a nationalistic protest against the Treaty of Portsmouth and the last a pacifist protest against the U.S.-Japan Mutual Security Treaty. Only the second instance, the Rice Riots, was class based but, as part of a nationwide wave of food riots, it did not generate fears of the Tokyo proletariat per se.[67] Even at the height of the interwar Red Scare, when state officials tried to persuade the public that imperial militarism was the only salvation from

Bolshevik threats at home and abroad, one cannot find the sort of implacable hostility that characterized the Parisian bourgeoisie and proletariat in the middle of the nineteenth century. And in the postwar period, the whole concept of class lost its political significance, as opinion poll after poll has shown that somewhere between two-thirds and three-quarters of the Japanese see themselves as a "middle mass," hardly a class in the Marxist sense at all.[68]

Against this, the exquisite class hatreds of Paris need little elaboration,[69] and all I adduce here is evidence of their impact on the city itself. The mélange of classes in prerevolutionary Paris gave way to an increasingly lower-class Marais, Belleville, and the rest of eastern Paris, and the June Days and 1848 intensified the standoff of the classes, with the bourgeoisie terrified of "an explosion of evil from the subterranean Paris of sewers and filth."[70] Haussmann's programs created socioeconomic "apartheid," and by 1871, class war "was written in the geography of the capital."[71]

The east-west class division of Paris has endured to this day, an objective and subjective cleavage with no parallel whatsoever in Tokyo. Gradually the bourgeoisie took control of space, and the homogeneity of the city proper increased. The postwar construction of the grands ensembles beyond the city's edge provided room for more and more of those pushed out by high rents.[72] Belatedly, President Mitterrand initiated a concerted effort to rebalance Paris: most of his "grand projects" were in the east.[73] And he did succeed in revitalizing significant parts of the east. But although concern has replaced hostility, it has not led to reconciliation: the revival of the Marais is largely a process of exclusionary gentrification, and the suburban rioting of October-November 2005 was explained at least in part in socioeconomic terms. Both municipal and state officials repeatedly bemoan the trend toward a Paris "for the very rich and the very poor,"[74] with deleterious effects on social solidarity and republican ideals — and crime rates.

The Deprived and the Depraved

Misgivings about the lower classes and other undesirables, in the Parisian context, have stemmed historically relatively strongly from the political dangers they pose. This is not to say, however, that considerations of common crime have been far from the minds of those with something worth stealing. There have been police structures in Paris for a millennium, and throughout the medieval period both royal and community (mostly craft-based) patrols, guard posts, and neighborhood barriers were common.[75] This machinery grew for both political and criminal reasons: the Fronde impressed the regime with the need for constant surveillance of the Parisians, as did the food riots.[76] Fear of crime swelled during the eighteenth century, when some one-third of Paris's population was poor — more in bad years. Riots increased, and the state became more and more preoccupied with social visibility and thus with control.[77]

This concern for public safety was obviously on Napoleon's mind when he put Paris and its police under state prefects, but such state control suggests that food riots and muggings were not the primary concern of crime control. In any case, a strategy of police control and expulsion was directed at the lower class throughout the nineteenth century.[78] The policing was of limited impact, but expulsion was a successful measure for removing putative criminals from Paris proper. Unfortunately, the predicted salutary effect on the lower class of removing them from the "evil urban influences" of inner-city slums (see fig. 28) was offset by the emergence of "instant slums" in the unregulated and unplanned suburbs.[79]

Since World War II, fearful social images of the capital have evolved. The revolutionary image has faded, and yet an apolitical, ethnically derived "fear of the banlieue" remains. Fear mixed with egalitarian republican virtue led to the construction of the grands ensembles in the early postwar period, which were soon derided as faceless, impersonal, and sterile. But "no unique or spectacular social problems" emerged there until their better-off elements moved out and left them to immigrants.[80] Then they became ghettoes, partly as the result of self-fulfilling prophecy. Police repression, official discussions of their "problems," and media depiction as ghettoes turned them into exactly that.[81] More recently came globalization, which according to many urban theorists results in "dual cities" of the very rich and very poor. I have argued elsewhere that — at least in Paris and Tokyo — the polarizing effects of globalization have been exaggerated, but the paucity of empirical evidence has, again, not prevented the continuity of negative images of Paris's margins.[82] To some extent the physical form of Paris has been altered in order to address these images: President Mitter-

Fig. 28. An inner-city Paris slum, early twentieth century.

rand in particular pushed the suburban rehabilitation of buildings, improvement of infrastructure, and facilities for social activities, and in recent years a number of grands ensembles have been demolished on the edges of the capital. Part of the motivation for this was political "fear of explosions of violence," but the riots of 2005 were attributed by then interior minister Nicolas Sarkozy not to radicalism but to "drug traffic" and "gang rule."[83]

In Edo and Tokyo, concern for antisocial behavior has wholly overshadowed the political as the source of whatever fears of the capital exist. Images of the capital are distinctive in two ways: this apolitical focus, and the gap between the image and reality of criminality. But after the early part of the Edo era, even these fears never rose to a level sufficient to induce the authorities to shape the city accordingly.

Edo arose from the turbulence of a century of civil war in which the common people had played a significant role. Among the first measures taken by the unifiers of the late sixteenth century was to disarm them, confine them to their villages, and open a great gulf between them and the warrior nobility, thus forestalling the elite-mass coalitions which drove so much insurgent activity in early modern Europe. But Ieyasu went further, and designed a city which was "user-unfriendly" to its criminal element. This element was apparently abundant: rapid growth, numerous slums, physical mobility, and unauthorized settlements on public land all offered "a convenient home to such forms of scum" as gamblers, gangs, and crooks of all kinds.[84] But it was not the easiest setting for illicit activity: the gates of the commoner quarters were guarded by residents and closed every evening at ten o'clock; a pass was needed for nighttime movement. There were patrols by commoner "peace officers,"[85] and the shogunal government had its own police as well. Finally, the authorities registered community residents regularly; groups of residents were collectively responsible for controlling criminal behavior.[86] There was considerable unorganized violence in Edo, and enough crime to create a negative image. But food riots were followed by increased relief, not increased police presence. The most famous figures of organized crime of that era were rural, not urban. When people expressed fear of the city, it seems more often to have been based on the frequency of fire and pestilence than crime or poverty.[87] But even here, Edo may well have been less unhealthy than contemporary Paris and London.[88]

After the Restoration, a concern about (and more rarely *for*) the poor — the urban poor in particular — grew rapidly, especially as Japan absorbed Western ideas on the subject. The city was seen as a "source of disease" in more ways than one,[89] and in the 1880s Governor Matsuda Michiyuki, along with other Haussmann fans, advocated expulsion of the poor from Tokyo. This idea never went anywhere, although city hall did take advantage of fires to pursue slum clearance.[90] Haussmann's influence can be seen in a small number of broad, straight avenues in the capital, but there is no evidence that social control was a motive.[91] The police were, however, concerned; by the 1920s, cities and crime were associated in the official mind — "Big cities are always hotbeds of crime" — and crime became one symbol of the city, not only in city hall but in a growing literature of urban crime.[92] But this literature did not rise to the heights of Paris's.[93] It may be that the frequency of slums and the level of human degradation there were insufficient to generate wholesale images of the immiserated city.[94] In any case, one foreign travel guide of the day described Tokyo as "huge, scattered, but orderly," with "a lack of discord incompatible with so big a city."[95]

In any case, social fears of the city survived the war and flourished in the chaos of immediate postwar Tokyo, when much of the city resembled a slum thrown up overnight. But stability — especially social stability — was quickly reestablished, although the police were then, and still are, preoccupied with urban crime. Thus fears of the capital have been shaped by the interpretations of the legal authorities and sociologists, not political or health care elites, and have not had an impact on the physical form of the capital.

There is more crime in city than country in Japan; people are aware of it, and they worry about it.[96] But the picture is mixed: crime rates have not correlated closely with rates of urbanization; some crimes are more frequent in rural areas; and neurosis, suicide, and mental illness are not clearly associated with urbanism.[97] And although juvenile delinquency and political crimes are more urban — with the latter especially common in Tokyo — arguments have been made that there is no causal connection, but rather that the provinces are exporting their least stable and most discontented youth to the cities and that politically disruptive elements come to Tokyo because that is where the targets of protest are.[98] Certain urban settings associated elsewhere with social pathologies and deviance also do not fulfill dire expectations. Japan, like France, built myriad grands ensembles, or danchi, after the war; they are as drab, sterile, and monolithic as France's (see figs. 29 and 30) and were also expected to become hotbeds of deviance. Inhabited by lower-income workers rather than a permanent underclass, they never have.[99] Moreover, Japan's "slums" (see fig. 31), although notorious, are not simply sloughs of despond or catchments for paupers but "an extremely important 'labor market' of highly mobile lower-class workers."[100] And those areas which used to be outcast ghettoes — often termed slums — are frequently nowadays provided, through compensatory government largesse, with some of the fanciest schools and other public facilities that urban Japan has to offer.

In other words, when the Japanese speak of fears of the social implications of cities in general and Tokyo in particular, they refer for the most part to the putative relationship between social change, community decay, and common crime. And Tokyo's police are, like Paris's, ultimately under state, not local, control.[101] But the "dual city" fears found in France are almost nonexistent in Tokyo, replaced by concerns that metropolitan growth might lead to "functional paralysis."[102] Efficiency, not social justice or danger, is the focus.

"The Other": Cultural Fear

With one exception: the culturally different. Social class, political cleavages, and religious faith have plagued Japan infrequently, but deviations from the comfortable — and almost universal — belief that We Japanese Are a Single, Homogeneous Race create great consternation. Such fears of the Other are found in France, too; the difference is that in Japan these fears do not have a geographic focus.

Both space and politics were essentially secularized in the late sixteenth century. What cultural fears have arisen have been based on three perceptions: of outcasts, or burakumin;[103] of the Korean minority; and of the wave of foreigners brought to Japan by the currents of globalization. The

⌃ Fig. 29. A suburban Tokyo danchi: Murayama, originally with 324 uniform apartment blocks (of which 160 have been replaced by 17 much taller ones, allowing more parking).

⌄ Fig. 30. A suburban Paris grand ensemble: Sarcelles in the 1960s. Or maybe this is Tokyo and the other is Paris.

Fig. 31. A Tokyo slum, early twentieth century.

first, although salient, is of little interest to us here: the burakumin are stereotypically ascribed with criminal and degenerate characteristics, but their numbers have shrunk as they marry out of their group; they are not distinctively urban, and they are ethnically Japanese — they have no visible stigmata. The Korean minority — the residue of empire — have been subjected to similar stereotypes, but their position in Japanese society has also improved: they, too, are marrying out and/or naturalizing; their neighborhoods have been devoured by urban redevelopment, and they, too, are indistinguishable from Japanese on the street.

This leaves the recent immigrants not of Korean or Chinese origin, who *are* visually distinctive. Such people — mostly from elsewhere in Asia, many illegally — have come to Japan to take on the "dirty, difficult, and dangerous" jobs that the Japanese are less and less willing to do. But they are not welcome: a government survey of 2004 reported that 87 percent of those surveyed said the country is less safe than it was ten years previously, and 54 percent of them said that this is due to the "increased number of illegal foreigners."[104] The stereotypes surrounding them are little different from those applied to Arab and African immigrants in France, but their relevance to the form of the capital is negligible.

In the first place, they are few: there are fewer than fifty thousand non-Korean, non-Chinese Asians in Tokyo's population of 12 million, whereas metropolitan Paris is almost 20 percent foreign-born, most of whom are African and Arab.[105] Second, Japan's immigration controls and ability to round up and deport foreigners are unmatched among the advanced industrial democracies.[106] Finally, Tokyo's foreigners (with the notably non-problematic exception of a concentration of Westerners in the embassy district) have not tended to cluster residentially. If it is difficult to picture, along Parisian lines, a book about Tokyo entitled *The Margins of City Life,* about the "uncertain," "confusing," and "threatening" interface of urban and rural, then a chapter title like "Marginal People, Peripheral Spaces, Fearsome Faubourgs" beggars the imagination.[107] Paris, and particularly its margins, have over the years been fearsome indeed. Sanguinary conflict between religious subcultures peaked on St. Bartholomew's Day, and between the religious and irreligious in the Revolution. This was overlaid in the nineteenth century by class hostilities, and the two were conflated in the Commune, as clerical France tried to annihilate secular, working-class Paris. In more recent decades, cultural fears have taken two forms, both directed at the Arab-African minority at the city's gates. In general, this group has been vested with the same images imposed on the nineteenth-century working class: degenerate, lazy, and criminally inclined. And, in particular, such phenomena as African female genital mutilation and Muslim headscarves are seen as a direct affront to the political culture of the French Republic. Once again the cultural, the political, and the spatial combine with particular efficiency to produce images with a potent impact on the city, especially in the violence against Algerians in the 1960s and the riots of 2005, attributed by many to ethnic discrimination and transmuted by many into ethnic fear. The skyline of (and body count in) Tokyo, by contrast, has been powerfully shaped by the absence of such a combination.

TORRID OR TEPID:

THE PASSIONATE AND THE IMPASSIVE

But as Tokyo has been relatively unscarred, either socially or architecturally, by cultural and political fears and their consequences, there is a perhaps related aspect to this: a puzzling lack of passion, either pro or con, in
views of the Japanese capital. Paris — with apologies to Harry Lime — had
four hundred years of warfare, terror, murder, and bloodshed, but it produced Victor Hugo, Baudelaire, the baroque city, the Seine on a sunny afternoon, and a city which has probably inspired more art of all kinds than
any other in human history. Tokyo had four hundred years of relative peace
and social order, and produced — a GNP.

This is a harsh commentary, and demands both qualification and sub-
stantiation. First, Tokyo is a lovable city, and I have spent many wonderful years there. There *are* those who have expressed exhilarated love for it,
and countless stories have been written in and about Tokyo.[108] There are
those at the other extreme, for whom cities like Tokyo are "a glimpse of
hell."[109] And no one who has ever attended the national high school base-
ball tournament would deny that the Japanese are capable of passionate
attachments. But if one compares Tokyo with Paris, the relative absence of
passion regarding the former is a deafening silence.

Accepting this commentary if only for purposes of examination, we
should begin, as elsewhere in this essay, by asking why such a thing might
be true. Five different possibilities come to mind. First, Paris is blessed with
unsurpassed architectural beauty, whereas Tokyo has little architecture at
all left from the past, and not much from the present of which to be proud.
Second, France — unlike Japan — is blessed, or cursed, with an anti-urban,
anticapital ideology; hence Paris has passionate enemies. Third, Paris is
clearly Paris; it may be more difficult to love *or* hate a vague or vanished city
like Edo, or one whose nature may be inauthentic, derived from foreign
sources. Fourth, Paris has a history of contending passions — at least as of
1989, the Revolution was clearly still not over.[110] And, fifth, returning to
a theme raised earlier, I would suggest that for all of the exquisite refinement of Japanese culture, Japanese views of cities have been — compared

to France's — far more pragmatic than esthetic, and economic rather than political. "Passionate pragmatism" or "economic passion" may not be oxymoronic, but they are close.

In the Eye of the Beholder

One need say little about the ease with which one can fall in love with the physical beauty of Paris. In the sixteenth century, Montaigne admitted that "Paris hath my hart from my infancy . . . the more other faire and stately cities I have seen since, the more hir beauty doth still usurpingly gaine upon my affection."[111] A century ago one could say, in all seriousness, that the architecture of Paris "involves the interest of France, and I would say even of the civilized world."[112] And today Paris's architecture is "a focus of continual controversy."[113] I have had a hard time finding observers who find Paris unlovely, except insofar as modern change has damaged its previous beauty.

And then there is Tokyo. It has its moments, including the lacy Gothic confection that is the New City Hall, and romantic old Tokyo Station. But already in 1920 its architecture represented "size without majesty, individuality divorced from all dignity . . . and convenience rather than fitness," and almost a century later, another guide saw a city "Westernized and modernized to the point of ugliness, much of it a drab concrete jungle."[114] Thus its champions must acknowledge that their love comes from other sources. To Edward Seidensticker, perhaps the city's foremost Western chronicler, contemporary Tokyo is of limited architectural interest; little about it is admirable (much less passion-inspiring), and the future "is unlikely to have either grandeur or harmony."[115]

Looking back, one can find Japanese artists who were absorbed in the city and its buildings, but their art contrasts dramatically with the impressionist effervescence of Parisian scenes like Seurat's *La Grande Jatte*. Koizumi Kishio and Kobayashi Kiyochika, for example, though rendering beautiful scenes of Tokyo, treated their subject with "ambivalence," "reticence," and "nostalgia" rather than passion.[116]

Perhaps because physical change has been so rapid and extreme, love for Tokyo has often been directed at a city which no longer exists. And whenever the city has rebuilt, it has done so under imperatives which subordinate the esthetic. The result, unsurprisingly, has been uninspiring architecture. But even as Japan has become rich, the ability to beautify the capital has not kept pace with the GNP. Tokyo's rivers have been paved over, the bay shrinks before the onslaught of the landfillers, and although architectural spectacles have been achieved, some are to many an average eye more weird than wonderful.[117] Visually wonderful parts of Tokyo — Kabuki-chō, for example — there are, but they are infrequent. More often, Tokyo is a churning, *socially* wonderful place confined within an architectural framework only a mother could love.[118]

Good Walls Make Good Enemies

It is not only passionate love that is in short supply among observers of Tokyo: real hate is missing too. Paris's enemies have included, at different times, the king, the provinces, the bourgeoisie, and the modern state, and Paris has reciprocated with enthusiasm. Images of the capital as a hell, a vampire, a black hole surface repeatedly, as does the more political "fortress of sedition."[119] And of course the enemies have their enemies, driven by the "consistent . . . conviction that the beauty of Paris is unique, fragile, and threatened."[120] As one might expect of the author of a book entitled *The Assassination of Paris,* Louis Chevalier typically fulminates against state technocrats and planners, developers, and architects — a veritable horde of barbarians already inside the gates, aiming to "Nanterrize" the city.[121] One need not share all this spleen — indeed, much of the anti-Paris fever has vanished over the last few decades, and I propose below that Paris has done rather well as postindustrial cities go — but it is both entertaining and illuminating to watch Paris's lovers and haters go at it.

Tokyo, in contrast, has dodged a number of such bullets — it has been described as a "destructive force" and a decadent source of "evil ways and dangerous thoughts."[122] But up until World War II, the critique was most often indirect or derivative, as noted.[123] Since the war, this diffuseness has continued: sometimes "urbanization" has been used as a blanket term for cultural, technological, social, and economic change overall.[124] Tokyo has also been a specific target of criticism, but the culprit is most frequently capitalism (especially its global variety) or the overcentralization of Japanese power, and the blame is put more often on the policies of a dirigiste "developmental state," with Tokyo as much victim as victimizer.[125]

No Object, No Affection?

If a "problem" is harder to hate than a flesh-and-blood (or bricks-and-mortar) city, it is also harder to love a city whose identity is difficult to pin down. Paris, as noted, does not have this problem: walls began the job, the octroi and the Périphérique enhanced it, civil wars and elections opened a gulf between capital and country, and both lovers and haters have had a full and precise idea of the object of their passions. Sometimes the city itself is the literary protagonist, and "photography, cinema, and popular song [have] mythologized Paris."[126] Tokyo, on the other hand, is more moving target than movable feast. Circumstances have conspired to deprive the city of a clear, stable image and its people of a clear identity, and even its devotees have tended to love a city that no longer exists, or a city that is attractive for reasons derived from non-native sources. This exciting, demanding, and rewarding city has never had the artists it deserves.

Edo began ahistorically; its swamps and fishing villages are hardly the stuff from which urban legends grow. It made up for this quickly, but identity did not come easily. Half the population, the warriors, were transients, and the commoner population never developed any spirit of autonomy.[127] Moreover, Edo was administratively fragmented — by design — into a conglomeration of quasi-independent pieces with no collective identity.[128] And — in a trend which accelerated after the war — Tokyo became increasingly a cobbled-together metropolis, many of whose parts, and most of whose people, are not really in Tokyo at all.

Dolores Hayden has argued that place-based identity is linked to memory, and memories are largely based on natural features, physical entities, landmarks, buildings, and so on.[129] In this regard, Tokyo is particularly deprived; Restoration, fire, earthquake, war, and obsessive, single-minded redevelopment have left a city singularly bereft of stable lieux de mémoire. One can visit in Paris the places Victor Hugo and Baudelaire wrote about, and Caillebotte painted; the Edo of Shikitei Samba and the Tokyo of Kafū and Kawabata are gone.

This is not to say that Japanese artists and writers have not tried to capture the city — rather that the object of their affections has proved elusive. It can be argued that there was no "city literature" at all until the 1920s.[130] Cities were treated literarily in their parts — the shops, bars, or gardens where stories were set — but not as urban wholes.[131] And in some cases the object of affection was a city that no longer existed: the paintings of Kiyochika, for example, portray a "love for the urban quality of Tokyo, a nostalgia for an Edo he never knew."[132] Another of Tokyo's famous devotees was Nagai Kafū, but he too was given to retrospection and — like Tanizaki — to shadows rather than bright lights. He loved Tokyo's slums and alleys and demimonde, especially those areas which recalled Edo and were being swallowed by the modern city. But he had a taste for the quiet and desolate, and none of the exuberance or passion of Toulouse-Lautrec or François Villon, who dealt with the same margins. He loved an idea, not a real city.[133]

And his idea of the city, like that of many early twentieth-century Japanese writers, was not wholly Japanese. Kafū's perceptions of Edo and Tokyo were mediated by the influence of French literature, and the "discovery" of the city in literature in the 1920s in particular owed much to foreign sources.[134] According to Unno Hiroshi, in the late nineteenth and early twentieth centuries the Europeans taught Japanese artists about the city.[135] Indeed, Japanese writers and painters often did a better job of portraying Berlin, Paris, or New York than Tokyo.

Whether authentic or derivative, a city literature blossomed in Tokyo in the 1920s; but it withered in the 1930s.[136] Perhaps it never really valued Tokyo at all, but only the modernism that flourished there. Perhaps the Japanese inability to find a truly "Japanese idiom" for European modernism made it "alienating and superficial."[137] In either case, it never had time to mature, folding like the nascent democracy of the same period under the increasing repression of the state. Might Tokyo have come to occupy a place in Japanese literature like that of Paris in French? A great literature or art of Tokyo might have emerged out of the 1920s excitement of the city, but the window slammed shut in the 1930s on all forms of freedom. Some authors turned inward, writing solipsistic novels, and some refocused away from the capital: in five short years, Kawabata Yasunari shifted focus from Tokyo, in

The Scarlet Gang of Asakusa (1930), to the far north in *Snow Country* (1935). And some — like Kafū and Tanizaki — simply moved away.[138]

No one immortalized Tokyo's great events, perhaps because they were so few. Tokyo has seen no revolution, no commune, no liberation. The city's birth, the Restoration, and modernization were all imposed from above; the earthquake was endured, not overcome; and the air raids were so devastating that they never generated a spirit similar to London's during the Blitz. Democracy came after the war, but it, too, came from above and outside. The people of Tokyo are hardworking, wonderful people, but there is almost nothing — won or lost — that they can look back on and say, with passion, "Our people did this, and it was heroic, and we're proud of it."

Many Parisians, of course, might wish that there had been somewhat fewer passionate events in their history. Blood has flowed freely in the streets, and for having escaped this Tokyoites may be grateful. But history has left Paris with an ample supply of the raw ingredients for passion; successive regimes have inscribed this history across the face of the capital; and the past memories and contemporary monuments together are capable of generating debate on any occasion. Paris has stood for something greater than itself — for beauty, freedom, even civilization (if the French are to be believed), or for degeneracy, insurrection, and rapacity — in which both its lovers and enemies passionately believe.

Esthetics and Economics

My final point is that in the evolution of Paris state guidance has unarguably played a role. And despite the lamentations of its devotees, Paris has really done rather well in subordinating the imperatives of the market and the whims of developers to the preservation of the architectural patrimony. Since World War II in particular, more and more has been sacrificed to the automobile, and buildings creep ever upward.[139] And on the edges Paris is seen as "following the example of US and Japanese cities which have spread their suburbs until they merge with those of other cities in a shapeless magma of highways, factories, and housing."[140] But overall the center of Paris has been marvelously preserved, with building heights limited, the Left Bank Freeway defeated, and La Défense sited outside the city, for esthetic and environmental reasons. The market has played a crucial role in the shaping of Paris, especially since Haussmann, but not at the ultimate expense of either political or esthetic values. The political values at work no longer involve beggaring the capital, but they do include Republican social solidarity, and the reshaping of Paris under Mitterrand and his successors has clearly aimed at balancing east and west and center and suburbs with this in mind. The evolution of Paris into a city of and for the wealthy has been decried again and again; it is difficult to forestall, but both the state and city hall are agreed on the point. One critique was blunt: "a two-speed economy, if that is the price we have to pay to allow Île-de-France to compete successfully with other European metropolises, would be a price unacceptable to the national community."[141]

It is a price, however, that one suspects the Japanese would be all too happy to pay. Indeed, cold economic rationality — primarily embodied in the private sector — has driven modern urban growth. So Tokyo *does* reflect a passion: first for national growth to catch up with the West, then for reconstruction (twice), and finally for globalization. But the capital, far from epitomizing this passion, has been sacrificed to it. Some Meiji voices called for the construction of a grand imperial capital, but they were soon drowned out by calls for "a rich country and a strong military." A capital with beauty was not in the libretto, and by the 1920s a travel guide named the Ginza, Tokyo's commercial heart, as its "busiest, noisiest, unhandsomest, and most flamboyant" street.[142]

In the immediate aftermath of World War II, Tokyo saw the breakneck erection of thousands of drab three- to six-story office buildings downtown and serried ranks of equally drab apartment complexes in the suburbs. As reconstruction progressed, and more money became available, newer (and often more attractive) buildings replaced them, but at the same time open spaces fell to the developer, as did whole neighborhoods, in a "gruesomely pragmatic, opportunistic and self-serving" process.[143] The only real exception to the primacy of the market is the center of the city, where buildings cannot rise so high as to look down upon the Imperial Palace. But this is small comfort as thickets of high-rises spring up in Shinjuku, Ikebukuro, Kichijōji, Shiodome, and elsewhere.

Someday the palace may be reposing in the middle of a low-rise plain on the floor of a concrete valley, because there is no sign that either noneconomic values or state priorities might rescue the capital. Tokyo is viewed largely as an international launching pad for Japanese corporations, and a beachhead for global corporations in Japan.[144] Tokyo has had neither the physical beauty, the passionate loves and enmities, the dramatic history, nor the esthetic and statist characteristics of Paris; it "is and has almost everything, and many a son of the city might say that it has lost the most important thing, its identity."[145] So has it suffered? Has Paris benefited? One could argue the opposite: passion incinerates as easily as it warms, and states oppress as often as they nurture. Paris basks in its beauty and its encomiums; would one ever say, "We'll always have . . . Tokyo?"[146] But, as we shall see in the next chapter, it has also paid a price.

7 CAPITAL, CONTEXT, COUNTRY

Paris and Tokyo not only look different; not only are they regarded differently by inside and outside observers; they also get along differently with the world around them. My initial impression is that all of Paris's relationships — with the French nation, the state, and its own suburbs — are more problematic than is the case in Tokyo. For Paris, these relationships have historically been frequently negative and occasionally intensely hostile, and both they and their less fraught Japanese analogues have arguably had implications for how the shapes of the two cities have evolved.

IMPRESSIONS: WHAT AND WHY?

Country and Capital

One might propose political, economic/demographic, and psychological reasons why the French have regarded Paris with a far more jaundiced eye than the Japanese have Tokyo. Some of the Parisian situation is easily understandable: in 1789, 1830, 1848, 1871, and 1968, Paris seemed to be at war with the rest of the nation. Some of the friction is less fair but no less frequent. Anyone hostile to the French state can easily turn against Paris: "The State having taken the name and the visage of the capital, Paris finds itself accused of the omnipresence of the State."[1] In Japan, too, there is a bit of this dyspepsia, since the Japanese state also in some ways seems to merge with the city. But the Parisian enmity is simply not there.

We have already (chapter 6) reviewed the zero-sum, Gravieriste literature on Paris. Such a literature does not exist for Tokyo; with a few Nativist or agrarianist interludes, the Japanese view of Tokyo brings to mind Pangloss more than Malthus. Urban growth in general and Tokyo's growth and prosperity in particular are a rising tide lifting all boats, not a tsunami.[2] Less tangibly, there is an atmosphere of provincial envy and capital disdain in France which I have never sensed as strongly in Japan. Whatever city-country dislikes may have typified Japan are historically less likely to have focused on Tokyo alone, for until a generation ago it had metropolitan rivals in Kyoto and Osaka, and provincials could complain as readily about the snooty coldness of the former and the crass money-grubbing of the latter as about the size and wealth of Tokyo. But this all pales before the pre-revolutionary "mutual dislike, disdain and distrust" of the French capital and countryside, which by the nineteenth century had become, on Paris's side, simple "contempt": "since the Revolution the provinces with impunity have sent to Paris their poor to nourish, their criminals to monitor, their pregnant daughters to deliver, and their bastard children to raise."[3]

State and Capital

Given the prominence of local notables in the French Parliament, it is perhaps unsurprising that negative provincial views of the capital lead to state-capital friction. Japan's Parliament is also weighted toward the provinces, but Japanese MPs have never simultaneously been small-town mayors. Three other factors come to mind: traditions of local autonomy and the evolution of war and capitalism; fear or its absence; and intergovernmental relations. All four support the impression that state-capital relationships have been far more adversarial in France than in Japan.[4]

The urban history of Europe is characterized by strong traditions of local autonomy, albeit frequently contested by feudal lords and monarchs, making for a generally contentious relationship between cities and states. In the case of France and Japan, the contrast is stark: except for one brief period in the sixteenth century, there has been almost no tradition whatsoever of autonomy or corporate identity in the Japanese city. "Such limitations on Tokugawa power as existed were limitations in terms of power, not in terms of legal theory."[5]

The historic evolution of war and capitalism, at least according to Charles Tilly and Wim Blockmans, also has hypothetical effects on city-state relations.[6] The stronger the urban merchant/financier class, particularly where it emerged before the creation of a strong state — as in France — the more leverage the city had with the (typically revenue-starved) state. Hence the proposition that bourgeois strength plus warfare made for strong cities and contentious state-capital relationships — as in France — and also its corollary: a weak merchant/financier class and peaceful times made for docile cities and smooth state-capital relationships, as in early modern Japan.

Thus the Japanese state has rarely fought with, and never feared, its capital. The French state has long feared Paris, not simply because it was contentious (so was Edo; so is Tokyo), but because its contention was aimed at the state. The result was centuries of policies designed to keep the capital divided, under state rule, and deprived of attractive amenities.[7] And the capital, under no illusions about the situation, has constantly feared the overweening power of the state.

The last possible source of more conflictual state-capital relationships in France than in Japan is the structure of state-local, or "intergovernmental," relations (IGRs) in each country. Both countries are highly centralized, albeit with some devolution of functions and powers in recent decades. But the uses to which central control has been put could hardly differ more. After the insurrection of Provost of Merchants Étienne Marcel in 1358, the crown subordinated this municipal post to the provost of Paris, an agent of the king.[8] Napoleon I established the position of prefect, a state official who governed Paris, and his system lives on in the prefect of police.

This subordination has continued, whether the state has been in pro- or anti-Parisian, or socialist or conservative, hands. Recently the "pros" have been ascendant, but even they are ambivalent about decentralization, which has unleashed myriad little municipal egotisms. But management of the capital "is and remains an eminent responsibility of the state. . . . [B]alkanization . . . is not . . . decentralization," and the superordinate role of the state is universally accepted.[9]

In Japan, in contrast, the state has traditionally had few intentions for the capital. The tradition of retaining ultimate control but doing little with it continued after the Restoration: the Home Ministry thoroughly controlled local governments but paid little attention to Tokyo as a city. After World War II, local government was democratized, state prerogatives were cut back, and national land use planning was instituted. But the urbanist Isomura Eiichi asserted in 1966 that "the government has no Tokyo policy,'" and Mikuriya Takashi, quoting him in 1996, remarked that "the situation has not changed in the slightest since then."[10]

The Japanese state has taken a somewhat more activist stance toward the city in the last few years, and the last two governors of Tokyo have taken a rather more confrontational position; but for the most part the state has continued to avoid using all the powers at its command. Thus although on the surface the state's influence over the capital appears similar to the French situation, the way IGRs are conducted in Japan seems less conducive to conflict. One might argue that Tokyo would have profited from a *greater* degree of provincial opposition: the rising tide of Tokyo might someday indeed inundate the entire nation.

The Suburbs: Capital and Context

Paris's strained relationships with the world around it extend to its immediate surroundings: the suburbs, or *banlieue*. The blasé, albeit positive, regard for Tokyo's suburbs offers a sharp contrast. An impressionistic tour of the history books and the contemporary media generates four possible sources, often interrelated, of this friction: the Parisian suburbs are regarded negatively for (*a*) their poverty and (*b*) their concentration of both literally and figuratively alien social groups; (*c*) they raise sociopolitical, economic, and demographic fears; and, until the election of Socialist Mayor Delanoë, (*d*) they have been largely opposed to Paris proper in a partisan political sense.[11] Not a single one of these factors has characterized Tokyo's suburbs.

The image of the Parisian banlieue in the eighteenth and early nineteenth centuries was still largely positive: a place of holiday recreation and second homes.[12] Then came Haussmann, and by century's end an economic gulf had opened between city and suburb. Chaotic development of subdivisions with no infrastructure, or simple illegal squatting in the Zone outside the wall, widened the gulf, as did housing policy: in contrast to public housing in Japan, Paris's was designed for the poorest segment of the population.[13]

Tokyo's suburbs are far less distinct from the city proper, merging with Tokyo and with each other in a metropolitan sprawl 100 miles across. Moreover, many are possessed of significant metropolitan amenities such as downtown department store branches.[14] At their turn-of-the-century inception, they were largely working class, but in the 1920s a middle-class flood began, and positive evaluations became dominant.[15] The huge danchi apartment complexes were disdained by many, but they consti-tuted a big step up for many new suburbanites.[16] They were also inhab-ited almost totally by "real Japanese," as opposed to the banlieue, which is stereotyped as the abode of foreigners, a terra incognita dominated a century ago by a proletariat deemed barely above the animal and today by swarthy, linguistically and religiously mysterious Others. But they are not only mysterious, they are dangerous, and have been for a long time. The prerevolutionary faubourgs were seen as hotbeds of insurrection, and the nineteenth-century Parisian bourgeoisie lived in fear of the lower or-ders inside and outside the wall.[17] Today new political fears focused on the immigrant Muslim population have filled the old bottle of antisuburban prejudice even as its social class vintage has drained out. Marginals and margins are equated; the suburbs are still seen as a "fragile point of the so-cial equilibrium."[18] Such views could have developed in Japan: during the Tokugawa era, social conflict and political protest were common on Edo's edges,[19] and during the Meiji era the suburban Tama region was renowned for its gamblers, thugs, and radicals. But the identification of margins and marginals never occurred.

After World War II, a period of leftist activism occurred, but neither was this ever identified with the suburbs. And, again, the partisan coloration of the national government was more stable and less polarized than that of France. National politics have been dominated for more than a century by right-of-center forces, which means that leftists in any locale have been consistently sidelined and thus less able to generate fear. And in the case of Tokyo, although the 1960s and 1970s saw the appearance nationwide of a large number of leftist mayors and governors, and a considerable number in the Tokyo suburbs, they never made confrontation with the state a major theme. None of the suburban Tokyo mayors was as disputatious with the state as was either leftist governor Minobe Ryōkichi (1967–79) or current conservative governor Ishihara Shintarō.

BESET OR BECALMED?
THE CAPITAL AND THE OUTSIDE WORLD

Neither Tokyo nor Paris has much in the way of formal relationships with the provinces beyond their suburban hinterlands; provincial views of the capital are thus relevant as mediated by the state. Hence discussion here has two foci: the capital's relationships to the state and to the suburbs. I look first at the history of intergovernmental relations in Japan and France and then at the state and the capital in particular. Last, I present a few exemplars: local government in the capital, city planning in the capital, and specific projects in the capital: giant housing complexes, new towns, and business centers.

Intergovernmental Relations

Both France and Japan have long traditions of control of local government from above, although in the French case this situation was preceded by centuries of rivalry and conflict. Moreover, the Japanese state, ever since the Tokugawa, has tended to "subcontract" local government to the locals, whereas the French state has assumed a far more hands-on posture. Consequently, Parisians have long chafed under state control in a way that Tokyoites have not; even after the democratizing reforms of the U.S. Occupation, it took decades before cities had the nerve to confront the state openly. Indeed, cities in both countries have been flexing their muscles more in recent decades as Japan and France have experimented with various forms of decentralization. But, in general, IGRs in Japan are far less messy than in France, which has more levels (state, *pays,* region, department, commune) than Japan (state, prefecture, municipality). With only one-third more territory than Japan, France has more than ten times as many municipalities.[20]

Local independence in the West goes back at least to the Middle Ages, when cities allied variously with rival lords and monarchs and seized whatever powers they could in the process.[21] Indeed, under natural law local government predates the state and as such has its own functions and rights — quite the opposite of Japan, where the state predates local government, which is simply the creation of the state.[22] After the Middle Ages, cities in general and Paris in particular gradually lost their autonomy to centralizing monarchs and absolutist states. Nonetheless, throughout the ancien régime, Paris was full of quasi-independent clerical, community, and mercantile jurisdictions which, although ultimately answerable to the king, exercised considerable power of their own. The French kings fought against this, and Napoleon I put state prefects over all local governments. Local government increasingly democratized during the nineteenth and twentieth centuries but was nonetheless rather simple: each level of government was nested spatially and functionally within the next, like Russian dolls, in a linear hierarchy of competences and jurisdictions; local plans were deduced from national plans.[23] In the 1960s, "decentralization" arrived on the agenda, and prefectural oversight of local government was reduced, but although "the coachman loosened the reins, the bit is always in place."[24] The 1960s and 1970s were a period of incessant institutional tinkering, in an effort to reconcile democracy and decentralization, on the one hand, with coordination, integration, and regional planning on the other.[25] By the 1980s, however, the tutorial powers of the prefect were sharply reduced relative to mayors and elected regional councils, and mayors really became masters in their own houses.[26] Even Paris was permitted a mayor.

The strongest characteristics of IGRs in France today are complexity and jealous independence. The mayor of a minuscule town in Île-de-France can in principle thumb his nose at prefects and at the mayor of Paris.[27] The power of the state to promote the regional cooperation necessary in a competitive Europe is limited, and the ability of Paris to coordinate with dozens of suburban governments whose affections for the capital are at best limited is still less.[28] The strongest characteristics of Japanese IGRs, historically, were wide leeway for local units despite a total absence of formal local autonomy. During the fifteenth and sixteenth centuries, a window opened: amid generalized civil war, a number of cities organized themselves and established independent urban governments, walls, moats, and militias.[29] They bore more than a little resemblance to European free cities but had fatal flaws. One was legal: many of them were recognized as such by the lords, who allowed them self-government but not formal independence; exemptions given could in principle be withdrawn.[30] Another flaw was temporal: Western cities were able, "in an era of more or less continual strife," to play lords off against kings and extract charters with real rights, but in Japan the vacuum of government lasted a relatively short time.[31] As the role of putative overlord took shape and armies grew, collisions with independent jurisdictions of all sorts were inevitable, and their outcome predictable: the last of the major free cities fell in 1580.[32] Under the Tokugawa, the condition of zero de jure local autonomy and wide de facto freedom of action continued. The lords had no autonomy except what was allowed by the state, and communities had no autonomy except what was allowed by their lords.[33] Villages were mostly free to choose their leaders as they wished, and as long as they paid their taxes and produced neither crime nor protest, the elites tended to leave them alone. The Meiji government's attitude was different. Centralized government was the goal, and simplification and subordination of local government was part of the plan. Prefectures and municipalities were put under the Home Ministry. Some elective local councils and offices were introduced over time, but the national ideal — as in France — was local administration, not local politics, and the ministry "prohibited the delegation of power to decide even the smallest details."[34] IGRs were thus a natural target of the American Occupation, which set out to decentralize and democratize. The Home Ministry was abolished, prefectural and municipal executives and councils were popularly elected, and local governmental powers were enhanced. But once the Occupation ended in 1952, the state tried to roll back these reforms. One tool was the constitution, which still restricted local government to those functions (including revenue) expressly allocated to it by the state. Another was "agent delegation," the power of state ministers to order local executives about as agents of the state, responsible for carrying out state mandates, which issued forth in a flood. A third was "administrative guidance," the informal and extralegal power of bureaucrats to demand action.[35]

The result of this was that, in the 1950s and 1960s, many observers saw local government as little better than it had been before the war: financially dependent on the state, and at its beck and call. But localities had more resources than they realized, as became apparent in the 1970s.[36] The immediate impetus to change was a dire environmental crisis, which led numerous citizens' movements and local governments — with great trepidation — to resist life-threatening state and corporate industrial projects.[37] What they found was that not only could they protest and survive, they could sometimes win. Revenue-sharing policies were so mechanistic that they could not be manipulated to punish recalcitrant cities;[38] initiatives might not be possible, but obstructionism was. The volume of delegated business was so manifestly excessive that localities could pick and choose what they would and would not do. Local MPs could be enlisted as lobbyists; municipalities could create coalitions. The state simply did not have the personnel to ride herd on a large number of noncompliant municipalities.

What have developed, then, are IGRs as a bargaining process, with the state often acting less as overlord than as umpire.[39] Gradually the state realized that the more it wants to do, the more it needs local government cooperation, which is conditional. The result — even before the elimination of agent delegation and administrative guidance around the end of the twentieth century — was a paradoxical combination of centralization and local autonomy which, I think, goes beyond what one finds in less subcontractarian, more hands-on France.

And the trend favors the cities. Because localities perform most welfare functions, growth of the welfare state has lessened state influence, and the current process of municipal merger (which entails greater local revenue powers) will reduce the number of financially nonviable (and thus utterly dependent) local governments.[40] The result will be simpler and more economical state administration, but not necessarily a stronger state voice.

The State Confronts the Capital

Edo was fabricated almost from whole cloth as the capital and creature of the Tokugawa shoguns, and for almost four hundred years the city made little attempt to get out from under them. Paris became France's capital under the Capetian monarchs, and by the time of Robert the Pious in A.D. 1000, "contestation" between the king and the bourgeoisie was already emerging.[41] A tradition of protest grew, as did royal efforts to control the city and limit its growth; nonetheless, in general an "alliance" endured between crown and capital under both the Capetians and the Valois.[42]

The situation changed under the Bourbons, and by 1789, the city's administrative autonomy had been whittled down decisively.[43] Nevertheless, Napoleon I represents a major turning point in Paris's history, as he brought it firmly under the control of his prefects, facilitating a punitive provincial stance toward the capital.[44] In the short run, the subjugation of the capital had its upside: the modernization of the form of the capital by Napoleon III and Haussmann. Paris had little say in the matter, but physically and architecturally it benefited mightily. But as we have seen, Haussmann's programs also aggravated class enmities. The split between state and capital climaxed in 1870–71 with the Commune;[45] the outcome was fire, bloodshed, and the Third Republic, in which the provinces eliminated Parisian hopes of independence. The surface was the Belle Époque; behind the gaslights, the housing and transportation situation deteriorated and the suburbs sprawled grotesquely.[46] Conditions did not change significantly after World War I: in 1919, the Departmental Council of the Seine proposed a plan which included industrial zone promotion, new towns, and better regional transportation. The Senate shot it down.[47] During the early postwar years little changed: the state's PADOG development plan, originally written in 1950, continued to straitjacket the capital. But with the advent of the Fifth Republic, two trends began: to enhance rather than constrain Paris; and to give the capital more autonomy. The first trend has progressed further and faster than the second, but both are clear.

The enhancement of Paris began with de Gaulle and Delouvrier and put grandeur once again at the top of the agenda; opposition was fading anyway as the importance of Paris to France's role in an increasingly integrated Europe became clear. One must not confuse enhancement with autonomy, but autonomy did increase. In 1975, municipal powers were expanded, and in 1977, Paris again had a mayor, Jacques Chirac, who won the post by defeating President Giscard's favored candidate.[48] Since then Paris's mayors have flexed their tongues, if not their muscles: Chirac railed against the augmentation of arrondissement powers by President Mitterrand, and his administrators objected to state exactions — the capital region pays more to the state than it receives — and tried to avoid state tutelage.[49] His successor, Bertrand Delanoë, has decried the "imperial and brutal behavior" of the state in deciding on uses for land freed up by the relocation of state ministries.[50] But it is difficult now to disentangle state-capital from partisan contention: Gaullist Chirac faced a Socialist president; Socialist Delanoë faced Chirac and now Sarkozy.

Overall, the state still plays a large role in the capital. It provides perhaps half of the city's revenue, almost that much of its operating budget, and covers more than two-thirds of the regional public transportation system's deficit.[51] It must approve the region's long-range development plan.[52] It is politically correct in France's republican tradition to reiterate state supremacy, just as it is politically correct in Japan to emphasize local autonomy. I suspect that there is more autonomy than meets the eye in Paris, and less in Tokyo. But Paris is still more in the state's grip.

If this comparison is accurate, for Tokyo it constitutes a stunning turnabout from the early days. During the Tokugawa era, the very idea of conflict between capital and state was meaningless. The Meiji Restoration was a further centralizing project which in a sense telescoped into a single generation everything that had occurred in France from Louis XIV through Napoleon I. An elected Tokyo Assembly was convoked in 1889, and from then on it remonstrated with both the state and with Tokyo's own executive (an imperial appointee) for more autonomy, to little avail: up until World War II, the home minister could veto anything the city government did, and for most purposes Tokyo government was part of the state.[53]

After the war, democratic reforms might have provided the capital with more muscle, but the first elected governor was not much of an activist and the state was concerned more with national than local reconstruction.[54] Indeed, when state intervention grew — particularly in planning for the 1964 Olympics — it was due less to state ambitions than to his successor's lack of accomplishment. The next governor, the leftist Minobe Ryōkichi (1967–79), adopted a confrontational posture toward the state, winning reelection in 1971 on an explicitly antistate platform. Minobe was brought low by the economic slowdown of the mid-1970s: the state forbade the capital to issue bonds which it needed to avoid financial collapse, and he acquiesced in a fiscal reconstruction plan which reversed many of his reforms.

But he had demonstrated that the state could be openly defied, and that there was, in fact, a lot of legal room for local policy innovation.

Minobe's successor was Suzuki Shunichi (1979–95); he was a far less confrontational man and saw eye-to-eye with the free-market economic policies of the state. The state backed away, and Tokyo took off economically. But Suzuki too struck a blow for local autonomy, in his way. Conservative candidates for governor had all been chosen by the national leaders of the Liberal Democratic Party (LDP); for coalitional reasons at the national level, the party rejected Suzuki's reelection bid in 1991. LDP members in the assembly, prefectural officials, and the people were all indignant; Suzuki ran as an independent, won in a walk, and increased the size of his support group in the assembly.[55]

Prefectural defiance of the state has continued since Suzuki's day. Governor Aoshima claimed financial exigency in canceling the 1996 World City Exposition Tokyo, despite commitments to build and/or participate by 122 other Japanese municipalities, the national government, 50 foreign cities, the United Nations, and 12 Japanese business consortia.[56] The Tokyo Assembly screamed, but as a directly elected official the governor has far-reaching powers, and his decision stuck. Aoshima was followed by the even more obstreperous Ishihara Shintarō, who has taken on the state and several other prefectures (over moving the capital), big business (over taxing the banks), and the U.S. government (over returning an air base in Tokyo). Thus far he has one win, one loss (the Americans are loath to depart), and one split decision (the courts nullified his bank tax, but the state made some concessionary changes in the tax laws) — not bad in a city which began as a simple appendage of the state. The explanation — especially in comparison to Paris — may be the absence of state fear of radical prefectural policy differences or political objectives, the absence of regional hostility, and the Japanese state's subcontractarian view of government.

Overall, this comparison suggests that legacy is not destiny. Despite European traditions of popular participation and urban autonomy, and Japan's history of urban subservience, it appears today as if the French president is more able to do things for, to, and in Paris than the Japanese prime minister and his agents can with Tokyo. The evidence of Paris's subordination to the state since 1789 is inscribed all over its face, as is the noninvolvement of the Japanese state in Tokyo. Edo and Tokyo have been and are largely laissez-faire cities — and they certainly look that way. But looking over the cityscape of Tokyo, compared with that of Paris, it occurs to one that there might be such a thing as too smooth a relationship.

Local Government, Regional Plans, Grand Projects

But before committing ourselves to such generalizations, it would be a good idea to look at some concrete outcomes of IGRs in Japan and France: the structure and status of local government, the regional-planning process, and the attempts of various governments to augment the capital's amenities with new towns and business centers.

As noted above, under the ancien régime Paris was governed by over-lapping and occasionally rival authorities: bourgeoisie, church, and crown. By the time of Louis XIV, the quasi-mayoral, bourgeois provost of merchants had become "the King's man," and the bishop of Paris was definitely a minor player, but royal power was still fragmented and potentially overshadowed by the Parliament of Paris.[57] Napoleon put an end to this situation, and Haussmann, with little municipal opposition to overcome, transformed Paris governmentally from a constellation of municipalities into a unified bourgeois city. He streamlined the city administratively and clarified its margins. But social segregation and political hostility grew; municipal governments became political weapons; and the role of the prefects in maintaining order fell somewhere between that of a fire department and a bomb disposal squad.

Given the political contention generated in and by Paris after Haussmann, it was not until the 1960s that anyone seriously considered giving the capital any more autonomy. But thereafter, in a series of reforms, Paris was hived off from the Department of the Seine into a separate department-cum-city (1964), the mayoralty was reestablished (1975), the power of the prefect was reduced (1982), and elected mayors and councils were established in the arrondissements (1982).[58] The enhancement of the arrondissements at the expense of city hall was, of course, a step against which Mayor Chirac railed, but they have turned out to be much like Tokyo's wards: tools of the city for carrying out its plans.[59] And the creation of a capital city doubling as a department has not in fact resulted in the chaos predictable from its surface appearance. The key is that the mayor is elected by the city council, thus assuring him of a majority there, and the city council doubles as the departmental council (headed by the mayor). Two budgets, two sets of functions, different bureaucracies, plus a number of public corporations and state agencies with their own budgets (the total income and expenditure of "Paris" is impossible to calculate) — somehow it works.[60]

And it works rather well: it probably helped that Paris's first mayor (for eighteen years) was Jacques Chirac, also a major national leader rather than a nonentity like Tokyo's first postwar governors. Aside from traffic and dog droppings, it is hard to argue that the city has not done well by its people. The major problems facing Paris today are actually the consequences of success: its evolution into a more and more expensive place to live. But the danger is fully recognized, and state, capital, and suburban governments — although still working through a legacy of disdain, fear, marginalization, and hypersensitivity — are focused on it with an unprecedentedly cooperative attitude.

Except for the cooperative attitude, none of the above holds for Tokyo: aside from fears that the whole capital city agglomeration might become too large, local government in Tokyo is relatively the picture of equanimity. This situation goes far back. From the beginning, control of Edo was a clear administrative hierarchy running from the state Council of Elders to the magistrates; the commoner *machi-nanushi,* responsible for from five to twenty neighborhoods; and "five-person groups" of neighbors at the bottom. Separate mechanisms governed religious properties, lordly estates, and state lands, but the ambiguities and jurisdictional rivalries that typified early modern Paris are absent.[61]

The Meiji Restoration ushered in a period of administrative experimentation which, in Tokyo's case, did not really end until 1943.[62] Tokyo's territory was divided, internally reorganized, and expanded; and official titles came and went. In 1889, the city of Tokyo was created within Tokyo Prefecture, with the governor doubling as mayor; in response to the city council's calls for independence, the two executive positions were separated in 1898, although the mayor was also an imperial appointee until 1926. By the 1930s, the city had expanded to incorporate almost all of the prefecture, and in 1943, they were merged to create essentially the Tokyo Prefecture we see today: a core of wards (now twenty-three), plus some two dozen suburban and, in the far west, rural municipalities.

Throughout the process, the Home Ministry kept firm control of the capital. The city council was a raucous bunch, but never challenged the state. Probably the most serious — or at least consequential — confrontation between state and capital came after the 1923 earthquake, when Governor Gotō proposed a sweeping reconstruction plan which was budgetarily gutted by Parliament. This reaction was not, however, a provincial rejection of the capital but rather an example of the distinctive IGRs of Tokyo: unlike Paris, where conflicts have tended to arise between different urban jurisdictions and between capital and state, in closely held Tokyo the rebuff reflected divisions within the state, both between bureaucrats and party politicians and among the ministries themselves.

Politics was not a major factor in Tokyo government in the early postwar period, except in a corrupt, backroom sense; in the 1960s, even this faded, as Governor Azuma Ryūtarō and his lieutenant, Suzuki Shunichi, focused on rational administration and cooperation with the state, wrapping postwar reconstruction in the banner of Olympic redevelopment.[63] The politicization of city government came with Governor Minobe, who opened up the closed legislative and executive shop to popular participation and openly confronted the state. Had it not been for the Oil Shock of 1973, he might have succeeded: a Japanese governor can claim a popular mandate far more credibly than either the mayor of Paris or the Japanese prime minister, and can often ignore his assembly.

Tokyo also has more fiscal independence than any other Japanese city. It complains about the wealth siphoned off by the state (perhaps $200 billion annually in personal and corporate income taxes in the 1990s), of which it receives little in return, but the upside of the situation is that three-quarters of Tokyo's revenues come from local taxes, and less than 10 percent from the state (compared to one-third in the average city).[64] The city is always vulnerable to economic downturns, but as long as it balances its accounts, governors can defy the state with considerable impunity.

Defiance, however, is not the default mode for local politics. There have been some contentious NIMBY issues, but with nothing approaching France's historical partisan divisions, interregional frictions, state intervention, or city-suburb cleavage, governments within the capital region have a record of relatively close cooperation — no doubt facilitated by the fact that the capital region contains fewer than three hundred governmental entities (Greater Paris has 1,309).[65] But perhaps more importantly, the state is more often a mother hen to local governments than an overbearing know-it-all. The face of Tokyo may be less resplendent than that of Paris, but it is more Tokyo's own.

This difference from France is especially visible in the process of national and regional planning. French national plans have historically had a paradoxically Parisian focus, hoping that if people and businesses could not get into Paris (or did not want to brave its infrastructural deprivations), they would go somewhere else. It finally dawned on the state that "somewhere else" could well be London or Brussels, and that wealth had to be produced before it could be redistributed. But even the most recent regional plan for Île-de-France stipulates a population ceiling, to be achieved by manipulating the number of schools and other public facilities there.[66] In Japan, by contrast, national land use planning has tended to fix the capital by changing the country, not the reverse. Ever since Japanese industry began to concentrate in the cities and along the Pacific coast in the late nineteenth century, Japanese regional planning has been a process of picking winners and paying off the losers. All of the postwar Zensō emphasized market-conforming regionalism in the (often misguided) hope that economic activities would follow the flow of infrastructural public works and prospect of tax breaks, subsidies, and concessionary loans.[67] And in many cases the market conformed to was not even economic, but political: public works flowing to the home folks helped reelect rural MPs, even if the fruits of their lobbying were highways to nowhere, airports without airplanes, and harbors without boats. Every Zensō had a new type of regional development — "New Industrial Cities," "Model Industrial Improvement Zones," "Technopolises," "Teletopias" — or regional growth pole concept,[68] but coping with the capital was often the furthest thing from anyone's mind — with the exception of the transportation lobby, which seems to entertain the dream that someday, with enough planes and trains, everyone in Japan can commute to Tokyo.

Narrowing the focus to regional planning, one finds in Tokyo consid-

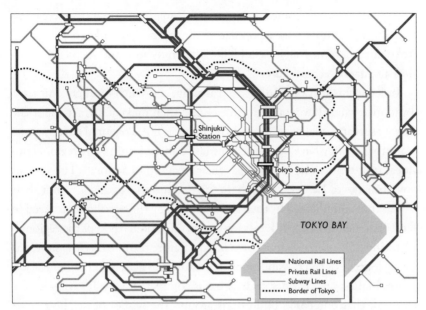

Fig. 32. Transit map of Tokyo: a transportation network which integrates the region without respect for boundaries.

erable freedom of action, and a view of the process which contradicts the state's. Tokyo planning agencies have long acknowledged in principle that the city is too big, too crowded, and too expensive. But when the state speaks of "unipolar concentration," it means concentration *in Tokyo;* when Tokyo does so, it refers only to the three-ward central business district, and when it agreeably proposes a "multipolar" solution, this refers only to a multipolar *region.*[69] And that, given the state's preoccupation with the provinces, is exactly what is coming to pass. An ever wider network of road and rail — especially the sort of concentric links in which Paris is so poor — knits the region together (see fig. 32); uniform schools and local tax rates make many neighborhoods equally attractive, and the developers are only too happy to create new commuter suburbs. Before the homes are even up, the metropolitan services that the new middle class wants are in place, and from one year to the next a patisserie or a Starbucks will replace a cabbage patch. There is an overarching plan, but it is a leisurely one, because the government furnishes infrastructure and waits on the market: "If you provide it, they will come." It has taken Tama New Town forty years to take shape, but now, with a population of 150,000, rail links to Tokyo and Yokohama, two universities, a Hello Kitty museum, and its own Parthenon, its future seems secure.

Indeed, this sort of "indicative planning," in which local governments announce what they would like to see and then make it attractive for the private sector to realize it, seems to be about as far as regional governments want to go. They have been unenthusiastic about joining any regional political unit which might diminish their freedom of action.[70] The various governments of Île-de-France share this "communal egotism,"[71] but their situation is complicated by their numbers and by the simultaneous need to fend off a state which, while talking decentralization, has kept the regional-planning process firmly in its own hands. Before the reforms, the state was unapologetic; of the possibility of consulting the people in the renovation of Les Halles, one planner said: "That is complete idiocy. It's truly idiotic to think that one could build Paris around the wishes of neighborhood people. Don't you see Paris is for everyone, not just for the Parisians, and certainly not just for the neighborhood associations? It is for France. Paris is for the world."[72] This is not to say that similar high-handedness does not characterize the Japanese state; the unilateral imposition in the 1960s of a new Tokyo international airport in the countryside of Narita was but one example. But the Narita airport ignited a firestorm of local governmental and grassroots opposition; it opened a decade behind schedule, is still incomplete and mired in contention, and taught the state a bitter lesson. The two international airports built since then have both been built on man-made islands offshore, following the BANANA principle: Build Absolutely Nothing Anywhere Near Anybody. The state remains exceedingly leery of exercising its powers of eminent domain. And in France? A second Seine-bank highway was planned, but canceled. Why? Because President Giscard said no.

To be sure, the situation in Paris has changed since then. With a mayor-gladiator, Paris was able in 1981 to stalemate a state proposal for a world exposition,[73] and twenty years later Paris was able to plan the redevelopment of the Les Halles area on its own. State-capital cooperation has grown, and the state's attitude toward Paris has improved tremendously. But the state's basically interventionist posture is unchanged, as can be seen in the state-prepared Île-de-France regional master plan of 1994.[74] Although re-affirming the grandeur and national and international importance of the capital, the plan follows in the tradition of earlier reports and plans: Paris must be limited and manipulated for state ends.[75] Interestingly, however, although the state-capital balance of power is different in France, there are indications that the Paris region is headed in the direction of Greater Tokyo: intraregional deconcentration and ever broader definition of the region. The Île-de-France Regional Council seems to have accepted a regional population ceiling of 12 million and an increased emphasis on commuting.[76] And there is a growing focus in state agencies like DATAR on the "Greater Paris basin" and on "cities within an hour": places like Rouen, Reims, Orléans, and Amiens could, with TGV (high-speed rail) service, become integrated with the capital, deconcentrating the region just as the new towns deconcentrated Paris. Such a development, they say, would prevent the "desertification" of the regional periphery. It could also conceivably create a metropolitan sprawl covering fully one-third of the entire territory of France.[77] And in 2009 a state committee proposed — over the screams of Paris — fusing Paris and the three "inner crown" departments of Île-de-France into "Greater Paris," and absorbing two departments from the neighboring Picardie region into Île-de-France.[78] Thus far, however, the specific projects resulting from the planning process have had what one might call a more disciplined effect on Paris than on Tokyo. This is perhaps unsurprising, given the greater role of the state in France and of local government and the private sector in Japan. Both countries have built new towns, but while most of France's surround Paris, Japan's new towns are scattered about, the result of national rather than regional planning, in order to give specific regions a shot in the arm. Only one, Tama, is really part of Tokyo.[79]

A similarly diffuse focus and disregard for the capital characterizes Tokyo's attempts to provide big business with the infrastructure it desires in an age of globalization. Ever more distant clusters of skyscrapers spring up from Tokyo's low-profile cityscape with no guiding principle except the location of train stations. The Waterfront City Subcenter is an exception,[80] but it has limped painfully toward completion. For many years, half-built or empty buildings dotted the site, and vacant land still spreads wide. I predict that the subcenter will see fine days; progress — and larger crowds — are visible every time I visit, and had Tokyo won the 2016 Olympics, it would certainly thrive. And, after all, Paris's equivalent center, La Défense, has taken forty years to reach its present vitality.

As for La Défense, its critics are not few today. But it does constitute a more coherent response to the exigencies of international economic competition and globalization than one sees in Tokyo, and shows more respect for its parent city as well. Paris's first high-rise experiment, the Montparnasse Tower (1973), is still regarded as a how-not-to-do-it lesson (even the grandiose development plans of Mayor Delanoë are all relegated to the gates of the city). In subsequent considerations of how the capital might better accommodate international business, the decision — first conceived in 1958 — was made to set up a new business district outside the city. The municipalities on whose territory it would grow were represented by half the members of the governing council of EPAD, the public corporation in charge of the project; the other half were state officials.[81] Given La Défense's critical role in Paris's future, it is curious — albeit logical, since the project was outside Paris proper — that EPAD did not include anyone from city hall.

La Défense is thus an example of the French state playing with Paris's future. As in other such cases, this has not necessarily redounded to Paris's detriment. Although La Défense's early years were as rocky as those of the Tokyo Waterfront, today the district has 1,500 corporate tenants, 150,000 workers, 20,000 residents, and a major transportation hub.[82] It has public art, stores, schools, and cinemas, and is a tourist, shopping, and work destination.

But is it more successful than the Waterfront? For its age, perhaps not. Was its growth smoother? By no means: once the initial plan for the Waterfront was agreed upon, its only real problem has been the Japanese economy, whereas for EPAD the budget, land use, public-private division of labor, personnel, and distribution of benefits all became grist for contention on an almost daily basis.[83] I predict that, in the end, the Waterfront will be fully developed and profitably used by corporations and citizens, but insofar as its goal was to become the corporate focal point of global Tokyo, it will fall short of La Défense. Is this a bad thing? Not necessarily: the ran-

Fig. 33. Barbarians at the gates (2): Global capital quarantined outside Paris; looking westward toward La Défense.

dom siting of corporate head offices, hotels, banks, department stores, and other international business services around Tokyo has not damaged the city because there is little to damage. And some private building complexes like Tokyo Midtown, Roppongi Hills, and Ark Hills are not unpleasant to regard. Central Paris, by contrast, has much to lose, and so perhaps the state's preemptive step of quarantining globalization in the suburbs is a vote in favor of the French planning process.

Baleful Banlieue, Home Sweet Hazure: *The Capital and the Suburbs*

Unless, of course, one is a suburban Parisian, in which case La Défense may look like just another Parisian problem being dumped over the city wall, like "its dead, its garbage, its poor, its foreigners."[84] Paris's suburbs — or the city's margins in general — have been a lively topic for centuries. But in the nineteenth century, as industry began to locate outside the city, and workers followed,[85] the city's bourgeoisie was only too happy to see them go. The capital's perceptions were hardening, and the goal was to keep Paris apart from outlying influences. The physical form of the metropolis is still characterized by fragmentation, with the periphery sliced apart by the pre-dominantly radial road and rail system.[86]

In the late nineteenth century and early twentieth, Paris began to at-tack its social problems, but in doing so aggravated the city-suburb split. The often ghastly îlots insalubres in the city were renovated one by one, but their residents could not afford the new rents. Social housing made its appearance, for the most part in the form of a belt of projects around the margins of the city, which simply enhanced the socioeconomic and politi-cal homogeneity of the Red Belt taking shape there.[87]

After World War II, the campaign to eliminate slums inside and outside the city continued,[88] and at last a frontal attack was launched upon Paris's acute housing shortage. The resulting strategy, unfortunately, emphasized monster low-rent housing projects, the grands ensembles, mostly in the suburbs. Huge complexes like La Courneuve, Aulnay, and Rose des Vents were erected, providing much-needed housing for thousands of families; as such they were successful.[89] But their architecture was Stalinesque, their locations were inconvenient (they were built where land was cheapest, that is, least accessible), and they soon fell victim to stereotypes of alienation, isolation, and poverty. Those who could, moved out, and were replaced by poorer and, increasingly, immigrant populations. Soon the grands en-sembles, and their image of drugs and crime, became for many "the single defining feature" of the suburbs, and today's officially designated suburban "quartiers en difficulté" are essentially the projects.[90]

To some extent this situation has changed, although reality moves faster than image. President Mitterrand brought a new respect for the suburbs, and the new towns brought in a large middle-class population.[91] Decen-tralization broke up the suburbs into seven departments, putting an end to the monolithic Red Belt.[92] Lip service, at least, is wholly devoted to co-operation between capital and suburbs, and construction of suburban rail lines (and the long-delayed Francilienne ring highway) continues. And the mayor claims that his six new high-rise developments at the gates of Paris will better integrate city and suburbs. Less enthusiastic observers worry that they will become "impassable walls,"[93] from which the Parisiens will be able to look down literally on the suburbs. But whichever image prevails, there is history to be overcome: much intrasuburban cooperation has been motivated simply by a common fear of Paris.[94]

In Tokyo, on the other hand, the question would probably be: Divisions? What divisions? "Tokyo" — twenty-three wards? one prefecture? four prefectures? seven prefectures? — is a pretty seamless whole physically and socioeconomically. From the very beginning, there was conscious, systematic integration of the periphery with Edo, with the shogunate providing tax breaks, tools, and low-interest loans to induce settlement as early as 1722, and allocating estates to the lords which ran in a continuum all the way from downtown to the distant countryside.[95]

This conscious, planned suburbanization continued after the Restoration, but it became predominantly the work of the private sector. As noted, to the extent that it planned Tokyo at all, the government focused on hygiene and other infrastructure. But its field of vision extended only as far as the Yamanote loop line: it built stations along the line as the termini for long-distance state-owned rail lines, and built a subway system to link the area within the loop. (There was, of course, no debate about integrating subway and rail.) It was left to private companies to run suburban lines out from these nodes; typically, they bought land in swaths radiating out from the stations and then built rail lines outward. They subdivided and sold the land, built the houses, set up bus companies to serve the suburban stations, and built department stores at the main stations in order to provide for all their customers' residential, sumptuary, and transportation needs. The suburbs grew from roughly 400,000 inhabitants at the dawn of the twentieth century to 1.2 million in 1920 and 2.9 million in 1930.[96] Some of the periphery, especially to the south and east, became industrial and working class, but most offered little employment,[97] and the image of the suburbs which became hegemonic was as middle-class bedroom towns. The suburbs were something to embrace, not keep at arm's length.

After World War II, the government — both state and prefecture — adopted a far more activist role regarding the suburbs. Again, for the most part Tokyo rebuilt itself: previous landowners pieced together whatever they could on their properties and improved them when they could — and private initiative (and resources) far outran the government. But the overall housing shortage, especially in the cities as migrants flocked to the re-vived industries, ushered in the age of massive public housing projects, the danchi. These were every bit as depressing as France's grands ensembles, and equally criticized, and in the short run they were socioeconomically similar, but soon their courses diverged: the danchi population tended to see them as way stations on an upward ladder, while people in the grands ensembles began to internalize their negative images. And while those who left the danchi were replaced by a similar class of people, the grands en-sembles became home to progressively more deprived groups.

It is interesting to muse about the fate of Paris's suburbs had France not experienced the immigrant problem that has arisen in recent decades. Is the banlieue today a suburban problem, or an ethnic problem? If ethnic Koreans and other foreigners had flocked to the danchi, would the Japa-nese situation parallel the French? It is possible. But Paris's suburbs are still a bottle — a Molotov cocktail, perhaps — of long-standing, problematic marginality. Once its contents were socioeconomic; now they are ethnic. But in both cases the tendency of the capital is to shun them, a tendency which remains to be overcome.

CONCLUSION

In the twenty-first century, both Japan and France are trying to integrate their capital cities fully into their regions and into the nation as a whole and to promote them not only as places to live, work, and visit but also as major contributors to the nation's progress in a competitive global economy. Tokyo does so by following, not overcoming, its historical path. Although the situation has ameliorated much in recent decades, Paris — and espe-cially its physical face, which bears the enduring evidence of the past — has had a far more conflicted relationship with its nation, its national govern-ment, and its suburban environment than has Tokyo. My initial impres-sions are largely borne out by detailed observation, and this observation has also provided some suggestions as to why this is so. Five interrelated, possibly explanatory themes can be abstracted from what we have seen.

First, France does seem to be characterized by a relatively defensive view of the world, a Malthusian, zero-sum insecurity and lingering mistrust of

Others. This is not to say that the Japanese easily suffer Others — far from it. But the scope of insularity, that is, the line between Us and Them, although more sharply drawn in Japan, is more narrowly drawn in France. The Japanese really do not see themselves as one with the rest of the human race, and a major influx of ethnically different people would create great social problems. But I am interested in describing the Tokyo which is, not that which might otherwise be. And so it is relevant here that essentially the entire Japanese population fits within the scope of Japanese cultural insularity, while the kind of fear and distrust the Japanese focus on foreigners can in France be applied to those from other villages, regions, or even neighborhoods.

Second, these relationships suggest a different view of centers and peripheries, and margins, in France and Japan, and a French inclination to clarify margins and make distinctions. The Japanese center looks down less on the periphery, and the periphery is less defensive; the Japanese are more likely to tolerate or even celebrate margins, or "shadows." Where ambiguity exists, as in French intergovernmental relations today, it is often the by-product of the confrontation with the past, and it motivates efforts to reimpose clarity.

Third, France is still living out a legacy of warfare, civil strife, and fear. Provincial hostility to Paris, the Parisian bourgeois fear of the proletariat, and the mutual enmities of capital and state are well substantiated.[98] And, of course, they are inscribed on the physical face of Paris, from the monuments of the winners to the more subdued memorials to Commune martyrs in Père Lachaise Cemetery. We have noted that part of the grandeur of Paris lies in the clash of symbols, in the material evidence of a tumultuous history, in the violent confrontation there of great ideas and human causes. And we note that Tokyo is by contrast a pallid place. It has a dashing statue or two, and a low-key memorial to the Forty-seven Rōnin, and little else. One might respond that Tokyoites never had to recoil in terror from the tumbrels of the Revolution or the anti-Communard executioners of 1871 either. Might there be a connection between orderly and ordinary, between tragic and magic?

Fourth, I suggested above that, compared to the West, political authority in Japan has tended to be exercised "softly," in a hegemonic cultural

» Fig. 34. Overstated commemoration? Orderly ranks of Parisian architecture climbing toward Montmartre and the counterrevolutionary memorial of Sacré-Coeur.

˅ Fig. 35. Understated commemoration: the graves of Japan's most romantic heroes, the Forty-seven Rōnin.

context of compliance and allegiance, more than through "hard," coercive means. The relationships of Paris and Tokyo are consistent with such a proposition. Both states have been historically preoccupied with control of the capital, but the French state has been far more hands-on, holding a more aggressive and manipulative view of control. And it has had reason to do so, for two reasons: first, a European tradition of urban autonomy, lacking in Japan, which made collisions with the late-coming state inevitable;[99] and, second, the Greco-Roman democratic tradition, which made conceivable, and legitimized, conflict between the people and lords, monarchs, states, and city halls over the very fate of the political community.

In Japan, by contrast, the state has long chosen to play the role of general contractor, or umpire, as if it were confident that loyal subjects, citizens, interest groups, local governments, and even private capitalists could, with maximum education and minimal oversight, be trusted not to embrace insubordinate ideas. Many critics of the modern history of Paris have decried the freewheeling, rapacious role of the market and of private developers, and the state's putative sacrifice of the city on the altar of capitalism. But compared to Tokyo, Paris is a model of dirigisme, and the relatively unchanging face of central Paris makes it clear that capitalism or no capitalism, there is a *force majeur* at work in Paris which makes Tokyo seem utterly laissez-faire by comparison.

Finally, the capital is seen in very different ways in Japan and France. Views of Paris, relatively speaking, have long been intrinsic, as if the capital were an end in itself. Some have seen it as good, some as evil. Today positive views predominate. This is not necessarily an unmitigated good: some people have warned that the resistance of Paris to change is turning it into an exclusive enclave for tourists and the rich, or a museum. But in any case, Paris seems to stand for something, and to stand up for itself.

The Japanese view of Tokyo, by contrast, seems to be much more instrumental and contingent. It has been less of a given, with which states and provinces must contend, than a means to some other goal. For the Tokugawa, Edo was the physical manifestation of their sociopolitical system, and an instrument of rule; in our day, it has tended to be seen as more of a money machine, a vehicle for national and then global economic success. The French state has tended to treat the capital as something to be nurtured (or disciplined); the Japanese government's view seems to have been: Set it up and let it run. Neither of these views is unique or absolute. But comprehending the relationships of Paris and Tokyo to the world around them is easier if one allows for the possibility that Tokyo has long been subordinated to other, more important national ideas, whereas Paris has often seemed to *be* the idea of France.

CONCLUSION

A city mirrors its past. Sometimes — especially in the enduring center of Paris — it looks more like its crystallization. The center of Tokyo looks more kaleidoscopic. Both impressions are misleading. The past is fluid — the French Revolution and the Meiji Restoration, for example, are shape-shifters — and even if the bricks and mortar do not change, their meaning — and hence the essence of the city — does. But neither the past nor the present is entirely up for grabs. The city's past matters, and it can be seen systematically in the form and functioning of today's city, both in what is there and what is not. And since pasts differ, cities differ, even cities with as many commonalities as Paris and Tokyo — ultramodern, global, capitalist cities, the capitals of centralized states. In these final pages, I recap a few of these differences in form and function/relationship, some of the ways that Paris and Tokyo strike one, and engage one, so differently. I have raised a number of possible reasons for the differences I see — perhaps not really *causes* in any rigorous sense, but historical and contemporary factors which are at least *consistent with* the differences between the capitals, and therefore perhaps worthy of more rigorous critique.

FORM

Most of my initial impressions of Tokyo and Paris seem to stand up under detailed examination, at least in a relative sense. One can find in Paris everything that one does in Tokyo, and vice versa. But the French and the Japanese clearly prefer not to do some things that they can, at least not nearly so often as the others do.

Organization and Order

Thus Tokyo is indeed more plastic, impermanent, and disorderly than Paris, but more organized than it appears. Once the Romans left, Paris for 1,000 years grew haphazardly; since Henry IV, it gradually has become a planned, unchanged, and physically homogeneous city par excellence. Architectural gems abound, but "the solo, no matter how inspired and powerful, never escapes the ensemble of laws, often secret, which regulate the symphony."[1] That symphony has a historical leitmotif: the interior boulevards of Paris follow the outline of one ancient wall, the Périphérique follows another, and the entire transportation system, even today, dances to a theme of exclusion and self-absorption.

Whether all this is good or bad is continually debated. Is Paris becoming a fossilized city, encased in amber, while new towers around its edges recreate the old wall? Is architectural harmony a reflection of some esthetic/political dictatorship? How can Paris ever build the concentric highways and rail lines which would create a harmonious region, not just a city?

Tokyo is, by contrast, frustrating. Tokyo took the opposite path from Paris, beginning life as a planned city and becoming an amoebic helter-skelter. There are architectural gems in Tokyo, too, but no sense of context, of coherent urban fabric, no visible conductor for the symphony: it is as if the Meiji regime erected over the gates of the city the slogan *Fais ce que vouldras* — Do as you please. There is certainly no political dictatorship over the form of the city, nor an esthetic one either; if there is a visible hand, it is that of commodification.

Not that this concerns the Japanese too much. History does survive, in a street plan which reflects that of Edo, and in place-names which imply the past and create lieux de mémoire even if the original physical structures are long gone. The ensemble of laws which regulates the symphony is more secret in Tokyo, but no less present. What we see — albeit with some difficulty — is not chaos but the juxtaposition of microorders without any apparent macroordering principle. Tokyo has, in fact, four different ordering principles: *religion,* seen in the Chinese cosmological siting of the castle and its environs; *defense,* seen (as in fig. 11 on p. 65) in the moats which regulated first the form of the city and more recently the courses of highways and rail lines; *topography,* seen in the contrast between regular flatland and meandering upland street layouts; and *social control,* manifest in the gridlike pattern of the commoner quarters (Zone F in fig. 11). These organizing principles may be as invisible or implicit as the Imperial Palace, but they are no less there. And although the resulting cityscape is disorderly, society is not, in relative contrast to Paris. Most Tokyoites work in the frantic, ephemeral global city, but they live in a different city, one that has much of a small town about it, in neighborhoods that are "forever tied to the past."[2]

The Center: Open Is Not Empty

The center of Paris is hardly empty. Street by street, *place* by *place,* it rewards the visitor with a visual feast of architectural splendor. Nor is Tokyo's; it is resolutely nonmonumental and closed, but, in the words of Augustin Berque: "There is no empty center in Tokyo. There is, even less, 'anarchic' urban development in Japan. Terms signifying 'absence of authority' contradict the logic of an urbanization which obeys very precise and perfectly identifiable forces (financial and political) of which the Emperor represents the hierarchical pinnacle."[3] In other words, central Tokyo took shape as the spatial conjunction of three modern forces: the emperor system, the centralized state, and industrial capital.[4]

The empty center is nonetheless a danger, albeit not in a way Roland Barthes ever imagined. Central Tokyo is depopulating; its neighborhood associations are atrophying,[5] and it risks becoming a nighttime wasteland. The Tokyo and Paris central business districts are about the same size, and their daytime populations — about 3 million people — are roughly the same, but whereas central Paris's nighttime population is about three-quarters of this figure, central Tokyo's is only about one-fifth.[6] The Waterfront Subcenter and other developments are premised on the assumption that this trend can be partly reversed, and the 2006 law restricting large-scale commercial, entertainment, medical, and educational developments in the suburbs is designed to sustain the urban center.[7] Whether such efforts can prevent Barthes' words from taking on new truth remains to be seen.

Middle and Margin: The Fixed and the Fuzzy

Paris is not what it used to be — literally. As recently as the 1950s the city was "distinctly delimited"; one entered through a "gate," and though there was no mark on the ground, "the line was clearly drawn in spirit."[8] The definition of the capital has diffused since then, albeit not so much as Tokyo. Is "Paris" the central business district (or "tourist Paris")? The twenty-arrondissement city? The inner ring of suburbs, both rings, or the entire Paris basin?[9] And east-west internal differentiation has also diminished.[10]

Nonetheless, Paris is still a more segregated and polarized metropolis than Tokyo. The Paris-banlieue cleavage "remains pregnant," and although the new Éole and Météor suburban rail lines will help, they do not address the need for integrating the suburbs with concentric lines.[11]

And segregation also persists within the city. In Paris, transformation tends to take the form of comprehensively planned development of large pieces of land — La Défense, Place d'Italie, Front de Seine, Bercy-Tolbiac, Beaubourg, and most recently Batignolles — which create a compartmentalized city.[12] Oddly, it is the French state, despite its dirigiste emphasis on social solidarity, which has ended up with the more exclusionist, segregated capital.

Also oddly, it was in Edo that the state set out to create an exquisitely segregated capital, but neither the Tokugawa state nor its successors ever adopted the hands-on urbanism needed to maintain segregation in the face of "insurgent" land use. Today "Tokyo" is even more of a moving target than is Paris, and neither Tokyo Disneyland nor the New Tokyo International Airport is even in Tokyo.[13] Internally, too, the Tokugawa ideal gave way more than two hundred years ago. The Meiji regime tried to reestablish some distinctions, but the pace of private-sector economic growth after the quake and the war outran policy, and the heterogeneity of Tokyo neighborhoods increased, with the three major types of cityscape — downtown (*shitamachi*), uptown (*yamanote*), and suburb — going from categories to a continuum.[14] As all this ferment did not lead to great con-

centrations of poverty, crime, minorities, disinvestment, or decayed housing, it flew mostly under the radar of governmental or popular concern.[15]
Nor did it lead to segregated enclaves of wealth. High-rent districts exist,
but there is no Tokyo parallel to the hundreds of private, gated, or chained
lanes and culs-de-sac seen in Paris.

Plans Seen and Unseen

My initial impression of Tokyo was, with exceptions, of a random sprawl
compared to Paris. But it seems far more accurate to say that Tokyo is also
planned, albeit implicitly, in the sense of being rule-governed. The overall
street layout of Tokyo is still, in many areas, that of Edo. But large-scale,
comprehensive plans — in Meiji, in 1923, in 1945, in the 1990s — have a long
history of failure in Tokyo.[16] Even those which are arguably successful have
taken a very long time to gestate (Tama), remain unfulfilled (the Waterfront), or have left relatively little behind (the 1964 Olympics). Piece-by-
piece, market-conforming, and often indirect means have worked better:
economic incentives, satellite cities, regional development programs, and
transportation policy.

Another governing principle of Tokyo's growth has been the subcontractarian nature of Japanese government: a much larger share of planning
has been done by the municipality and by the private sector than in Paris.
The westward movement of Tokyo has been largely municipally driven,
and the city has the resources and autonomy to engage the state in a planning duel. And much planning has simply been by default, with the government letting individuals determine the use of their own land. Indeed,
one might say that land use and architecture are in some ways more democratic, or populist, processes in a Japan, with no tradition whatsoever of
citizen participation, than in Republican France.[17]

Another factor governing the form of the capital is the emperor. The
avenue from the palace to Tokyo Station and the low skyline reflect his
role. And a final guiding principle in Tokyo's growth is the market. But
this is not the market in the neoliberal Western sense. Meiji Japan was the
first "developmental state," which rigged the market to create incentives for
the pursuit of state goals.[18] These included national defense and national
economic growth; a capital city which would impress foreigners, facilitate

the accumulation and productive use of capital, and generate and trade commodities was a means to these ends. It is not that the Japanese are distinctively *free*-market, or that they are distinctively materialistic; what has shaped Tokyo is capitalism guided by a state little interested in urbanism, linked to a distinctively pragmatic culture — of which more below. What the state has imposed on Edo and Tokyo is an implicit and social, not an explicitly planned and visual, order.[19] Despite the frequent assertions that the market is running roughshod over the growth of Paris, France has chosen to plan Paris explicitly and to transform it broadly. Tokyo tries to work around the centripetal forces in polity and economy, while Paris tries to counter them.[20] Thus the dispersal of ministries and the creation of commercial/industrial centers outside the capital at La Défense, Rungis, and to the south dwarf in scale and planning detail the growth poles of Greater Tokyo. Like the new towns, they are intended explicitly to impact the market, bringing price stability, regulation of the market, and a multiplier effect, as many newly occupied offices, apartments, or warehouses represent freed-up space in central Paris.[21] Parisian planning is more statist and public, less municipal and private than in Tokyo; it is more explicit, and there is more of it.

Transforming the Capital

All of which is not to say that the Japanese are incapable of transforming their cities. What is of more interest is how manipulation of the capital in Japan differs qualitatively from what we see in France. There are three ways in which manipulation of urban form differs: in Paris, it is more monumental, more physical, and more public/statist; in Tokyo, less monumental, more social or behavioral, and more private or municipal. Second, the driving forces behind urban transformation in Paris are relatively esthetic and intrinsic, whereas in Tokyo they are more economic and instrumental. Third, urban transformation in France is motivated relatively strongly by domestic considerations; in Japan, by international considerations.

Of the monumentalism of Paris I need add little. "Seeing is believing" is as true today as it was for the Romans. And it does not cease: "The impetus toward prestige and grandeur gains momentum,"[22] and more monuments are under way. Even though Paris did not win the 2012 Olympics, Batignolles will happen: the state is committed to it and, as with La Défense and Bercy-Tolbiac, will put in whatever is needed to realize it. Unflagging state support in all three cases is the same.

How different it is in Tokyo, where one must hunt for visible historical monuments. And one must know the celebratory calendar to know when the commemorative festival of a neighborhood takes place. Certainly the tides of history have played a role in this material amnesia. Natural disasters and construction materials also played a role. But there is more to it than this. The "architecture of authority"[23] has simply not played a major role in Japanese history, and commemorations have been left to the people who attach place-names, put up roadside shrines, and celebrate local rituals — and to organized interests in the private sector.

It is this last which really sets Tokyo apart. Tokyo's "vitality is largely economic," and much of the city is a privately built monument to consumption.[24] But there is more going on here. It is a mistake simply to say, Well, all advanced capitalist societies have become "societies of the spectacle,"[25] and Japan is simply furthest along. The incredible mercantile display of the Tokyo street and the flood of commercial stimuli "exist for themselves."[26] They have transcended their capitalist or commercial qualities and acquired intrinsic value; Japan is not so much supercapitalist as supracapitalist; capitalism has become noneconomic for the Japanese, as it was for Max Weber's Protestants.

This partnership between commerce and society transforms Tokyo every evening when the lights come on. When the state tries to transform the capital, its record is far less impressive. The city itself has managed some striking achievements, foremost among which is the New City Hall. But state-initiated projects include Tama New Town — successful on its own terms but contributing little to the deconcentration of Tokyo — the Cross-Bay Highway (an overpriced money-loser), and Narita Airport, a policy snafu from the very beginning. Far more successful have been West Shinjuku and the more recent, private Ark Hills, which attracted 26 million visitors in its first six months.[27]

The second distinctive aspect of the transformations of Tokyo and Paris focuses on the difference between the esthetic and the pragmatic. Lewis Mumford argued, in the context of urbanism, that man faces a choice be-

tween devoting himself to the development of his own humanity or sur-
rendering to the "almost automatic forces" of economics and technology
and yielding to a "dehumanized alter ego."[28] Henri Lefebvre answered that
the choice had already been made, that city space has become a product,
marketed and evaluated according to efficiency, function, and profit.[29] A
comparison of Paris and Tokyo suggests that Lefebvre spoke too soon: over
and over, decisions about the future of Paris have been motivated by noneconomic factors.[30]

Japan, on the other hand, would warm Lefebvre's heart. Tokyo is a living
testament to the priority of pragmatism over esthetics. Such masterpieces
as the Imperial Hotel were unceremoniously torn down and replaced by
better moneymakers, and Tokyo Tower, the symbol of postwar optimism
and technological achievement, is slated to be superseded by a new tower,
twice as tall and more efficient for broadcasting.[31] And many of the romantic neighborhood names of Edo were changed to numbers in the interests
of administrative standardization. As this last suggests, however, there is
again more going on here than the simplistic victory of capitalist economic
values. There is a pragmatic, instrumental strain in Japanese culture which
is clearly visible in the city. I do not know where it comes from, but it begs
inquiry. It is one of the "roots of difference" between Paris and Tokyo
which I address below, but I did not propose it initially; rather, it emerged
during my examination of the cities.

It is also visible elsewhere. Thomas C. Smith has seen it in two instances: the first was the cold-eyed birth control which aimed to optimize
the relationship between family size, sex balance, and landholdings in
early modern Japan; the second was Japan's "aristocratic revolution," the
ruthless post-Restoration abolition of the warrior aristocracy by a samurai
regime — perhaps the only example of a class which liquidated itself.[32] Another example is 1945, when the Japanese, starkly aware of the total, devastating bankruptcy of fifteen years of military adventure, turned 180 degrees
and, in John Dower's words, "embraced defeat."[33]

In any case, Tokyo is a pragmatic, instrumental city. Transformations
tend to be for the purpose of clearing the decks for something else —
usually something more profitable. Paris, too, has been changed for public
health, public security, and economic reasons, but also for grandeur for its

own sake. A century later, the pragmatic step for traffic-choked Paris would have been highways along both sides of the Seine. That has not occurred, and will not.

The last way in which Tokyo's self-transformation differs from Paris's lies in the realm of domestic as opposed to international considerations. In a sense the globalization of Japan began in A.D. 645, when the government adopted a wide variety of political and cultural practices and institutions from China. Japan's receptivity to the new and different has waxed and waned since then, but in the modern era it has been married to an acute sensitivity to what foreigners think of Japan, and an intense desire for respect. The first characteristic, borrowing, does not set Japan apart — after all, how much of contemporary American culture was here in 1492? But the shaping of the country in general and the cities in particular in explicit emulation of the outside world are distinctively Japanese. During the Meiji era, everything from Western architecture to Western dancing was adopted in order to impress the foreigners with Japan's modernity. The Ende-Bockmann plan for Tokyo, and the baroque plans for Japan's colonial capitals, were explicitly Western. And today Tokyo has its own Eiffel Tower, Statue of Liberty, and Parthenon.[34] If foreign considerations may have gone too far in Tokyo, one can argue that they have not gone far enough in Paris. Paris is in competition with Brussels, London, and Frankfurt; it is behind; and it is losing ground.[35] Bad traffic, oppressive government regulation, strikes, labor force inflexibility, provincial opposition to urban development — the list goes on. As a result, France has fewer European corporate headquarters of American and Japanese companies than the United Kingdom, Germany, Belgium, or Holland. To be sure, the French posture has changed — the new Île-de-France master plan "places the region deliberately in a worldwide competition."[36] And high-speed rail lines, highways, airports, and conference centers are only the most directly relevant changes in the region; all of the cultural amenities mentioned above are also among the assets Paris brings to the competition. But there is a limit, and Paris is unwilling to transform itself to such an extent that it compromises its quality of life and esthetic values, whereas Tokyo will do just about anything to make itself more attractive to international business.

RELATIONSHIPS

If the form of a city is fluid, mirroring a changing past and present, then its relationships are even more so. In general, Paris's relationships today are dominated by efforts to come to terms with its past; Tokyo's represent much more continuity with its own. In the most general sense, Paris seems to be in the process of integrating and balancing itself with France, with the state, and with its suburbs, albeit not without reluctance and not without state constraint. Tokyo, on the other hand, seems to be taking advantage of its own autonomy, its good relations with its neighbors, and an otherwise preoccupied state to drift in the direction of swallowing Japan.

Capital and Country: Balancing or Devouring?

The French have traditionally feared inundation by Paris more than the Japanese have feared Tokyo. Even with the improvement in provincial attitudes toward Paris, "deconcentration" in France has meant extensive functional devolution to regional and local governments. The economic and demographic weight of Paris in France has declined, and the provinces are less focused on Paris; for more and more of them, the focus of economic attention is elsewhere in Europe.[37]

Indeed, there are those who say ominously that the provincial-capital divide will be solved rather by the "gradual dissolution of the notion of province in the featureless expanse of 'Greater Paris.'"[38] But no one who has compared Tokyo and Paris will be too exercised by this view. Japan fears Tokyo less, but has more to fear from it; the technophiliac and largely laissez-faire urbanism of the Japanese state leads daily to the spread of the capital metropolis, and the state has not contested the notion of an ever larger, multipolar region rather than a really deconcentrated nation.[39] A small number of large regional cities are holding their own, and many prefectural capitals are too. But Tokyo's symbolic domination continues, the geographic expanse of its region grows, and the planners' tendency to cite Tokyo as an issue but not address it directly continues.[40]

The domination is figurative — consumer styles and media sources all seemingly emanate from Tokyo — and it could become literal, for two reasons. One is the ever increasing scope and efficiency of the Japanese transportation system. The other is the fact that the population of Japan has begun to shrink, the result of years of subreplacement birth rates. The question is, will this depopulation be equally spread throughout the country, or unbalanced? If the latter, with the capital continuing to attract people from a nation with an ever smaller population, and the younger, employed population of Tokyo required to cover the spiraling welfare bills of an ever larger and rural aged population, Tokyo may truly move into a zero-sum relationship with the rest of the country, with possible political consequences.

The Capital and the State

As the demonization of Paris has faded, so has its victimization by the French state. The "Paris versus France" literature has declined; the state is more solicitous, the regions are more confident, and Paris can, with its own mayor, speak more effectively for itself. But an autonomous Paris is not on the horizon. For one thing, there have been second thoughts about decentralization. Even the Left has realized that, in terms of regional planning and social justice, decentralization is a Frankenstein's monster,[41] and decentralization has been accompanied by a litany of assertions by the state that it intends a "strong dose" of intervention whenever social solidarity, interregional equity, and coordinated pursuit of national goals are "menaced."[42] Japanese bureaucrats may agree, but it is politically incorrect to say so; lip service is unfailingly paid to local autonomy.

Thus the French state reserves — and flaunts — its right to intervene in Paris. Moreover, individual presidents have continued the practice of treating Paris as their personal canvas. Tokyo is almost bereft of similarly individual-linked monuments, with a few exceptions like Masashige, Hachikō, and the ubiquitous Mori buildings.

Thus, while Paris and France wrestle over decentralization, statism, and a fraught history, Tokyo sails on with state acquiescence in its consensually accepted role as the center of everything. Indeed, it would be good for Tokyo and for Japan if there were a little more opposition to, or at least concern for, Tokyo by the state, which has tended for the last century to sacrifice the rest of the country to the needs of the capital. On the other hand, Tokyo's form is more populist, if not democratic: it has no ghettoes,

no gated communities, and lively local governments and neighborhood associations. Is it possible that the quality of citizenship is higher in Tokyo
than in the cradle of *liberté, égalité, fraternité?*

Tokyo's relationship to the state also seems headed toward greater autonomy. The state itself is partly the cause of this: despite regional planning and billions of dollars worth of pork barrel funding for the provinces,
it is the policies of the developmental state which dictate the functional
primacy of the capital.[43] Add postwar reforms and activist governors, and
Tokyo's freedom of action expands: in recent decades, it has developed its
own "Monroe Doctrine" toward the state, adopted an alternative, regional
solution to the "Tokyo Problem," and carried out its own grands projets.[44]
The economic crisis and the rapid turnover of prime ministers and turbulence of the party system during the 1990s meant less and less state attention to the capital. Even the state's plan to move the capital to another city
was halfhearted and abortive.[45] Tokyo's autonomy, by default or by design,
is real.

Capital and Context: The Suburbs

The same relatively bland picture of smooth relationships, regional enrich-
ment and integration, and functional efficiency again characterizes Tokyo's
position in its region.[46] Paris also presents a picture of improvement, but
with significant reservations rooted in history.

In the first place, despite the obstacle of decentralization, Paris has become better integrated with its region. Led by the new towns and such satellite commercial centers as Roissy and Massy-Saclay-Orly, Greater Paris is
taking on a life of its own, expanding and becoming multipolar, like the
Japanese capital region. The road and rail infrastructure has improved, especially links within the suburbs, and physical mobility has increased, again,
especially within the suburbs.[47] In a sense, La Défense not only deconcentrated central Paris but, by extending the grand axis past the city limits,
broke Paris's shell, setting off a process which now touches La Défense itself:
corporate leaders BP and Esso have sold their properties there and moved
farther out of town.[48] These trends make relationships with the suburbs less
touchy and collective improvement easier. And Mayor Delanoë has pursued
a strategy of cooperation which one suburban mayor has described as "a

revolution."[49] But two caveats remain. First, there are lingering problems that may be intractable. The Paris transportation system is nowhere nearly as complete as Tokyo's.[50] The average Métro line still goes only a couple of stops beyond the city limits, and there is not yet any complete concentric highway or rail line in the far suburbs, although a "Super Métro" with stations at its intersections with the radial rail lines, and a loop rail line in the Grande Couronne are on the drawing board.[51] The Périphérique and the apartment complexes still wall off the city, and Delanoë's towers and Sarkozy's elevated railroad would do so further, and one may rest assured that the new apartments, offices, hotels, and restaurants will not be at the disposal of the less privileged.

The other lingering problem is the banlieue. Things may have improved there, but a "foreign world" with a "taste for violence" lurks beyond the Périph', and, paradoxically, the increasing integration of Paris with the suburbs may enhance the potential for collision: as Paris's corporate and media functions overflow into the Plaine St-Denis, they encounter "a population which is very far from this universe."[52] In 2004, a National Agency for Urban Renovation with a €20 billion to €30 billion budget was established to oversee a five-year "Marshall Plan for the Banlieues" comprehending more than six hundred deteriorated neighborhoods: 200,000 dwellings are to be demolished, 200,000 more renovated, and a further 200,000 built.[53] But massive as the plan is, it is unlikely that it will neutralize the suburbs once and for all in the eyes of Paris. And the riots of 2005 exacerbated the situation terribly. While the minister of social cohesion was calling upon people "not to have a one-sided view of the suburbs," then–interior minister Nicolas Sarkozy was calling the suburbs' residents "scum" in need of "an industrial-strength cleanup."[54]

The second caveat is that there can be too much of a good thing. One good thing, to the French state, is decentralization. It was much easier when Paris was part of the Department of the Seine; eight departments are a handful, and 1,200 mayors are more so, especially since every revenue-seeking mayor "wants business; no one wants housing."[55] Another good thing is regional integration itself, at least when it implies the integration of an ever larger region. Christian Sautter, author of the 1994 master plan for Île-de-France, has spoken up for a regional "urban galaxy" with productive, livable planet-cities orbiting the Parisian sun.[56] He observes that a Paris left to the market might become "Manhattan-sur-Seine," while limits on growth will simply create an ultradense, ultraexpensive city. If any entity could control the future of Île-de-France as he proposes, it is the French state. The state continues to claim its prerogatives in this realm, but whether it can do so in the context of decentralization remains to be seen.

So a Japanese future may beckon Greater Paris. And what is that future? The Gare du Nord, Europe's busiest rail hub, handles 560,000 people per day; Shinjuku, Tokyo's busiest, handles more than 3 million. The Métro and the RER together carry 3.3 million passengers per day; the Tokyo subways alone carry 7.4 million. The Tokyo subway system runs for 750 kilometers; the Métro, 302 kilometers. Trains and subways in the Tokyo region alone log 175 billion passenger-kilometers annually; the entire French rail system, 67 billion.[57] Different plans for Greater Paris specify somewhere in the vicinity of a half dozen growth poles; the "multimodal metropolis" plan for Tokyo now includes twenty-two.[58]

And how does Tokyo contemplate this situation? With equanimity. Neither housing nor unemployment, nor social integration, is seen as a critical challenge, and the image of the suburbs continues to be overwhelmingly positive. Tokyo's meaning, and its reach, will expand, particularly so long as corporations subsidize their employees' tickets on the bullet train.

Perhaps one should mute one's criticism of this process; after all, the relationships between Tokyo and its suburbs are far less conflictual than those of Paris. And Tokyo has been the driving force of an era of growth which has brought the Japanese people undreamt-of prosperity. But the growth of the region does have a negative demographic impact on the center of the city, and the Tokyo commuting experience is intensely stressful. And there is a deadening feeling to travel across the Tokyo cityscape which "monotonous" does not begin to capture. Surely, for all the sacrifices they have made and all the work they have put in, the Japanese deserve better.

THE ROOTS OF DIFFERENCE

I have adduced a number of possible explanations why Tokyo and Paris look and act as they do. All are really, at most, possible correlates; little offered here really justifies the imputation of clear causality. Almost all apply — at best — in a relative sense: neither the French nor the Japanese are exotic or inscrutable, and neither can be reduced to unique essences. But I hope that, together, they begin to capture — without overdetermining — the complexity of these two cities.

On the basis of everything which has preceded, I have collated the most apparently useful ideas into four groups. One combines the most abstract factors: holism and dualism, Cartesianism and organicism, permanence and impermanence, and fatalism versus will in the culture — plus one wild card, the Japanese strain of pragmatism which appeared along the way as investigation proceeded. Second is the fear-and-loathing factor: the history of violence and enmity which characterizes Paris's, but not Tokyo's, history. Third is the role and history of authority and power in Japan and France. Fourth and finally there is the role of the outside world: the distinctive difference in French and Japanese responses to and incorporation of foreign factors in urbanism.

Order, Clarity, Eternity

The form and functioning of Paris is consistent with the suggestion that there is in French culture a stronger degree of dualism and a desire to make distinctions than is the case in Japan. Walls; clear borders of all kinds; invidious distinctions between city and country, artifice and nature, and inside and outside; a desire to draw lines; mistrust of margins; and an esthetic of wholes — all these Parisian affinities contrast with Tokyo's sprawl, shadings, and shadows, the acceptance of spatial and temporal ambiguity, and a willingness to let lines appear where they may, or may not. Where might it all come from? Religion — syncretic, inclusive, and focused on evanescence — is a tempting answer in Japan, but the huge variety of urban forms and functions in Judeo-Christian civilization warns us away. And where does it lead? Perhaps to the clarity of Paris's form and the nebulous nature of Tokyo's, and perhaps to other things as well. Something there is — in the city — that does not like a wall: "borders in cities usually make destructive neighbors," and Paris and its suburbs have been among the most destructive of neighbors.[59]

Within Paris as well the difference between clarity and ambiguity persists; a deductive, logical, Cartesian purpose has been at work quite at odds with the organic, inductive forces which have driven the evolution of Tokyo: disorder, no, but no ordering by any superordinate, visible hand. Once Paris was so, but the superimposition of the modern state on voluntarist, Enlightenment principles had very different urban implications than its superimposition on a more passive political tradition of implicit authority.

Also within Tokyo — but throughout Japan as well — there is an air of impermanence wholly at odds with the Parisian attempt to defy time with architecture. Certainly some of this difference is due to building materials and techniques, to natural disasters and war, and to land prices. But the Japanese could and did build with stone, and impermanence still characterizes this age of permanent construction materials. What occurred some time ago is that impermanence and transience were "folded into" the Japanese view of architecture,[60] and into the view of the city as well. Social arrangements turned out to be better vehicles for aspirants to permanent power. In Paris no one relied so on social arrangements to regulate society: elaborate institutions and physical symbols were needed to demonstrate God's eternal glory and the power of the state in both past and present.

Thus voluntarism and fatalism respectively seem to characterize French and Japanese urbanism. Counterexamples can of course be found, and one cannot push this too far, since a ruthless pragmatism has also characterized Japanese urbanism. The public sector has largely left the evolution of Japanese cities to the cities themselves — with the exception of the modern transportation system — but the people, and an activist private sector, have more than filled the vacuum. Thus the form of Tokyo today appears unguided, but is not. The two combine, and complement each other, with an inconsistency not seen in Paris. The inconsistency does not bother the Japanese,[61] but Tokyo might have benefited along the way from slightly more state guidance. In a sense, the form of Tokyo today reflects the General Will better than does that of Paris, but I am not sure how good a thing that is.

Conflict and the Capital

I have noted repeatedly how the form and functioning of Paris reflect a past typified by both sociopolitical and cultural hostilities. The first includes wars, walls, revolutions and rebellions, and the fear and demonization of both foreign invaders and domestic insurrectionaries. All of these factors have faded, but their consequences are still visible in the spaces of the city, in sharp contrast to the absence of violent conflict in the history, and on the face, of Tokyo. Paris's monuments alert us to the importance of historical factors relative to diaphanous cultural ones: regardless of any hypothetical French preference for borders and dualism, when Paris was not threatened, it was not walled. On the other hand, Paris is not threatened today, but it is still walled. In any case, on the basis of body counts, I would describe Paris as a city of darkness, and Tokyo as a city of light: Japan's capital has centered on the culturally vivifying emperor; Paris's center was the home of the guillotine.

A second form of hostility found in Paris but not Tokyo is cultural: French culture seems historically to be based more upon a fearful, zero-sum worldview,[62] and an ambivalence about cities, than that of Japan. Japanese villages certainly have a history of fighting intensely with each other. But there is a French fear of other communities in general and of the capital in particular that does not typify Japan.[63] Insecurity regarding foreigners and the outside world, yes; but not toward other groups or entities in Japan.

As I have suggested, a little less homogeneity and harmony might have benefited Tokyo. I would not be surprised if Paris's violent past accounts partly for the passions with which it is regarded by both its champions and its adversaries. Paris's physical form makes statements about, and reflects the struggle for, ultimate values; the capital is an end in itself. Tokyo, by contrast, has seldom moved anyone to passion, and it has never stood for anything intrinsic: it has been a tool of the shogunate, then the Meiji state, and now the market. Perhaps it could have been different: there are perhaps three windows out of which a passionate, committed Japanese urbanism might have emerged. The first was in the free cities of the sixteenth century, but they were crushed by the state-builders. The second was the energetic popular culture of Edo, which disappeared in the turbulence of the Restoration and modernization. The third was most short-lived of all: the *modan* ("modern") 1920s and 1930s. But this florescence wilted with the demise of democracy, and its leaders decamped both literarily and physically from the capital.

Authority, Architecture, and the Capital

Power is central to the differences between Paris and Tokyo in three ways. First, authority has historically influenced architecture, cities, and the shape of the capital in France in ways that it rarely has in Japan, and this posture has critically influenced Paris's relationships with nation, state, and suburbs. Obviously Ieyasu shaped Edo in an expressly political way, the Meiji regime shaped some parts of Tokyo, and Tokyo Prefecture has made a spectacular statement with its New City Hall. And, again, the form of Tokyo's center is intimately related to imperial power. But authority has tended to manifest itself in Tokyo by omission and in Paris by commission, and when Tokyo has tried to make monumental changes — the self-conscious, foreign-inspired monuments to contemporary *kokusaika,* or "internationalization," come to mind — it has not notably succeeded.

The second connection between power and the capital lies in the sweep of history: the greater historical frequency in France of major political ruptures and discontinuities, and the consequent need for legitimization of new regimes. What ruptures did occur in Japan were disguised: the transition from imperial to feudal rule was formally legitimized by the throne; the return to imperial rule was simply a "restoration," and even wartime defeat elided into the postwar era under the sitting monarch. Moreover, even short of rupture, French political culture has been cleft more deeply than Japanese: class and partisan political divisions, in particular, have riven modern France in ways Japan has never experienced.[64]

History also reveals the very different roles played by the people in the evolution of Paris and Tokyo. Japanese urban history has been one of "cities without citizens" and, consequently, cities without autonomy. But although weak autonomy may influence Tokyo's relationships to state and suburbs in ways very different from Paris's, the absence of a hands-on state like France has meant that the actual form of the city has in many ways been more strongly influenced by the people than has Paris.

A third possible political influence on the capital is political values. The contrasts between democracy and autocracy, dirigisme and subcontractarian rule, and republican and developmental-state values are all consistent with the differences we have seen between Paris and Tokyo. In their influence on the contemporary capital, particularly the way it functions, it is developmental versus republican values that hold center stage. Paris, and the French state, have placed great emphasis on secular education, social integration and equality, the ominous gentrification and exclusivity of Paris, and the need for "an economy with a human face" instead of a "neo-American" economy. The tone implies that some things are simply *wrong* for France.[65]

In Tokyo, contrarily, it is hard to believe that anything could be completely wrong. Anything that contributes to the GNP is ipso facto consistent with state goals. This is a society in which the old is expected to give way to the new, via the wrecking ball. Japan *has* built a welfare state, and it *does* promote interregional equity through revenue sharing and the pork barrel. But for our purposes, it is most significant that the only spatial correlate of such considerations is the urban-rural continuum and that the preferred solution is a rising tide, led by Tokyo, which will raise all provincial boats. The question — so absurd that it would never even be asked in Paris — is whether any agency is either willing or able to control this tide.

Paris, Tokyo, and the Wider World

Neither Tokyo nor Paris is an island. The world beyond the borders of France and Japan has played a role in the shaping and behavior of our two capitals in two ways. First, the wider world is the source of Others, of people with different, sometimes puzzling, sometimes frightening characteristics; the city, as the primary arena for interaction with them, is inevitably influenced thereby. The Japanese and the French are little different in this regard: an intense insularity can be found in both countries. The stereotypes of immigrants held by the French would come as no surprise to Japanese.[66]

Indeed, everything I have said about Japanese collectivism, inclusivity, and acceptance of margins and rejection of distinctions holds true only among Japanese. But the situation in Paris and Tokyo differs dramatically, partly because French insularity targets not only Others, but other French, whether disdainful Parisians, hostile proletarians, or resentful provincials; and partly because the foreign Others whom the Japanese would resent if they were there are not, as in Paris, present in large numbers or concentrated in certain spaces. Insularity can have a dramatic impact on urban form and policy, as American white flight, exclusionary zoning, and gated communities have shown. Paris, though by no means as extreme, has parallels with the United States. Tokyo has had the luxury of ignoring such considerations, at least since the Korean and outcast ghettoes began to fade. There are cultural and ethnic Others in Tokyo, but they have accommodated themselves to the form and functioning of the city rather than influenced them.

The second way in which the wider world impinges on the capital is through direct foreign impact; today, perhaps most obviously, through globalization. Indeed, some observers argue that the forces of globalization are dissolving national differences, that states are retreating, and that the universal force of postindustrial capitalism will submerge the sorts of differences I have sketched out above. I think this greatly overstates the case: Japan may have embraced globalization, but Paris has tried to hold it at arm's length. Both have in fact limited its impact — Paris physically, Japan socially. And neither has fallen victim to the theorized socioeconomic "dualization" of the global city.[67]

Still, Japan has globalized with a will, beginning 1,500 years ago. In the nineteenth century, Japan wanted to modernize, industrialize, and win foreign respect, and it learned how from the West. Its borrowings included Western urban forms and architecture, although the fad faded. Since World War II, Japan again has needs — for a start, it must import about half of its people's total caloric needs, and almost all natural resources — and it is perhaps unsurprising that Tokyo and its people have to a large extent been sacrificed to the needs of this economy. One occasionally fears for the integrity of Japanese culture in its pursuit of foreign approval, especially when one witnesses the parade of imitation foreign monuments so common in Tokyo.

But Tokyo's future is not forgone. Tokyo may have been saved, and Japan saved from Tokyo, by the bursting of the speculative economic bubble in 1990: since that time Japan has "de-globalized," with foreign corporations pulling out, the foreign presence in the Tokyo stock market shrinking, Japan's banks retrenching, and Japan's share of international currency and securities markets declining.[68] The economy has recovered, and gradually opened in a wide variety of areas, and dependence on exports has increased; but in a broader sense, Japan may be headed for a period of greater international reticence. Like France, Japan has attempted to create a sort of capitalism with a human face, a capitalism without losers. Perhaps the Japanese see the way the rest of the world is headed, and do not want to go there, and are willing to pay a price — fifteen years of stagnation, for a start — to go somewhere else, specifically, to a future of social cohesion and stability and protection from foreign practices and social groups. In the last few years, Japan has discarded a long-standing low profile in the world, inciting friction with its neighbors in ways unthinkable twenty years ago. Is all this a momentary recoil from globalization, or a lasting trend? If the former, then the eventual inundation of Japan by Tokyo may be in sight. If the latter, then the face of Tokyo will reflect it in years to come.

I find Paris's global future less problematic in terms of the shape of the city. France seems to recognize more clearly the negative implications of globalization, to challenge them forthrightly, and to give precedence to esthetic and republican values.[69] Free-rein globalization may have promised greater wealth and a more flamboyant cityscape, and Paris's global role may "slip away," rather than follow "the soaring trajectory it might have done."[70] But just as Paris has been shaped by sensitivity, but not subservience, to the international, it appears today to stand by its own principles *and by so doing* play its global role: "no city anywhere has taken more seriously its duties to look and behave throughout as if the eyes of the world were on it and the honor of the nation at stake."[71] But it does so by being a universal — even if not a global — city.[72] Tokyo actually performs the same duties, but it has done so by being all too often — on the surface — what it thinks the world wants it to be. And yet, at the same time, Paris is, in its own eyes and its own appearance, for everyone; way down deep, Tokyo is only for the Japanese.

NOTES

Introduction

1. Savitch 1988, 290–93.
2. Mosher 1997, 8.
3. Levine 1994, 388; Renaud 1993, 129; Scheiner 2006.
4. Sudjic 1992, 5.
5. This overview draws heavily upon, among others, Bergeron 1989; Braudel 1986; Evenson 1979; Francastel 1984; Garssey 1980; Horne 2002; Lavedan 1975; Marchand 1993; Mollat 1971; Noin and White 1997; Pinon 1999; Rouleau 1997; and Jones 2005.
6. Davies 1982.
7. Noin and White 1997, 23.
8. Higonnet 2002.
9. Cornu 1972, 94. Arrondissements are administrative subdivisions of the city, similar to boroughs.
10. *Le Monde,* May 5, 2004; October 15, 2004.
11. Sassen 1994a, 1994b; Mittelman 1996.
12. This overview draws heavily upon, among others, Dōmon 1999; Fujino 2002; Haga 1980; Kodama and Sugiyama, 1969; Masai 1989; Mikuriya 1996; Naitō 1985; Nishikawa 1972; Ogi and Jinnai 1995; Tamai 1987; Ishizuka 1991; and Wakita 1994.
13. The name in all likelihood refers to the entrance to Hibiya Inlet at the head of Tokyo Bay.
14. Nouët 1990, 18; Yazaki 1968, 173.
15. Totman 1983.
16. Cybriwsky 1998, 57.
17. If Paris's population in 1801 is set at 100, by 1896 it was 463 (Sennett 1977, 133).
18. Shigematsu 1986; White 1995.
19. Masai 1989, 12.

20. Fortune 1863.
21. Masai 1989, 195.
22. Fujino 2002.
23. Fujitani 1996.
24. Kawamoto 1996, chap. 24.
25. *Japan Times International,* June 16, 1973.
26. Sōmu-shō 2003; INSEE 2004.
27. Sudjic 1992, 20–21.
28. Sōmu-shō 2003; INSEE 2004.
29. Sassen 1991, 170; *Le Monde,* October 15, 2004; Tokyo-to 1991, 88.
30. Tokyo-to 1991, 88; Clubs Convaincre 1990, 24.
31. Camp 1990; Secretariat 1991, chaps. 19, 24.
32. In other words, I will try to say more than simply *post hoc, ergo propter hoc.*
33. Sennett 1977, 43.
34. Agnew, Mercer, and Sopher 1984, 277.
35. Tracy 2000, 2.
36. Francastel 1984, 9.
37. Mumford 1938, 5.
38. Maki 1987, 25.
39. Visible: Mumford 1938, 4; coordination: Francastel 1984, 11; precondition: Benevolo 1993, xv.
40. Jones 2005, xvii; Agnew, Mercer, and Sopher 1984, 186.
41. Francastel 1984, 10–11.
42. Zukin 1995, 7.
43. Olsen 1986, ix; Yokoyama 1991, i–iii.
44. Agnew 1987.
45. Ibid., 6, 25, 58.
46. M. Berry 1998, 405.
47. Halbwachs 1980, 130.
48. Symbolic landscapes: Karan and Stapleton 1997, 57–74; (de)legitimize: Kertzer 1988.
49. There is in the scholarly literature considerable discussion of the nature of and differences between "history" and "memory," in which I will attempt not to get involved (see, for example, Halbwachs 1980; Dienstag 1997; and Nora 1996, 3).
50. Gildea 1994, 10.
51. Nora 1996, xv, xvii.
52. Such impressions are hardly novel with me; see Sacchi 2004, 13, 75; and Mansfield 2009, viii.
53. Roncayolo 1990, 53–56; M. Weber 1958, 16, 49; Kurasawa 1968.
54. Holton 1986, 148–49; Hammond 1972, chap. 8.
55. Tilly 1990, chap. 1.
56. Hammond 1972, 9, 31–34; Roncayolo 1990, 27–29; Scargill 1979, chap. 9, 253; Hohenberg and Lees 1995, 23; Mumford 1961.

57. A propos of this argument, see Scargill 1979, chap. 9; B. Berry 1973, xii, xv, chap. 5; Silver 1993, 339; Berger and Dore 1996, 4 and passim; and Harvey 2003, chap. 2.
58. See, for example, Pagano and Bowman 1995, 2–5, chap. 7.
59. Tajbakhsh 2000, 2, 16, 76, 125.
60. White 1998; see also Savitch and Kantor 2002.

1. Views of the Capital

1. Coaldrake 1996, 253; Ogi and Jinnai 1995, 11–12; Scargill 1979, 251.
2. Kerr 2001, 240–42.
3. Lynch 1960, 10.
4. Halbwachs 1980, 131; Fiévé and Waley 2003, 29; Donald Richie in J. Friedman 1986, 94.
5. Fujino 2002, 2.
6. Kurokawa in Golany 1998, 21.
7. Ogi and Jinnai 1995, 15–16.
8. Rouleau 1997, 372.
9. Barthes 1982.
10. Maeda A. 1989, 80; Blakely and Stimson 1992, 1–20.
11. Maki 1987, 44.
12. Russell 1983, 35.
13. Noin and White 1997, vii.
14. *New York Times,* September 11, 2005.
15. Cybriwsky 1998, 35.
16. Ibid., 13.
17. Russell 1983, 20.
18. Clammer 1997, 25
19. Keene 1988.
20. Fujita 1993, 96.
21. Noin and White 1997, 1, 255.
22. Vale 1992, 54; Higonnet 2002, 160.
23. Augé 1992, 89–93.
24. After Cybriwsky 1998, chap. 5.
25. Popham 1985, 71–72; Clammer 1997, 28; Richie 1999, 32.
26. Edward Seidensticker, quoted by Ishida Yorifusa in Hein et al. 2003, 44; see also Richie 1999, 36; and Maki 1987, 47–48.
27. Masai 1989, 78; Cybriwsky 1998, 146, 150.
28. Maeda A. 1989, 455.
29. Karan and Stapleton 1997, 57–74.
30. Donald Meinig, quoted in Karan and Stapleton 1997, 57–60; Cybriwsky 1998, 149, chap. 5.
31. Russell 1983, 222; Ferguson 1994, 69; Gravier 1972; Renaud 1993; Rey 1996.
32. Cornu 1972, 13.

33. Sennett 1977, 156; Ferguson 1994, 39; Cornu 1972, 48; Sharpe and Wallock 1983, chapters by Theodore Reff and Michele Hannoosh.
34. Berman 1982, 147; Sennett 1977, 129.
35. Marchand 1993, 379.
36. Marchand 1993.
37. For a fuller discussion of this critique and of Sorai's many contemporaries and reformist successors, see Nishikawa 1972; Gluck 1985; McEwan 1962; Harootunian 1988; and Najita 1987.
38. Nishikawa 1972, chap. 3.
39. See Gluck 1985.
40. Keene 1984, 399; Seidensticker 1965; Maeda A. 1989, 93–100; S. Katō 1983, 95–103; Gluck 1985, 185.
41. Richie 1999, 31, 63.
42. Tamanoi 1998. 116.
43. Wakabayashi 1998, esp. chaps. 3, 4.
44. Isoda 1983.
45. Gurōbaru Shakai 1994.
46. Shinohara 1977, 197; Hara 1989, 75.
47. Sharpe and Wallock 1983, 223.
48. H. Smith 1979, 84–85.
49. See, among others, Merlin 1991, 30; Maspero 1994, 136; Ferguson 1994; Chevalier 1958; Garrioch 2002; and Tombs 1981.
50. Noin and White 1997, 11.
51. After Unno 1983, 149.
52. Unno 1983.
53. Seidensticker 1965, 20, 40–42, 67, 140.
54. Isoda 1983, 84–85, 110.
55. Gurōbaru Shakai 1994.
56. See Maspero 1994.
57. Burton 2001, 8, 29; Merriman 1991, 61; Jordan 1995, 98.
58. Noin and White 1997, 207–22.
59. Marchand 1993, 371.
60. Doublet 1976, 91; Benoit et al. 1993, 296.
61. Noin and White 1997, 8.
62. Marchand 1993, 371.
63. Ibid., 335–38; Haegel 1994, 191.

2. Form and Pattern in the City

1. Berque 1994a, 587–88.
2. Claval 1981, 511; Hammond 1972, 225, 230, chap. 17.
3. I will pursue this below, while acknowledging the autonomy of many ecclesiastical, guild, and professional institutions in medieval and early modern Paris, and the extralegal immunities of the nobility.

4. Maki 1987, 89.
5. Richie in J. Friedman 1986, 94–96; Tanizaki 1977.
6. Japanese gardens are "composed of a series of viewpoints with no integrating perspective," and the architectural tradition is typified by "objects which are erected without connection to their built environment and often even in confrontation with it" (Stewart 2002, 211; Hein in Fiévé and Waley 2003, 342; Kurokawa in Golany 1998). The "sense of integration itself is an alien concept, a sort of beauty which the Japanese do not look do find" (Popham 1985, 181).
7. Kurokawa in Golany 1998; Maki 1987, 64; Ogi and Jinnai 1995, 20. The heyday of the castle town, exemplified by Edo, contradicts this generalization, but it appears (see chap. 4) that integrated urban planning was a short-lived phenomenon in both the Heian and Edo periods.
8. Lynch 1960, 127; Berque 1994b, 85–89; Keene 1988, 18.
9. Tanizaki 1977.
10. Keene 1988, 7–9.
11. Richie 1999, 44–50; Berque 1994b, 87–89.
12. Gropius and Tange 1960, 6.
13. Kawazoe 1979, 9–10; Berque 1994c, 138, 190; Kurokawa in Golany 1998, 8.
14. Ishida T. 1970.
15. Maki 1987, 26.
16. Francastel 1968, 6; Maki 1987, 27, 31; Ogi and Jinnai 1995, 12–13.
17. Lehan 1998, 234.
18. Noin and White 1997, 45; contrast with Gropius and Tange 1960, 4; Stewart 2002, 10.
19. Mumford 1961, 394; 1938, 131.
20. Frequency of fires: Dōmon 1999, 91; Kaempfer 1999, chap. 12; Meireki Fire: Kodama and Sugiyama 1969, 187; Nouët 1990, 105–6.
21. Ishizuka 1991, 37.
22. Kodama and Sugiyama 1969, 321–22; Ishizuka and Ishida 1988, 25.
23. Screech 2000, 102; Ward 1985, 63.
24. Kurokawa in Golany 1998, 21.
25. Nishikawa 1973, 270–71.
26. The foregoing is from Totman 1995, 110–12.
27. Wheatley 1971; Agnew, Mercer, and Sopher 1984, 10–11, chap. 1.
28. Wheatley 1971, 267, 282, 225.
29. Claval 1981, 494–95; Wheatley 1971, 481.
30. Desmarais 1995, 103, chap. 2.
31. Preston and Simpson-Housley 1994, 331.
32. Francastel 1968, 21; Mumford 1938, 61.
33. Wheatley 1971, chap. 5.
34. Maki 1987, 95; Naitō 1985, 115–19; Naitō 2003, 24, 34.
35. Richie 1999, 134.
36. Kurokawa in Golany 1998, 7–10.

37. Yamasaki in Fiévé and Waley 2003, 347, 362, 365.
38. I would also note that La Défense is *outside* Paris proper.
39. Koschman 1978, introduction.
40. I would argue that the warfare of the late sixteenth century never rose to the level of European religious wars, and that neither the subordination of the emperor in 1185 nor his "restoration" in 1868 belongs in the same taxonomic box with 1789.
41. Smith in M. Friedman 1986, 32; Berque 1997b, 38–40, 198; Mumford 1961, 88–91.
42. Mumford 1961, 88–91.
43. Hussey 2006.
44. I disagree here with the view (McClain et al. 1994) that the king's power in Paris and the shogun's power in Edo were analogous in scope (see White 1988).
45. "Soft": Gluck 1985; Garon 1997; "myth," "mind molding": Koschman 1978, introduction.
46. This paragraph and the next draw on Ward 1985, 1; Nishikawa 1973, pt .2, 62–66; Coaldrake 1996, 8–9, 17, 38, 279–82; Ogi and Jinnai 1995, 95; Yamasaki in Fiévé and Waley 2003, 347, 362, 365; Berque 1997b, 92; and Mumford 1961, 88–91.
47. Ancient Egypt, for example, was protected by desert, sea, and mountains (Nishikawa 1973, 27). See also Tracy 2000, 229; Waterhouse 1993, 28–29; Blakely and Snyder 1997, 4; and Claval 1981, 29–30.
48. Scargill 1979, 151.
49. Mumford 1938, 88; 1961, 356–62.
50. Watanabe in Sutcliffe 1984, 405.
51. Perrin 1979.
52. Marshal Vauban (1633–1707) was Louis XIV's chief military engineer; he perfected the star-shaped fortress with thick earthworks.
53. White 1995.
54. Wheatley and See 1978, 105; Ponsonby-Fane 1979; Rozman 1973, 13.
55. This discussion draws on Naitō 1985; Kodama and Sugiyama 1969; Nishikawa 1972; Nouët 1990; Wheatley 1971; Murai 1964; Masai in Golany 1998.
56. Ishizuka and Ishida 1988, 37; Maeda A. 1989, 68; Sorensen 2002, 59.
57. Fujino 2002, 140; Ishizuka 1991, 3, 221; Kodama and Sugiyama 1969, 314.
58. Ishizuka and Ishida 1988, 25; Kodama and Sugiyama 1969, 321–22.
59. Terry 1920, 128.
60. Hein et al. 2003, 245; Sorensen 2002, 7–8.
61. Mollat 1971, 26–33.
62. Rouleau 1997, 23, 30.
63. Francastel 1968, 10; Pinon 1999, 30.
64. Rouleau 1997, 42–48.
65. Ibid., 51, 59; Pinon 1999, 30.

66. Rouleau 1997, 59, 62; Mollat 1971, 104.
67. Horne 2002, chap. 2; Francastel 1968, 12–14.
68. For this period, see Francastel 1968, 15, 22, 29; Mollat 1971, 105, 146–47, chap. 8; and Rouleau 1997, 114–49.
69. See Francastel 1968, 32, 42; Sutcliffe 1971, 262–70; Rouleau 1997, 149–205; Lacaze 1994, 67–68; and Mollat 1971, chap. 11.
70. Francastel 1984, 141.
71. Horne 2002, 96–97, 152.
72. Mollat 1971, 469.
73. Ibid., 466.
74. Mumford 1938, 221.
75. Chevalier 1994, 29–31, 199; Cornu 1972, 171; Sutcliffe 1971, 285; Marchand 1993, 290–94.
76. Chaslin 1994, 71; Cohen and Fortier 1988, 40.
77. Braudel 1986, 225–26.
78. Ferguson 1994, 19.
79. Hammond 1972.
80. Horne 2002, x.
81. Benevolo 1993, 72–74, 124–30.
82. Roncayolo 1990, 96.
83. Benevolo 1993, 140–45; Jordan 1995, 25–31.
84. Murai 1964, 29–37.
85. Yazaki 1968, 283–84; Mikuriya 1994, 107–8; Fujino 2002, 52–57.
86. Esherick 2000, 4. See also Rozman 1973, 20, 26, 27; Ponsonby-Fane 1979, 38, 52; Piggott 1997, 83, 132–35; Yazaki 1968, chaps. 1, 2; Mimura in Golany 1998, 40; Nishikawa 1973, 54, 84; and Wheatley and See 1978, 113, 115, 128, 139–40. A yamen was any government office or official residence.
87. Hall 1968, 171.
88. Naitō 1985, 115–18; Naitō 2003, 24, 34. Strictly speaking, the palace was 90 degrees out of kilter, with its back to Mount Fuji in the west, not the north (as called for in the Chinese model).
89. Tamai 1987, 112–20.
90. Richie 1999, 24.
91. Maki 1987.
92. Greenbie 1988, 60.
93. Popham 1985, 15. See also Golany 1998, xix; Kurokawa in Golany 1998, 5.
94. This discussion draws on Jinnai 1995; Maeda A. 1989; Popham 1985; Sorensen 2002; Maki 1987; Tamai 1987; and Masai 1989. On land use, see Kodama and Sugiyama 1969, 165; Ogi and Jinnai 1995, 94; and Nishiyama 1997, 79. The remaining 20 percent of the city was occupied by Buddhist temples and Shinto shrines.
95. Yazaki 1968, 129–30.

96. Maki 1987, 108.
97. Popham 1985, 95–97.
98. Jinnai 1995, 23.
99. Mumford 1938, 486–89.
100. Roullier 1989; DATAR 1994.
101. Kornhauser 1976, 77–78.
102. Bergeron 1989, 3–8; Lavedan 1975, 72; Mollat 1971, 11, chap. 1; Pinchemel 1979, 43–44.
103. Kurasawa and Machimura 1992, 63.
104. Benevolo 1993; Francastel 1984; Lavedan 1975; Desmarais 1995; Friedrichs 1995.
105. Noin and White 1997, 32.
106. Evenson in Sutcliffe 1984, 266–68.
107. Kawazoe 1979, 9–10; Naitō 2003, 67.
108. Lavedan 1975, 292, 299.
109. After Kabayama and Okuda 1985, 117–20.
110. Francastel 1984, 19.
111. Tracy 2000, 589.
112. See ibid., 591. The Louvre and the Bastille were originally parts of the city's exterior defenses, but their nature was transformed after the city walls expanded.
113. Cohen and Fortier 1988, 86; Parker 1996, 43.
114. After Mumford 1961; 1938, 84.
115. *Min fuzai no toshi.*
116. Fiévé and Waley 2003, 6.
117. Fujita 1993, 86–87; Nishikawa 1973, 177–81.
118. Fujitani 1996, 132.
119. White 1995. I disagree with Bodart-Bailey (in Fiévé and Waley 2003). I see the defensive configuration of the castle town as aimed at elite, not popular, threats. The only real threats to the regime came from hostile elites, and those occurred in the seventeenth century (Kodama and Sugiyama 1969, 185–86).
120. Sorensen 2002, 8.
121. Hinago 1986, 31, 39; Naitō 1979, 11–12, 21–22.
122. Coaldrake in Hinago 1986, 14; Nouët 1990, 58.
123. Fujita 1993, 87.
124. Nishiyama 1997, 24–26; Kōjiro in M. Friedman 1986, 40.
125. Bodart-Bailey in Fiévé and Waley 2003, 105–10.
126. Nishikawa 1973, 156–73.
127. Brinkley, quoted in Terry 1920, 150–51.

3. From Center to Periphery

1. Maki 1987; Cybriwsky 1998, 8–11; Maeda A. 1989, 418–19; Seidensticker 1991:46; Jinnai 1995, 99.

2. Jinnai 1995, 99; Cybriwsky 1998, 8–11.
3. Mumford 1961, 304; Waterhouse 1993, 5–6; Claval in Agnew, Mercer, and Sopher 1984, 42; Tanizaki 1977; Greenbie 1988, 104; Maeda A. 1989, 80; Kurokawa in Golany 1998, 8–10.
4. Kim et al. 1997, 19; Smith in Umesao et al. 1986, 37.
5. Distinction unclear: Berque 1997b, 50; agrarian "coexisted" with urban: Smith in Umesao et al. 1986, 37.
6. Benevolo 1993, 1–2.
7. Sennett 1990; Hughes in Swan 1991, 20–21; Sibley 1995, 26–27; Waterhouse 1993, chaps. 4, 6; Lefebvre 1991, 253; Frugoni 1991, 3–11, 55, 112; Mumford 1938, 68; Benevolo 1993, 217; Fumagalli 1994, 1–12, 121–28.
8. Gilloch 1996, 11.
9. Blakely and Snyder 1997, 1. The Romans, for whom citizenship included all those in the empire, were an exception.
10. M. Weber 1958, 82–83.
11. Mumford 1961, 66; Tracy 2000.
12. Berque 1996, 38, 40; Hayashiya 1982, 6–11.
13. Hayashiya 1982, 6–10.
14. McClain et al. 1994, 42–45.
15. Rouleau 1985, 103.
16. Tax collection in Paris was indirect, "farmed out" for a fee to private collection agents, the Farmers-General.
17. Such lands, or *tobichi,* were also administratively under the jurisdiction of the place where the landowner lived.
18. Mumford 1961, 37, 44–46, 63, 304; Ellin 1997.
19. Yokoyama 1991, 35.
20. Tracy 2000, 72, 192–99; Mumford 1938, 14–17; Fumagalli 1994, 76–77.
21. Tracy 2000.
22. M. Berry 1994, xv.
23. Except briefly during the sixteenth century; see below (and chapter 7).
24. Merriman 1991. Until the nineteenth century, it was common for wealthy families to live on the first and second floors of buildings, with progressively poorer people renting the higher floors.
25. See Masai in Golany 1998, 58; Maeda A. 1989, 42; Minami 1978; McClain et al. 1994, 28; Cybriwsky 1998.
26. Popham 1985, 53–55.
27. Ellin 1997, 7–13.
28. Nishikawa 1973, 169, 182–86.
29. After Jinnai 1995. By contrast, for example, see Kyoto, the plan of which reflected a Chinese-style politico-cosmic order.
30. Berque 1994c, 364.
31. Scargill 1979, 249. The quotation about stratification applies to Osaka (Karan

and Stapleton 1997, 106, 111, 129, chap. 6), but I suspect it to be equally true of Tokyo.

32. Nishikawa 1972, 228; Stewart 2002, 41; Masai in Golany 1998, 61.
33. Kim et al. 1997, 8.
34. McCargo 2000, 73.
35. Richie 1999, 134–35.
36. Greenbie 1988, 66.
37. Gropius and Tange 1960, 19.
38. Screech 2000, 112, chap. 3.
39. Nishikawa 1973, 150.
40. Jordan 1995, 14.
41. Francastel 1968, 46–47.
42. Bestor 1989, chap. 7; Greenbie 1988.
43. Dōmon 1999, 49–52; Kodama and Sugiyama 1969, 148–53.
44. Nouët 1990, 73; Jinnai 1995, 15, 86.
45. Masai 1989, 104–6; Hall 1968, 178.
46. Nishikawa 1972, 303.
47. Yazaki 1968, 158–66; Nishikawa 1972, 327.
48. Naitō 1985, 129; Haga 1980, 53; Fujino 2002, 13–14.
49. Tracy 2000; Friedrichs 1995, 42.
50. See Marcuse in Ellin 1997, 102.
51. Benevolo 1993, 3, 6–8; Noin and White 1997, 38; Mumford 1961, 129, 205–6, 238–42; Pinon 1999, 26–28.
52. Mumford 1961, 50; Lavedan 1975, 80; Waterhouse 1993, 150; LeClère 1985, 47.
53. Pinon 1999, 54,135. The following discussion also draws upon Garssey 1980; Cohen and Fortier 1988, 54, 76; Francastel 1984, 34–40; Desmarais 1995, 194–202; Lavedan 1975, 102–4; Sutcliffe 1971, 3; Jones 2005, 13, 47, 111, 292, 479.
54. Francastel 1984, 40, 76.
55. Pinon 1999, 97–98.
56. Ibid., 101–6.
57. Cohen and Fortier 1988, 112, 128; Lavedan 1975, 185–93; Rouleau 1997, 227–29, 249, 266.
58. Lavedan 1975, 486; www.fortifs.org.
59. Jordan 1995, 284–85.
60. Wheatley and See 1978, 78, 109, 129–32, 156; Hayashiya 1982, 175.
61. Nishikawa 1972, 161–64.
62. This description of Edo Castle draws on Naitō 1979, 79–84; Masai 1989, endpaper; Murai 1964, 85–87, 91; Coaldrake in Fiévé and Waley 2003, 131.
63. Tracy 2000, 412–14; Parker 1996, 143.
64. Masai 1975; Naitō 1979, 79–84.
65. Nishikawa 1972, 65–67.
66. This history of the rail system draws on Tokyo-to 1991, 20–34; Masai 1989, 153–55, 191–92; Seidensticker 1983, 79, 177; Sorensen 2002, 73; Cybriwsky

1998, 41. The main line to the north was not extended to Tokyo Station until after the 1923 earthquake; however, one could come from the south, change at Tokyo, go four stops, and board a train to the north.

67. Masai in Golany 1998, 70.
68. See Evenson 1979, 12, 87; Soulignac 1993, 116–29; Jordan 1995, 107; Rouleau 1985, 110–15; Sutcliffe 1971, 81–83.
69. Lavedan 1975, 451.
70. Jones 2005, 358.
71. Evenson 1979, 92; LeClère 1985, 566–67.
72. Evenson 1979, 92; Sutcliffe 1971, 85.
73. Soulignac 1993, 118–20; Noin and White 1997, 57, 153.
74. White 1998.
75. Evenson 1979, 114–16; Doublet 1976, 161.
76. Soulignac 1993, 129–30.
77. Franc 1971, 137–44.
78. Actually it runs inside the city line, by as much as a kilometer in one spot. Paris proper also includes the Bois de Boulogne and Bois de Vincennes parks, but as a city it is closely enclosed by the highway.
79. Fiévé and Waley 2003, 67.
80. Yazaki 1968, 452.
81. Masai 1989, 145, 165–66, 179; *Asahi Shimbun,* January 27, 2000.
82. Burton 2001, 131–32.
83. Garssey 1980, 222–23.
84. Rouleau 1997, 400, 320–21.
85. Stovall 1990, 1.
86. Sennett 1977, 297.
87. Franc 1971, 213.
88. Nishikawa 1972, 2, 182–98; Yazaki 1968, 150.
89. Murai 1964, 81–82; Nishikawa 1972, 324–26; Kaempfer 1999, 358.
90. White 1982, 267–69.
91. Fujino 2002, 103–4, 164; Ishizuka 1991, chap. 2.

4. The Manipulated City

1. Rouleau 1997, 289.
2. Greenhouse 1992.
3. Savitch and Kantor 2002, 104–8.
4. Golany 1998, xlv.
5. Hein in Fiévé and Waley 2003, 309–10; Muramatsu 1991, 210–11.
6. Hein in Fiévé and Waley 2003, 311.
7. Ishida T. 1970. See also Ashihara 1989.
8. On the above, see Katz 1998; Karan and Stapleton 1997, 48; Golany 1998, xxxix, xlii–xliii; Stewart 2002, 172.
9. Bergeron 1989, 48–50; LeClère 1985, 111.

10. Pinon 1999, 53–56.
11. Francastel 1984, 126.
12. Noin and White 1997, 44; Francastel 1984, 160.
13. Garrioch 2002, 209–12; Boyer 1994, 11–12.
14. Russell 1983, 168.
15. Pinon 1999, 143.
16. Ibid., 182.
17. Cornu 1972, 36–50; Pinon 1999, 15–19.
18. On these objectives, see Rouleau 1997, 337; Francastel 1984, 158–59; Cornu 1972, 55–60; Olsen 1986, 44–47; Pinon 1999, 184–90.
19. Sutcliffe 1971, 33–42; Merriman 1994, 279; Lacaze 1994, 77.
20. Harvey 2003, chaps. 5, 6.
21. Francastel 1984, 165.
22. Hohenberg and Lees 1995, 328.
23. Merriman 1994, 292–94.
24. Noin and White 1997, 45, 53.
25. Evenson 1979, 272–75; Rouleau 1997, 443–50.
26. Marchand 1993, 258–70.
27. Savitch 1988, 133–34; Hohenberg and Lees 1995, 358.
28. For this period, see Horne 2002, 382–83; Gravier 1972, 95–107; Noin and White 1997, 61–63; Sutcliffe 1971, 230–31; Lacaze 1994, 81–82; Claval 1981, chap. 14; Evenson 1979, 287–310, 327–40.
29. Gravier 1972, 95.
30. Plan d'Aménagement et d'Organisation Générale (General Plan for the Administration and Management [of the Paris Region]).
31. Evenson 1979, 337–45.
32. Pinon 1999, 273.
33. Franc 1971, 174; Colloque de Créteil 1990, 9; Evenson 1979, 329.
34. Délégation à l'Aménagement du Territoire et à l'Action Régionale (Delegation for Territorial Management and Regional Action). See Gravier 1972, chap. 7; Savitch 1988, 135; Marchand 1993, 317.
35. Marchand 1993, 315.
36. Its full name was the Master Plan for Management and Urbanism of the Paris Region, or Schéma Directeur d'Aménagement et d'Urbanisme de la Région Parisienne. For detailed discussion, see Evenson 1979, 280–85, 340–44; Marchand 1993, 306–12; Merlin 1991, 35–39; Savitch 1988, chap. 4; Colloque de Créteil 1990, 175; Lacaze 1994, 89–90; Clubs Convaincre 1990, 40–41; Benoit et al. 1993, 268; Bergeron 1989, 247; Mollat 1971, 20.
37. Franc 1971, 169.
38. Colloque de Créteil 1990, 90–96; Cornu 1972, 232; Savitch 1988, 105–6.
39. Pinchemel 1979, chap. 5.
40. Zones d'Aménagement Différé, Zones d'Aménagement Concerté, and Zones à

Urbaniser en Priorité (Differentiated Management Zones, Concerted Management Zones, and Priority Urbanization Zones). See Pinchemel 1979, 96; and
Savitch 1988, 135.

41. Marchand 1993, 326; Pinon 1999, 303; Noin and White 1997, 71.

42. Merlin 1991, 100–108. The master plan of 1994 can be found online at www
.ile-de-france.equipement.gouv.fr.

43. The following draws on Levine 1994, 385; Marchand 1993, 363–70; DATAR
1994, 14–15 and "Documents annex/es" section 12; Clubs Convaincre 1990,
19–20, 27; Soulignac 1993, 167, 173; and Colloque de Créteil 1990, 174, 181–92.

44. Ascher et al. 1993, 93–95, 135–52.

45. www.ile-de-france.equipement.gouv.fr.

46. INSEE 2004, 17.

47. Plan Local d'Urbanisme. See www.paris.fr/fr/urbanisme/plu.

48. www.ile-de-france.equipement.gouv.fr.

49. McClain et al. 1994, 455–56; Coaldrake 1996, 140.

50. Rozman 1973, 288; Naitō 2003, 108; Kodama and Sugiyama 1969, 188; Fujino
2002, 11; Haga 1980, 5–14.

51. Wakita 1994, 3, 6, 143–49; Kawazoe 1979, 165–69; Fiévé and Waley 2003,
129–43.

52. Yokoyama 1991, 219; Sorensen 2002, 81.

53. Fujino 2002, 100; Kabayama and Okuda 1985, 86; Berque 1994c, 312; Ishizuka
1991, 3–8; Tokyo-to 1991, 4–7; Stewart 2002, 22.

54. Ogi and Jinnai 1995, 44–64; Tokyo-to 1991, 8–10; Berque 1997b, 60–62.

55. Ishizuka and Ishida 1988, 10–13; Fujino 2002, 117–18; Ishizuka 1991, 8–13,
16–20.

56. Sorensen 2002, 111, chap. 3; Stewart 2002, 41.

57. Ishizuka and Ishida 1988, 88–91, pt. 2, sec. 4.

58. Ishida Y. 1999, 185; Ishizuka 1991, 17.

59. Seidensticker 91, 10–11; Tokyo-to 1991, 24; Kodama and Sugiyama 1969, 328;
Fujino 2002, 135–40.

60. Seidensticker 1991, 11; Fujino 2002, 138; Ishizuka and Ishida 1988, fig. 3; Kawamoto 1996, 258; Mikuriya 1996, 57–60. One should note, however, that these
changes were intended to cope with fire, not to enhance the quality of city life.

61. Tucker in Hein et al. 2003, 161–62; Stewart 2002, 111; Buck in Esherick 2000.

62. Sorensen 2002, 142.

63. Garon 1997.

64. Kornhauser 1976, 148; Tokyo-to 1991, 46–50; Fujino 2002, 168–69; Ishizuka
and Ishida 1988, 26–27; Sorensen 2002, chap. 5; Mikuriya 1994, 174–75.

65. Calder 1988, chap. 9.

66. *Shuto-ken Seibi Hō*. Mikuriya 1994, 180–82; Fujino 2002, 179–81; Hall in Sutcliffe 1984, 433–38; Ishizuka and Ishida 1988, fig. 7.

67. Sudjic 1992, 92.

68. Samuels 1983, chap. 5.
69. In full, *Zenkoku Sōgō Kaihatsu Keikaku. Asahi Shimbun,* February 2, 1972; May 15, 1977; Gurōbaru Shakai 1994, 65–70, 244; Economic Planning Agency 1972, 2.
70. Itō 1990, 41.
71. Fujita and Hill 1993, 207–8.
72. Komiya and Yoshida 1979, 28–35.
73. Itō 1990, 42ff.; Inoue et al. 1992, 45.
74. Tokyo-to 1991, preface, 66; Komiya and Yoshida 1979, 52.
75. Itō 1990, 39–63; *Asahi Shimbun,* February 14, 1977; May 15, 1977; Sorensen 2002, 249–53; Komiya and Yoshida 1979, 60; Tokyo Shisei Chōsa Kai 1992, 27.
76. "Overflow": Itō 1990, 122. Governor's actions: Tokyo Shisei Chōsa Kai 1992, 35–36; Mikuriya 1994, 233.
77. Sorensen 2002, 249–61.
78. Tokyo Shisei Chōsa Kai 1992, 28–30; Kokudo-chō 1994, introduction; Fujita and Hill 1993, 7; Itō 1990, 124–34.
79. Karan and Stapleton 1997, 7–8.
80. Tokyo Shisei Chōsa Kai 1992, 31–34; Tokyo-to 1991, 98.
81. Berque 1997b, 187.
82. *Japan Times Weekly,* December 25, 1995; Ministry of Land 1998; Kokudo Kōtsū-shō 1998.
83. *Japan Times,* May 19, 2003; Sakurai Yasuyoshi, personal communication, February 10, 2005.
84. Sorensen 2002, chap. 10; Inoue et al. 1992, 176–77.
85. Popham 1985, 156–60; Seidensticker 1991, 302.
86. Hara 1989, 66–68.
87. Ibid., v, 146–49; Berque 1997b, 185–86.
88. *Rinkaibu Fukutoshin;* Tokyo Shisei Chōsa Kai 1992, 38–40.
89. Lefebvre 1996, 207; Waterhouse 1993, 221; Rouleau 1997, 403–5.
90. Marchand 1993, 303–5.
91. Établissement Public d'Aménagement de la Défense. Evenson 1979, 296–99; Cornu 1972, 207–12; 257–67. For an intimate but engaged account, see Senneville 1992.
92. Sassen 1994b, 95; Savitch 1988, 147.
93. Marchand 1993, 303–5.
94. Senneville 1992, 24.
95. Savitch 1988, 147–55.
96. Iwata 1998.
97. Tokyo-to 1991, 68–69; Fujita and Hill 1993, 58; Tokyo Shisei Chōsa Kai 1992, 41–45; *Japan Times,* January 1, 2005; Cybriwsky 1998, 215–16; *Japan Times Weekly,* May 17, 1975.
98. www.toshiseibi2.metro.tokyo.jp/newtown.

99. Merlin 1991, 26–29.
100. Pinchemel 1979, 79.
101. Roullier 1989.
102. On this process, see Merlin 1991, 65–73, 85.
103. Lacaze 1994, 93–98.
104. Pinchemel 1979, 83, 90.
105. www.idf95; www.ors-idf.org.
106. Benoit et al. 1993, 297.
107. Ibid., 62, 87; Merlin 1991, 47–52.
108. Lacaze 1994, 262–63; Savitch 1988, 153–58.
109. For an enthusiastic treatment of this project, see www.parisjo2012.fr.
110. Municipalities are empowered by the state to set up their own SEMs. On SEMs, see Renaud 1993, 82–91; Berque 1994c, 450; on Les Halles, see Savitch 1988, 138–42.
111. Evenson 1979, 194, 287–90.
112. Renaud 1993, 87.
113. Sorensen 2002, 191–94.
114. One could add the Roppongi Hills and Tokyo Midtown developments as well.
115. McClain et al. 1994, 460–62.
116. Cohen and Fortier 1988, 6.
117. As spelled out in the enabling law, Solidarité et Renouvellement Urbains; see www.urbanisme.equipement.gouv.fr/actu/loi_sru/sru.pdf.
118. Both of these initiatives are discussed at www.leparisien.com, January 27, February 19, March 9, 2009; *New York Times,* March 17, 2009. For reference, the Montparnasse Tower is also about 700 feet tall.
119. Berque 1994c, 288.
120. Sacchi 2004, 223 and passim.
121. B. Berry 1973, 172–75.
122. Fujita and Hill 1993, 111 (emphasis added).
123. Karan and Stapleton 1997, 75.

5. Monuments and Commemorations

1. LeClère 1985, 688–89.
2. Mumford 1938, 433–40.
3. Farrar 2001, 10.
4. Horne 2002, 124; Lavedan 1975, 326.
5. Fortune 1863, 88, 201–2.
6. "Antimonumental": Henry Smith in M. Friedman 1986, 24–25; "lack of physical statement": Fiévé and Waley 2003, 29.
7. Richie 1999, 50–51.
8. Lefebvre 1991, 221.
9. Miyamoto in Takahashi and Yoshida 1990, 63–80, 190.

10. Nora in Gilles 1994, 8–9.
11. Dower 1999.
12. Gluck 1985; the phrase is Sheldon Garon's (1997).
13. E. Weber 1976.
14. White 1988; Stewart 2002, 188.
15. Richie 1999, 20, 35.
16. Nouët 1990, 219.
17. Claval in Agnew, Mercer, and Sopher 1984, 33–37; Hammond 1972, 177, 235; Friedrichs 1995, 252; Brill in Altman and Zube 1989, 16.
18. This passage is a distillation of ideas from Berque 1997b, 94–95; Murai 1964, chap. 8, 146–50; Naitō 2003, 91; Maki 1987, 46; and Fujitani 1996.
19. Kertzer 1988.
20. Outside Tokyo one should also note the very popular nineteenth-century American educator William S. Clark, whose statue stands in Hokkaido.
21. Gerhart 1999, ix–xiii, 141.
22. Clammer 1997, 69; see also Maki 1987, 202, 226; and Karan and Stapleton 1997, 51.
23. Fiévé and Waley 2003, 14; Fiévé in Fiévé and Waley 2003, chap. 5.
24. Waley in Fiévé and Waley 2003, 385, 389.
25. Haga 1980, 18–19; Kurushima in Takahashi and Yoshida 1990.
26. Ogi and Jinnai 1995, 15–16.
27. Farrar 2001, 3–8.
28. Desmarais 1995, 215–20; Lavedan 1975, 171–73.
29. Francastel 1984, 109; LeClère 1985, 292–93.
30. Jordan 1995, 30, 39; Francastel 1984, 144; Russell 1983, 163–64.
31. Gilles 1994, 239.
32. Quoted in Pinon 1999, 142.
33. Jordan 1995, 38; Agulhon in Nora 1992, 875–79.
34. Agulhon in Nora 1992, 879.
35. Olsen 1986, 171.
36. Michalski 1998, 8–9, 27–28; Gilles 1994, 187.
37. Harvey 1985a, 240; Burton 2001, 182, 266; Jones 2005, 375.
38. Law of 1887: Pinon 1999, 265; strengthened in 1913: Lavedan 1975, 548.
39. Michalski 1998, 79.
40. Noin and White 1997, 203; Ferguson 1994, chap. 1.
41. Michalski 1998, 49.
42. Ibid., 167–70.
43. Kaplan 1995.
44. Piggott 1997, chap. 1.
45. Fiévé and Waley 2003, 5–6.
46. The hall is 57 meters long, 51 meters deep, and 49 meters high, and yet is only two-thirds the size of the original building (Ward 1985, 34–37).

47. Nishikawa 1973, 88–99.
48. Frois in Coaldrake 1996, 11.
49. M. Berry 1982, 189–93 and passim; Sansom 1961, 312, 341, 346.
50. Naitō 1985, 51; Gerhart 1999, 104; Yazaki 1968, 193–95.
51. Duus 2001, 968–69.
52. Screech 2000, 118.
53. Ibid., 34, 113.
54. Haga 1980.
55. Gerhart 1999, xiv.
56. Ibid., 3; Totman 1983, 111.
57. Wakita 1994, 193–95; Sorensen 2002, 31; Nouët 1990, 50; Kawazoe 1979; Haga 1980, 185, 204.
58. Ishizuka and Ishida 1988, 72; Jinnai in Miao 2001, 55–60; Sorensen 2002, 25; Smith in M. Friedman 1986, 28–34.
59. Terry 1920, 186.
60. Murai 1964, 175–86.
61. Fujitani 1996, 35, 41, 59, 68.
62. Ibid., 132, 17, passim; Terry 1920, 109–235.
63. Keene 2002, 211–12.
64. Fujitani 1996, 17.
65. Coaldrake in M. Friedman 1986, 68.
66. Sorensen 2002, 63–66; Ishizuka 1991, 64–76.
67. Smethurst 1974; Garon 1997; Gluck 1985.
68. Ishizuka 1991, 149–58.
69. Maeda A. 1989, 204.
70. Schulz in Fiévé and Waley 2003, 286; see also Mikuriya 1994, 164; Ishizuka 1991, 30; Fujita 1993, 101–5.
71. Murai 1964, 108, 191.
72. Coaldrake 1996, chap. 9.
73. Cybriwsky 1998, 73–77; Yokoyama 1991, 221–23; Stewart 2002, 39.
74. Stewart 2002, 42.
75. Fujitani 1996, 124–25.
76. Cybriwsky 1998, 93.
77. Sudjic 1992, 237; Seidensticker 1991, 228.
78. Coaldrake 1996, 266, chap. 10; see also Hara 1989, 29–32; Seidensticker 1991, 290.
79. Coaldrake 1996, 269.
80. Kerr 2001, 245.
81. Richie 1999, 43.
82. Sorensen 2002, 8.
83. Machimura in Kim et al. 1997, 159.
84. Jones 2005, 180.

85. The same may be said of the "wastefully rather than tastefully splendid" temple and garden complex which formerly stood in Shiba Park (Terry 1920, 168).
86. This solemn, dignified, and unprepossessing mini-Arlington, four wooded acres outside the palace moat, is the interment site for some 350,000 sets of remains repatriated from World War II combat zones.

6. The Capital Envisioned

1. Holton 1986; Preston and Simpson-Housley 1994, chap. 13.
2. Olsen 1986, 3.
3. Frugoni 1991; Agulhon in Nora 1992, 869; Griotteray 1962, 2; Schorske in Handlin and Burchard 1963, 96–100; Lefebvre 1996, 22; Lehan 1998.
4. Wright in Skinner 1977, 34.
5. Mote in Skinner 1977, 102; Skinner 1977, 269.
6. See also Kodama and Sugiyama 1969, 4; Nosco 1990; Wakabayashi 1998; S. Matsumoto 1970; and Nishiyama 1997.
7. H. Smith 1978, 47–51.
8. Holton 1986, 1.
9. Jacobs 1961, 444; Lefebvre 1970, 145.
10. Wakita 1994, 125–29.
11. For a fuller discussion of kokugaku, see Haga 1980, 181; Nishikawa 1973, 213–16; Najita 1987, 172–73; McEwan 1962; and Harootunian 1988, chap. 5, 243–44.
12. Holton 1986, 1, 10–15; Schorske in Handlin and Burchard 1963, 96–101; Mumford 1938, 7–8; Lefebvre 1996, 119; 1970, 8, 10; Higonnet 2002; Benevolo 1993, chap. 6; Marchand 1993, 21–24; Lehan 1998.
13. Higonnet 2002, 261–75; Schorske in Handlin and Burchard 1963, 96–101; Gilloch 1996, 1, 139.
14. Sutcliffe 1984, 13.
15. Ishizuka 1991, 149; Havens 1974; Ishida T. 1966; Shinohara 1977, 197; Ozaki 1919.
16. Vlastos 1998, chap. 6; Havens 1974, 105–7.
17. Watanabe in Sutcliffe 1984, 427; Tamanoi 1998, 152.
18. Tamanoi 1998, 145–50.
19. Havens 1974, 255–59.
20. Tamanoi 1998, 116, 128–29, 196.
21. Ozawa 1994, 159–62.
22. On the "Tokyo Problem," see Gurōbaru Shakai 1994, passim and 91–93; Komiya and Yoshida 1979, 9, 14, 16–20, 56–60, 101; and Inoue et al. 1992, 165–68.
23. *Japan Times,* May 26, 2006.
24. Marchand 1993, 8.
25. Corbin in Nora 1996, 428, 432, 437.

26. Gravier 1972; Rey 1996; Franc 1971; Chevalier 1994; Cornu 1972; Griotteray 1962; Tombs 1981; Robb 2007. See also — in the counteroffensive genre but with a less inflammatory title — Marchand 1993.
27. H. Smith 1978, 47–50.
28. Dōmon 1999.
29. Tamanoi 1998, ix, 139.
30. Vlastos 1998, chap. 6; Yamakawa 1931, 13.
31. White 1973, 1982; Dore 1967.
32. Mikuriya 1994, 117–29.
33. Roncayolo 1990, 165.
34. Pinchemel 1979, 60.
35. Russell 1983, 47.
36. McClain et al. 1994, 385, 463, chap. 17; White 1995.
37. Jordan 1995, 91–95, 110.
38. White 1991.
39. Ishida Y. 1999; Ishizuka 1991.
40. Watanabe in Sutcliffe 1984, 413.
41. Ohashi 1973, 1976; Keisatsu-chō 1971.
42. Doublet 1976, 172.
43. Francastel 1968, 11.
44. Jordan 1995, 21.
45. LeClère 1985, 204–8; Garssey 1980, 85; Francastel 1984, 101–5; Horne 2002, 60–61; Hussey 2006, 87.
46. LeClère 1985, 386–89; Jones 2005, 121–25.
47. Francastel 1984, 102; LeClère 1985, 203.
48. LeClère 1985, 389–92; Horne 2002, 105–9.
49. Garrioch 2002.
50. Mollat 1971, 376; LeClère 1985, 425–27; Jones 2005, 230.
51. Garrioch 2002, 318–19; Mollat 1971, 482–84; Jones 2005, 272–76.
52. LeClère 1985, 437–38.
53. Mumford 1938, 117.
54. Jordan 1995, 101, 109; see also LeClère 1985, 487–92; Horne 2002, 221–25; Marchand 1993, 49; Rouleau 1985, 117; and Maspero 1994, 168.
55. Marchand 1993, 69.
56. Jordan 1995, 188; Merriman 1994, 281–84; Tarrow 1994, 76; *New York Times,* September 24, 1995.
57. Jones 2005, 321; Burton 2001, 137.
58. LeClère 1985, 576; Mollat 1971, 512–13.
59. On these events, see LeClère 1985, 524–26, 604–9; Mollat 1971, 509–542; and Horne 2002, 340–41.
60. Horne 2002, 408. On the postwar period, see also Noin and White 1997, 34, 65; Cornu 1972, 199; and Gildea 1994, 190.

61. Seidensticker 1983, 10.
62. Ishizuka 1991, 222.
63. Bowen 1980; Scalapino 1962; Ike 1950; Ishizuka 1991, 49–50, 222.
64. Gordon 1991, 1, 31–32.
65. With one exception: the replacement of Tokyo's paving stones with asphalt, which is harder to tear up and throw at the police.
66. White 1995.
67. Lewis 1990.
68. Murakami 1982.
69. Hussey 2006.
70. Harvey 1985a, 181.
71. Socioeconomic "apartheid": Horne 2002, 239; Harvey 1985a, 183–87; class war: Tombs 1981, 3.
72. Cornu 1972, 200, 243, 253.
73. LeClère 1985, 684–89.
74. Benoit et al. 1993, 272–75.
75. LeClère 1985, 182–84; Geremek 1987, 23–29.
76. Bergeron 1989, 58; Merriman 1994, chap. 3; Roche 1987, 271–74; Kaplan 1984; LeClère 1985, 241–44, 330.
77. Garrioch 2002, 48, 127; Roche 1987, 49.
78. Lacaze 1994, 72, 79.
79. Stovall 1990, 41, 169; Soulignac 1993, 55.
80. Evenson 1979, 238–49; Lacaze 1994, 26–30.
81. Maspero 1994, 268.
82. Effects exaggerated: White 1998; negative images continue: Colloque de Créteil 1990.
83. Fear of violence: Rey 1996, 100, chap. 4; riots of 2005: *Le Monde,* November 21, 2005.
84. Nishiyama 1997, 38–39; Naitō 1985, 81–95.
85. Naitō 2003, 84–85; Cooper 1965, 152–53.
86. Nishikawa 1972, 303; Naitō 2003, 80.
87. Kodama and Sugiyama 1969, 240; Naitō 1985, 87.
88. Compare Jones 2005, 202–6, with Hanley 1983.
89. Seidensticker in Fiévé and Waley 2003, 293.
90. Ishizuka and Ishida 1988, 8–11.
91. Jinnai 1995, 128–30, 193; Yokoyama 1991.
92. Unno 1983, 183.
93. Higonnet 2002, chap. 4.
94. Dore 1967, 40–44; Ishizuka 1991, 89, 124–30; Yazaki 1968, 450–51.
95. Terry 1920, 122–23, 134.
96. See, among others, Satō 1965a, 1965b; Hōmu 1974; and Maeda S. 1957, 54.
97. Katō M. 1965; Nasu and Hashimoto 1968.

98. Satō 1965a; Tokyo Katei Saibansho 1970.
99. Sorensen 2002, 187.
100. Kurata 1970, 159–60, 171–78; Fowler 1996, 13.
101. Seidensticker 1991, 169. One should note that, unlike France, this is the situation in all Japan's prefectures (*Japan Times,* 1989, 52–55).
102. Inoue et al. 1992, 5.
103. Actually, the descendants of the outcast class, which was legally abolished in the Meiji era. They account for perhaps 1 or 2 percent of the population.
104. *Japan Times,* September 19, 2004.
105. www.stat.go.jp/data/kokusei/2000/gaikokuu/oo/zuhyou/aoo1-1.xls; http:// encyclopedia. laborlawtalk.com/Paris#immigration.
106. Cornelius 1993, 21.
107. Merriman 1991, 9, 59.
108. Unno 1983, 53, 90, 110–12, 237.
109. Shinohara 1977, 197.
110. Kaplan 1995.
111. Quoted in Baedeker 1924, xxxii. See this guide for a typically adoring foreign appreciation of Paris.
112. Charles Lortsch, quoted in Evenson 1979, 159.
113. Evenson 1979, 124.
114. In 1920: Terry 1920, 143; almost a century later: Reiber and Spencer 2004, 98–102.
115. Seidensticker 1990, 348 and passim.
116. H. Smith 1988, 44; Koizumi 2003, 28, 53.
117. The Pompidou Center fills this description just as well, but I still think the generalization is fair.
118. Our two travel guides, from 1920 (Terry, 144) and 2004 (Reiber and Spencer, 98–100), concur on this point, citing the social animation and exhilaration of the city.
119. Savitch 1988, 284.
120. Evenson 1979, 124.
121. Chevalier 1994, 12 and passim.
122. Vlastos 1998, 20–24; Gluck 1985, 9, 178.
123. Gluck 1985, 32–36, 177–80; Najita and Harootunian in Wakabayashi 1998, chap. 4; Havens 1974, 295.
124. Keisatsu-chō 1971, 1.
125. "Developmental state": Johnson 1982. See also Inoue et al. 1992, 4–7, 42, 168–69; Ito 1990, 8–11; and Komiya and Yoshida 1979, 22–27.
126. Literary protagonist: Harvey 2003, 25–57; mythologized: Jones 2005, 404.
127. Nishikawa 1973, 150–51.
128. Sorensen 2002, 37.
129. Hayden 1995.

130. Unno 1983, 8, 96.
131. Sharpe and Wallock 1983, 30.
132. H. Smith 1988, 11, 24; Maeda A. 2004, chap. 2.
133. Kawamoto 1996, 38, 41, 76, chap. 16, 222, 444; H. Smith 1978, 68. See also Tanizaki 1977.
134. Kawamoto 1996, 220; Unno 1983, 8.
135. Unno 1983, 53, 61, chap. 3.
136. Ibid. 1983, 45; Maeda A. 2004, esp. 13. On the florescence of the 1920s, see also Mansfield 2009, chap. 6.
137. Unno 1983, 24–25; Stephen Snyder, quoted in Kawabata 2005, xxx; Freedman in Kawabata 2005, xxxv.
138. Sharpe and Wallock 1983, 223; Unno 1983, 97, 250.
139. Lavedan 1975, 533.
140. Franc 1971, 221.
141. Colloque de Créteil 1990, 103.
142. Terry 1920, 140–44.
143. Coaldrake in M. Friedman 1986, 71; Ogi and Jinnai 1995, 14–15.
144. Iyotani 1993, 3.
145. Seidensticker 1991, 344.
146. Actually, one would, albeit rarely: a Google search for this phrase turned up about seventy sites, almost all related to reviews of the film *Lost in Translation*. But my point stands — a search for the original phrase returns almost 180,000.

7. Capital, Context, Country

1. Griotteray 1962, 125.
2. Inoue et al. 1992, 183.
3. Horne 2002, 120; Higonnet 2002, 310–13; Franc 1971, 40. On Parisian parochialism, see also Harvey 2003, 30–32; and Jones 2005, xix.
4. Marchand 1993.
5. Steiner 1965, 11–14; White 1988.
6. Tilly and Blockmans 1994, 6–22.
7. Marchand 1993, 384; Lacaze 1994, 33.
8. Franc 1971, 26–27.
9. Colloque de Créteil 1990, 29–31 (quoted) and passim; Rouleau 1997, 230. See also Evenson 1979, 159; and Clubs Convaincre 1990.
10. Mikuriya 1996, 92, 105–9.
11. See, for example, Genestier 1994.
12. Rouleau 1985, 72, 124, 128.
13. Noin and White 1997, 105.
14. Berque 1997b, 86–87, 111–12.
15. Watanabe in Sutcliffe 1984, 413, 422.
16. Kurasawa 1968, 119–22; Tokyo-to, Minami-Tama 1972.

17. Merriman 1991, 61; Jordan 1995, 98.
18. Rey 1996, 7.
19. White 1992, 72.
20. France has about 200,000 square miles and 36,000 communes (of which 22,500 have fewer than 500 inhabitants); Japan, about 150,000 and roughly 2,000. Japanese villages and urban neighborhoods actually have semiformal subunits, and the largest cities have wards, but Paris also has its arrondissements, so the relative complexity remains (see Mabileau 1994, chap. 2; Gravier 1972, 204; Ehrmann 1983, chap. 4, 291–94; and *Japan Times,* February 21, 2006).
21. Hohenberg and Lees 1995, 41; Braudel 1986, 161; Jones 2005, 29, 53.
22. Steiner 1965, 118–19.
23. Ascher et al. 1993, 152–55.
24. Griotteray 1962, 121–22; Franc 1971, 86–87.
25. Doublet 1976.
26. Mabileau 1994; Secretariat 1991, xix; Mazey 1990, 150–61; Frears 1983, 60–64; Gurr and King 1987, 89.
27. Ascher et al. 1993, 152–53.
28. DATAR 1994, 28; Noin and White 1997, 2.
29. On this interlude of populist urbanism, see Hall 1968, 172; Hayashiya 1982, 62–65; Nishikawa 1973, pt. 3; 1972, 75–95, 161ff.; and Wakita 1994, 18, 105.
30. Nishikawa 1972, 133; Wakita 1994, 13–17, 25–26. Japan had no concept of "rights" at all, and the word itself had to be invented in 1868 (Steiner 1965, 16).
31. Steiner 1965, 16–18.
32. Nishikawa 1972, 143; 1973, 144, 168.
33. Steiner 1965, 14.
34. Ibid., 26.
35. Abe et al. 1994, 35–36.
36. Steiner 1965; Yamamoto 1970; Samuels 1983, 83–85. On the transformation, and contemporary IGRs, see Muramatsu 1991; Samuels 1983; and Hoshino 1994.
37. McKean 1981; White 1984.
38. Shibata 1993.
39. Allinson and Sone 1993.
40. Lessened state influence: Muramatsu 1991, 134–37. On the merger process, see *Asahi Shimbun,* March 28, May 13, 2001; February 11, October 3, October 29, 2002; November 17, 2003; and *Japan Times,* February 1, July 9, December 4, 2003.
41. Francastel 1984, 31–33.
42. Mollat 1971, 136; Francastel 1984, 71–73; LeClère 1985, 219–32; Lavedan 1975, 160. The kings hedged their bets, however: both the Louvre and the Bastille anticipated both internal and external enemies.

43. LeClère 1985, 406–7.
44. Marchand 1993, 21; Corbin in Nora 1996, 438–47.
45. Burton 2001, 95; Marchand 1993, 107–24; Tombs 1981, 2–4, 34.
46. Corbin in Nora 1996, 450–59; Bergeron 1989, 232; Marchand 1993, 205–40, 400.
47. Marchand 1993, 240.
48. LeClère 1985, 558; Haegel 1994, 61, 65, 104–7.
49. Chirac: Marchand 1993, 335–38; Haegel 1994, 191; administrators' objections: Marchand 1993, 388–89; Renaud 1993, 96, 211, 223.
50. *Le Monde,* January 28, 2005.
51. Renaud 1993, 70–73; Greenhouse 1992.
52. Lacaze 1994, 232. The 1994 master plan for the Île-de-France Region can be found at www.idf95.
53. Seidensticker 1983, 30–31; Steiner 1965, 44–45; Ishizuka 1991, 76, 78; Mikuriya 1996, 2–3; Fujino 2002 passim, 148–50.
54. For this period, see Mikuriya 1994; 1996; and Tokyo Shisei Chōsa Kai 1992.
55. Tokyo Shisei Chōsa Kai 1992, 250–54; Mikuriya 1994, 18–19; 1996, 78–81. There are also indications that, as with Minobe, the state wanted to put a local grandstander in his place.
56. *Japan Times International,* May 8, 1995.
57. Friedrichs 1995, 54; LeClère 1985, 237–40, 314–17; Lavedan 1975, 180; Mollat 1971, 293.
58. The Île-de-France region today consists of eight departments: Paris, an "inner ring" of three, and an "outer ring" of four. Renaud 1993, 39–42.
59. Ibid., 46–47.
60. Haegel 1994, 128; Secretariat 1991, chap. 19; Renaud 1993, 57–61, 120–34, 172.
61. Naitō 1985, 102–4; Nouët 1990, 99–100; Murai 1964, 43; Fujino 2002, 15–16.
62. On the process, see Kodama and Sugiyama 1969, 288–322; Yazaki 1968, 333–35; Ishizuka 1991, 9, 42; Steiner 1965, 61; and Seidensticker 1991, 43, 88–95, 132–33.
63. Tokyo Shisei Chōsa Kai 1992, 243–44.
64. Shibata 1993, 183–86.
65. Four prefectures, about 45 urban wards, and 250 municipalities; Paris has 8 departments, 20 arrondissements, and 1,281 municipalities. Savitch 1988, 279; www.iaurif.org.
66. Préfecture Île-de-France 1995.
67. Calder 1988, chap. 6; Gurōbaru Shakai 1994, 245; McCargo 2000, 66.
68. *Asahi Shimbun,* October 10, 1971; *Japan Times,* October 7, 1972; Yazaki 1970, 28; Calder 1988, chap. 6; Itō 1990, 75–83; Kokudo Kōtsū-shō n.d.
69. Tokyo-to 1991, 104.
70. *Japan Times,* December 4, 2003.
71. Doublet 1976, 117.
72. Quoted in Savitch 1988, 255.
73. Kaplan 1995, 177.

74. Noin and White 1997, 61–63; Lacaze 1994, 232.
75. Marchand 1993, 332–34; Cornu 1972, 171–75.
76. Renaud 1993, 248–52.
77. Benoit et al. 1993, 68–72, 159.
78. *Le Parisien,* February 26, 2009.
79. Tsukuba Academic City, to the north, is quite separate; indeed, its university and research institutes are staffed largely by commuters from Tokyo, thus hardly "deconcentrating" the capital.
80. Hara 1989; Inoue et al. 1992; Iyotani 1993; Mikuriya 1994.
81. Senneville 1992, 12.
82. www.ladefense.fr.
83. Senneville 1992.
84. *Le Monde,* November 12, 2004.
85. Stovall 1990, 25–28.
86. Rouleau 1985, 56.
87. Evenson 1979, 220–23; Mollat 1971, 527–31; Pinon 1999, 223–40; Soulignac 1993, 63.
88. Evenson 1979, 235–36.
89. Marchand 1993, 286.
90. Noin and White 1997, 112, 196; Marchand 1993, 282–85; Colloque de Créteil 1990, 138; Soulignac 1993, 198; Maspero 1994, 32; Keating 1991, 151–52.
91. Noin and White 1997, 109; Lefebvre 1996, 35–36.
92. Noin and White 1997, 203.
93. www.leparisien.fr, January 27, 2009.
94. Doublet 1976, 141–44; Lacaze 1994, 126–30; Cohen and Fortier 1988, 177, 189; *Le Monde,* November 12, 2004.
95. Fujino 2002, 24–37.
96. Sorensen 2002, 124–25.
97. Ishizuka 1991, 138; Karan and Stapleton 1997, 83.
98. Hussey 2006; Robb 2007.
99. It is instructive that when the first shoots of urban autonomy emerged in Japan, the would-be state-builders crushed them utterly.

Conclusion

1. Cohen and Fortier 1988, 18–27.
2. Cybriwsky 1998, 1. On this "hidden order," see also Berque 1994c, 587; 1997a, 19, 26; 1997b, 3; and Maki 2008.
3. Berque 1994c, 373.
4. Machimura in Kim et al. 1997, 155; Seidensticker 1991, 298–99.
5. These informal organizations, given the subcontractarian quality of Japanese government in general, are an important part of urban service delivery and social organization in Japan (Inoue et al. 1992, 156–59; White 1982; Bestor 1989).
6. *New York Times,* October 28, 2003.

7. *Japan Times,* May 26, 2006.

8. Cornu 1972, 8–9.

9. Savitch 1988, 25–29; Doublet 1976, 99.

10. Agulhon in Nora 1992, 898–903.

11. Haegel 1994, 197; Burgel and Burgel in Cohen et al. 1996, 332; Clubs Convaincre 1990, 38; *Le Monde,* October 2, 2003.

12. Rouleau 1985, 320–28.

13. Fujino 2002, 184.

14. White 1982, appendix.

15. Karan and Stapleton 1997, chap. 6; Berque 1994c, 364–72; White 1973. Again, this is not to say that areas like Sanya do not exist, but that they are fewer and farther between, less physically "slumlike," and less behaviorally pathological than are their Parisian counterparts. By one estimate (*Le Monde,* January 10, 2005), fully one-eighth of Parisian households are in "extreme poverty."

16. Ishizuka and Ishida 1988. The last date refers to the attempt to move the capital.

17. Which has an explicit tradition of state expropriation dating back to Napoleon (Aldrich 2005).

18. Johnson 1982.

19. Stewart 2002, 182.

20. After Lang 2003, 25–26; and Ascher et al. 1993, 30.

21. Lacaze 1994, 122.

22. Savitch 1988, 302.

23. Coaldrake 1996, 11.

24. Richie 1999, 29, 38, 82.

25. Deborde 1994.

26. Richie in M. Friedman 1986, 97.

27. *New York Times,* October 28, 2003; *Far Eastern Economic Review,* November 27, 2003. A similar private initiative has transformed Shiodome.

28. Mumford 1961, 4.

29. Lefebvre 1991, 26–27; Boyer 1994, 408.

30. Vale 1992, 19–20.

31. *New York Times,* December 30, 2008; *Japan Times,* December 30, 2008.

32. T. Smith 1961 and 1977.

33. Dower 1999.

34. Kerr 2001, 224.

35. Lacaze 1994, 330–35; Sudjic 1992, 235, 241; Noin and White 1997, 252–53; Marchand 1993, 372–77.

36. Benoit et al. 1993, 25.

37. Paris: Benoit et al. 1993, 56; elsewhere in Europe: Hohenberg and Lees 1995, vi; Ascher et al. 1993, 66–67, 76.

38. Corbin in Nora 1996, 462–63.

39. Isoda 1983; Richie 1999, 134.
40. Berque 1997b, 181; Kokudo-chō 1994; *Asahi Shimbun,* July 7, 2002. The region also anticipates the completion, within ten years, of two additional circumferential highways, one 30–40 kilometers outside central Tokyo, the other 80–120 kilometers out.
41. DATAR 1994, 3, 9; Colloque de Créteil 1990.
42. Piore and Sabel 1984, 303–7; Cornu 1972, 33; Ascher et al. 1993, 56–58; DATAR 1994.
43. Hill and Fujita 1995, 188–92; Nakamura 1996, 16–28.
44. Mikuriya 1994, 146–55.
45. *Asahi Shimbun,* September 6, October 25, 2000; *Japan Times,* April 2, 2004.
46. With the brief exception of 1943–45.
47. Noin and White 1997, 144–50; *Le Monde,* December 12, 2003; Benoit et al. 1993, 95–97; 289, 295; Evenson 1979, 119–22; Marchand 1993, 316.
48. Benoit et al. 1993, 197.
49. *Le Monde,* November 12, 2004.
50. Benoit et al. 1993, 141.
51. *Le Parisien,* February 19, 2009.
52. Rey 1996, 7; *Le Monde,* November 17, 2003.
53. *Le Monde,* June 8, 2004.
54. Ibid., November 1, November 3, 2005. Sarkozy's actual words were "nettoyer au Kärcher." Kärcher is a firm that makes pressure-washing equipment.
55. Benoit et al. 1993, 248–57.
56. Sautter 1994, 86, and passim.
57. Passenger data for the Gare du Nord, Métro, and RER are from Noin and White 1997, 152–53; for Shinjuku, Masai in Golany 1998, 70; mileage data are from Iwai in Golany 1998, 239–40. Tokyo subway data are from Tokyo-to 2003, tables 117, 118. Japanese rail data are available at www.jreast.co.jp/e/investor/ar/2002. Note: Greater Tokyo has roughly 2.5 times the population of Île-de-France; Japan has roughly twice the population of France.
58. Cybriwsky 1998, 205.
59. Jacobs 1961, 257, with apologies to Robert Frost.
60. Richie 1999, 44–47.
61. After all, as Ruth Benedict (1958) famously noted, the Japanese have been described with perhaps more "but alsos" than any other society.
62. Hussey 2006.
63. Compare, for example, the sense of the village reflected in Beardsley, Hall, and Ward 1959; Embree 1939; Doŕe 1978; or R. Smith 1978; with Wylie 1964 or E. Weber 1976.
64. The weakness of class divisions in Japan is one factor which could be pursued causally in many further directions; I am not implying that the Japanese are Just This Way. The structure of feudal loyalties, the process of industrializa-

tion, government-stimulated nationalism, and the structure of Japanese corporations and unions all played a role.
65. DATAR 1994, 13; *Le Monde,* October 17, November 17, November 24, 2003;
Sudjic 1992, 75; Colloque de Créteil 1990, 16, 79–82.
66. Nishio 1990.
67. Arguments for and against this theory are reviewed in White 1998.
68. Kamo 1994, 6–7; *Far Eastern Economic Review,* December 1, 1994.
69. Ascher et al. 1993, 9, 13; Savitch 1988, 161.
70. Noin and White 1997, 14, 130.
71. Olsen 1986, 291.
72. Higonnet 2002, 434.

BIBLIOGRAPHY

Abe, Hitoshi, et al. 1994. *The Government and Politics of Japan.* Translated by James White. Tokyo: University of Tokyo Press.

Abu-Lughod, Janet. 1999. *New York, Chicago, Los Angeles.* Minneapolis: University of Minnesota Press.

Agnew, John. 1987. *Place and Politics.* Boston: Allen and Unwin.

Agnew, John, and James Duncan, eds. 1989. *The Power of Place.* Boston: Unwin Hyman.

Agnew, John, John Mercer, and David Sopher, eds. 1984. *The City in Cultural Context.* Boston: Allen and Unwin.

Aldrich, Daniel. 2005. *Leviathan or Agile State?* Ph.D. diss., Harvard University.

Allinson, Gary. 1975. *Japanese Urbanism.* Berkeley and Los Angeles: University of California Press.

Allinson, Gary, and Yasunori Sone, eds. 1993. *Political Dynamics in Contemporary Japan.* Ithaca: Cornell University Press.

Altman, Irwin, and Ervin Zube, eds. 1989. *Public Places and Spaces.* New York: Plenum.

Anderson, Benedict. 1983. *Imagined Communities.* London: Verso.

Asahi Shimbun. Tokyo, daily. www.asahi.com.

Ascher, François, et al., eds. 1993. *Les territoires du futur.* Paris: DATAR (Délégation à l'Aménagement du Territoire et à l'Action Régionale).

Ashihara, Yoshinobu. 1989. *The Hidden Order.* Translated by Lynne Riggs. Tokyo: Kōdansha.

Augé, Marc. 1992. *Non-lieux.* Paris: Seuil.

Baedeker, Karl. 1924. *Paris and Its Environs.* Leipzig: Karl Baedeker.

Balzac, Honoré de. 1901. *The Works of Honoré de Balzac.* Vol. 13. Philadelphia: Avril.

Barthes, Roland. 1982. *Empire of Signs.* Translated by Richard Howard. New York: Hill and Wang.

Beardsley, Richard, John Hall, and Robert Ward. 1959. *Village Japan.* Chicago: University of Chicago Press.

Benedict, Ruth. 1958. *The Chrysanthemum and the Sword.* Tokyo: Tuttle.

Benevolo, Leonardo. 1993. *The European City.* Translated by Carl Ipsen. Oxford: Blackwell.

Benoit, Philippe, et al. 1993. *Paris 1995: Le grand desserrement.* Paris: Romillat.

Berger, Suzanne, and Ronald Dore, eds. 1996. *National Diversity and Global Capitalism.* Ithaca: Cornell University Press.

Bergeron, Louis, ed. 1989. *Paris: Genèse d'un paysage.* Paris: Picard.

Berman, Marshall. 1982. *All That Is Solid Melts into Air.* New York: Simon and Schuster.

Berque, Augustin. 1994a. "J'en ai rêvé, c'était Tokyo." *Annales de l'École des Hautes Études en Sciences Sociales* 3.

———. 1994b. "Des thermes à Nanterre." *Le Débat,* no. 81 (September).

———, ed. 1994c. *La maîtrise de la ville.* Paris: EHESS (Éditions de l'École des Hautes Études en Sciences Sociales).

———. 1996. "Ville, nature et politique en Europe et au Japon." In *Villes et jardins.* Liège: Éditions du Centre d'Études Japonaises de l'Université de Liège (CEJUL).

———. 1997a. *Japan: Cities and Social Bonds.* Translated by Chris Turner. Yelvertoft Manor, Northamptonshire: Pilkington Press.

———. 1997b (September). "La ville européen vue du Japon." Paris: EHESS (École des Hautes Études en Sciences Sociales)/CNRS (Centre Nationale de Recherche Scientifique). In the author's files, Department of Political Science, University of North Carolina.

Berry, Brian. 1973. *The Human Consequences of Urbanization.* New York: St. Martin's.

Berry, Mary Elizabeth. 1982. *Hideyoshi.* Cambridge: Harvard University Press.

———. 1994. *The Culture of Civil War in Kyoto.* Berkeley and Los Angeles: University of California Press.

———. 1998. Review of *Architecture and Authority in Japan,* by William Coaldrake. *Journal of Japanese Studies* 24, no. 2:401.

Bestor, Theodore. 1989. *Neighborhood Tokyo.* Stanford: Stanford University Press.

Blakely, Edward, and Mary Gail Snyder. 1997. *Fortress America.* Washington, D.C.: Brookings Institution.

Blakely, Edward, and Robert Stimson, eds. 1992 (October). *New Cities of the Pacific Rim.* Monograph 43, Institute of Urban and Regional Development. Berkeley: University of California.

Bowen, Roger. 1980. *Rebellion and Democracy in Meiji Japan.* Berkeley and Los Angeles: University of California Press.

Boyer, M. Christine. 1994. *The City of Collective Memory.* Cambridge: MIT Press.

Braudel, Fernand. 1986. *Espace et histoire.* Vol. 1, *L'Identité de la France.* Paris: Arthaud-Flammarion.

Burton, Richard. 2001. *Blood in the City.* Ithaca: Cornell University Press.

Calder, Kent. 1988. *Crisis and Compensation.* Princeton: Princeton University Press.

Camp, Sharon, ed. 1990. *Cities: Life in the World's 100 Largest Metropolitan Areas.* Chart, with statistical appendix. Washington, D.C.: Population Action International.

Cassella, William. 1991 (September). "An American Looks at the Tokyo Metropolitan Government." Draft article in author's files, Department of Political Science, University of North Carolina.

Chaslin, François. 1994. "Le moment Pompidou." *Le Débat,* no. 80 (May).

Chevalier, Louis. 1950. *La formation de la population parisienne au XIXe siècle.* Paris: Presses Universitaires de France.

———. 1958. *Classes laborieuses et classes dangereuses à Paris pendant la première moitié du XIXe siècle.* Paris: Plon.

———. 1994. *The Assassination of Paris.* Chicago: University of Chicago Press.

Chōfu-shi, Sōmu-bu, Kikaku-shitsu 1971. *Chōfu Shimin no Ishiki Chōsa Sho.* Tokyo: Chōfu-shi.

Clammer, John. 1997. *Contemporary Urban Japan.* Malden, Mass.: Blackwell.

Claval, Paul. 1981. *La logique des villes.* Paris: LITEC.

Clubs Convaincre. 1990. *Les Paris pour L'Île-de-France.* Paris: Syros-Alternatives.

Coaldrake, William. 1996. *Architecture and Authority in Japan.* New York: Routledge.

Cohen, Jean-Louis, and Bruno Fortier. 1988. *Paris: La ville et ses projets.* Paris: Babylone.

Cohen, Michael, et al., eds. 1996. *Preparing for the Urban Future.* Washington, D.C.: Woodrow Wilson Center.

Colloque de Créteil. 1990. *Île-de-France: Pouvons-nous éviter le scénario catastrophe?* Paris: Economica.

Cooper, Michael, ed. 1965. *They Came to Japan.* Berkeley and Los Angeles: University of California Press.

Cornelius, Wayne. 1993 (June). "Controlling Latin American Migration to Industrialized Countries: The US and Japanese Experiences." Paper prepared for the National Convention of the Japan Association of Latin American Studies, Tokyo.

Cornu, Marcel. 1972. *La conquête de Paris.* Paris: Mercure de France.

Cybriwsky, Roman. 1998. *Tokyo.* New York: Wiley.

DATAR (Délégation à l'Aménagement du Territoire et à l'Action Régionale). 1994 (April). *Débat nationale pour l'aménagement du territoire.* Paris.

Davies, Simon. 1982. *Paris and the Provinces in Eighteenth-Century Prose Fiction.* Oxford: Voltaire Foundation.

Deborde, Guy. 1994. *The Society of the Spectacle.* Translated by Donald Nicholson-Smith. New York: Zone.

La Défense. Official website. www.ladefense.fr.

Desmarais, Gaetan. 1995. *La morphogenèse de Paris.* Paris: Harmattan.

Dienstag, Joshua. 1997. *Dancing in Chains.* Stanford: Stanford University Press.

Direction Générale de l'Urbanisme, de l'Habitat et de la Construction. 2000. *Loi, solidarité et renouvellement urbains.* Paris: Ministère de l'Équipement. www.urbanism.equipement.gouv.fr/actn/loi_sru/sru.pdf.

Dōmon Fuyuji. 1999. *Edo no Toshi Keikaku.* Tokyo: Bungei Shunjū.

Dore, R. P. 1967. *City Life in Japan.* Berkeley and Los Angeles: University of California Press.

———. 1978. *Shinohata.* New York: Pantheon.

Doublet, Maurice. 1976. *Paris en procès.* Paris: Hachette.

Dower, John. 1999. *Embracing Defeat.* New York: Norton.

Duus, Peter. 2001. "Presidential Address: Weapons of the Weak, Weapons of the Strong — The Development of the Japanese Political Cartoon." *Journal of Asian Studies* 60, no. 4:965.

Economic Planning Agency. 1972 (October). *New Comprehensive National Development Plan.* Revised. Tokyo: Economic Planning Agency.

Ehrmann, Henry. 1983. *Politics in France.* Boston: Little, Brown.

Ellin, Nan. 1997. *Architecture of Fear.* New York: Princeton Architectural Press.

Ellul, Jacques. 1970. *The Meaning of the City.* Translated by Dennis Pardee. Grand Rapids, Mich.: Eerdmans.

Embree, John. 1939. *Suye Mura.* Chicago: University of Chicago Press.

Esherick, Joseph, ed. 2000. *Remaking the Chinese City.* Honolulu: University of Hawaii Press.

Evenson, Norma. 1979. *Paris: A Century of Change, 1878–1978.* New Haven: Yale University Press.

Farrar, Margaret. 2001 (September). "Monumentality and Democratic Citizenship." Paper prepared for the annual meeting of the American Political Science Association, San Francisco.

Ferguson, Priscilla. 1994. *Paris as Revolution.* Berkeley and Los Angeles: University of California Press.

Fiévé, Nicolas, and Paul Waley, eds. 2003. *Japanese Capitals in Historical Perspective.* New York: Routledge Curzon.

Fortune, Robert. 1863. *Yedo and Peking.* London: John Murray.

Fowler, Ted. 1996. *San'ya Blues.* Ithaca: Cornell University Press.

Franc, Robert. 1971. *Le scandale de Paris.* Paris: Bernard Grasset.

Francastel, Pierre. 1968 (April 23). "Paris: Un héritage culturel et monumental." *Notes et Études Documentaires,* no. 3483.

———. 1984. *Une destinée de capitale: Paris.* Paris: Denoël/Gonthier.

Frears, J. R. 1983. "The Decentralisation Reforms in France." *Parliamentary Affairs* 36, no. 1.

Friedman, John. 1986. "The World City Hypothesis." *Development and Change* 17, no. 1:69.

Friedman, Mildred, ed. 1986. *Tokyo: Form and Spirit*. New York: Abrams.

Friedrichs, Christopher. 1995. *The Early Modern City 1450–1750*. London: Longman.

Frugoni, Chiara. 1991. *A Distant City*. Translated by William McCraig. Princeton: Princeton University Press.

Fujino Atsushi. 2002. *Tokyo-to no Tanjō*. Tokyo: Yoshikawa Kōbunkan.

Fujita Hiroo. 1993. *Toshi no Ronri*. Tokyo: Chūō Kōron.

Fujita, Kuniko, and Richard Hill. 1993. *Japanese Cities in the World Economy*. Philadelphia: Temple University Press.

Fujitani, Takashi. 1996. *Splendid Monarchy*. Berkeley and Los Angeles: University of California Press.

Fumagalli, Vito. 1994. *Landscapes of Fear*. Cambridge, U.K.: Polity.

Garon, Sheldon. 1997. *Molding Japanese Minds*. Princeton: Princeton University Press.

Garrioch, David. 2002. *The Making of Revolutionary Paris*. Berkeley and Los Angeles: University of California Press.

Garssey, Maurice. 1980. *Paris: Vingt siècles d'histoire et de métamorphoses*. Paris: Pensée Universelle.

Genestier, Philippe. 1994. "La banlieue au risque de la métropolisation." *Le Débat*, no. 80 (May): 192.

Geremek, Bronislaw. 1987. *The Margins of Society in Late Medieval Paris*. Translated by Jean Birrell. Cambridge: Cambridge University Press.

Gerhart, Karen. 1999. *The Eyes of Power*. Honolulu: University of Hawaii Press.

Gildea, Robert. 1994. *The Past in French History*. New Haven: Yale University Press.

Gilles, John, ed. 1994. *Commemorations*. Princeton: Princeton University Press.

Gilloch, Graeme. 1996. *Myth and Metropolis*. Cambridge, U.K.: Polity.

Gluck, Carol. 1985. *Japan's Modern Myths*. Princeton: Princeton University Press.

———. 1998. "The Invention of Edo." In *Mirror of Modernity*, edited by Stephen Vlastos. Berkeley and Los Angeles: University of California Press.

Golany, Gideon, ed. 1998. *Japanese Urban Environment*. New York: Elsevier.

Gordon, Andrew. 1991. *Labor and Imperial Democracy in Prewar Japan*. Berkeley and Los Angeles: University of California Press.

Gourevitch, Peter. 1980. *Paris and the Provinces*. Berkeley and Los Angeles: University of California Press.

Gravier, Jean-François. 1972. *Paris et le désert français en 1972*. Paris: Flammarion.

Greenbie, Barry. 1988. *Space and Spirit in Modern Japan*. New Haven: Yale University Press.

Greenhouse, Steven. 1992 (July 19). "Why Paris Works." *New York Times Sunday Magazine*, 14.

Griotteray, Alain. 1962. *L'état contre Paris*. Paris: Hachette.

Gropius, Walter, and Kenzō Tange. 1960. *Katsura*. New Haven: Yale University Press.

Gurōbaru Shakai ni okeru Kansai-zō Kenkyū Kai. 1994. *Gozensō e: Kansai kara no Messēji.* Kyoto: Gakugei.

Gurr, Ted, and Desmond King. 1987. *The State and the City.* London: Macmillan.

Haegel, Florence. 1994. *Un maire à Paris.* Paris: Foundation Nationale des Sciences Politiques.

Haga Noboru. 1980. *O-Edo no Seiritsu.* Tokyo: Yoshikawa Kōbunkan.

Halbwachs, Maurice. 1980. *The Collective Memory.* Translated by Francis Ditter and Vida Ditter. New York: Harper and Row.

Hall, John. 1968. "The Castle Town and Japan's Modern Urbanization." In *Studies in the Institutional History of Early Modern Japan,* edited by John Hall and Marius Jansen. Princeton: Princeton University Press.

Hammond, Mason. 1972. *The City in the Ancient World.* Cambridge: Harvard University Press.

Handlin, Oscar, and John Burchard, eds. 1963. *The Historian and the City.* Cambridge: MIT Press.

Hanley, Susan. 1983. "A High Standard of Living in Nineteenth-Century Japan: Fact or Fantasy?" *Journal of Economic History* 43, no. 1:183.

Hara Takeshi. 1989. *Tokyo Kaizō.* Tokyo: Gakuyō Shobō.

Harootunian, Harry. 1988. *Things Seen and Unseen.* Chicago: University of Chicago Press.

Harvey, David. 1985a. *Consciousness and the Urban Experience.* Baltimore: Johns Hopkins University Press.

———. 1985b. *The Urbanization of Capital.* Baltimore: Johns Hopkins University Press.

———. 2003. *Paris: Capital of Modernity.* New York: Routledge.

Havens, Thomas. 1974. *Farm and Nation in Modern Japan.* Princeton: Princeton University Press.

Hayami, Akira. 1982 (September). "A 'Great Transformation.'" Paper prepared for the Third International Studies Conference on Japan, The Hague.

Hayashiya Tatsusaburō. 1982. *Rekishi no Naka no Toshi.* Tokyo: NHK (Nihon Hōsō Kyōkai).

Hayden, Dolores. 1995. *The Power of Place.* Cambridge: MIT Press.

Hein, Carola, et al., eds. 2003. *Rebuilding Urban Japan after 1945.* New York: Palgrave.

Higonnet, Patrice. 2002. *Paris: Capital of the World.* Translated by Arthur Goldhammer. Cambridge: Harvard University Press.

Hill, Richard, and Kuniko Fujita. 1995. "Osaka's Tokyo Problem." *International Journal of Urban and Regional Research* 19, no. 2:181.

Hinago, Motoo. 1986. *Japanese Castles.* Translated by William Coaldrake. Tokyo: Kōdansha, 1986.

Hohenberg, Paul, and Lynn Lees. 1995. *The Making of Urban Europe 1000–1994.* Cambridge: Harvard University Press.

Holton, R. J. 1986. *Cities, Capitalism, and Civilization*. London: Allen and Unwin.

Hōmu Sōgō Kenkyū-jo, ed. 1974. *Shōwa 49–nen Hanzai Hakusho*. Tokyo: Hōmu-shō.

Horne, Alastair. 2002. *Seven Ages of Paris*. New York: Knopf.

Hoshino, Shinyasu. 1994 (August). "Japanese Local Government and Global Economic Interdependency." Paper prepared for the NIRA–NAPA (National Institute for Research Advancement–National Association for Public Administration) Conference on Centralization and Decentralization in Japan and the United States, Georgetown University.

Hussey, Andrew. 2006. *Paris: The Secret History*. New York: Penguin.

Ike, Nobutaka. 1950. *The Beginnings of Political Democracy in Japan*. Baltimore: Johns Hopkins University Press.

Inoue Junichi et al. *Tokyo: Sekai Toshi-ka no Kōzu*. Tokyo: Aoki, 1992.

INSEE (Institut National de la Statistique et des Études Économiques). *Annuaire statistique de la France*. Paris: Ministère de l'Économie.

Ishida Takeshi. 1966. "Nihon ni okeru Toshika to Seiji." *Shisō*, no. 510 (December), 1609.

———. 1970. *Nihon no Seiji Bunka*. Tokyo: Tokyo Daigaku Shuppan Kai.

Ishida Yorifusa. 1999. *Mori Ogai no Toshi-ron to sono Jidai*. Tokyo: Nihon Keizai Hyōron.

Ishizuka Hiromichi. 1991. *Nihon Kindai Toshi-ron*. Tokyo: Tokyo Daigaku Shuppan Kai.

Ishizuka, Hiromichi, and Yorifusa Ishida. 1988. *Tokyo: Urban Growth and Planning 1868–1988*. Tokyo: Tokyo Metropolitan University Center for Urban Studies.

Isoda Kōichi. 1983. *Shisō to shite no Tokyo*. Tokyo: Kokubun Sha.

Itō Zenichi. 1990. *Tokyo to Chihō*. Tokyo: Chūō Keizai.

Iwai Hiroaki, ed. 1971. *Toshi Shakaigaku*. Tokyo: Yūhikaku.

Iwata, Kazuaki. 1998. "Tokyo's New Waterfront Transit System." *Japan Railway and Transit Review*, no. 16 (June): 15.

Iyotani Toshio. 1993. *Henbō suru Sekai Toshi*. Tokyo: Yūhikaku.

Jacobs, Jane. 1961. *The Death and Life of Great American Cities*. New York: Random House.

Jansen, Clifford, ed. *Readings in the Sociology of Migration*. Oxford: Pergamon.

Japan Times. Tokyo, daily. www.japantimes.co.jp.

———. 1989. *Yo no Naka Kō Natte Iru*. Tokyo: Japan Times, 1989.

Jinnai, Hidenobu. 1995. *Tokyo*. Translated by Nishimura Kimiko. Berkeley and Los Angeles: University of California Press.

Johnson, Chalmers. 1982. *MITI and the Japanese Miracle*. Stanford: Stanford University Press.

Jones, Colin. 2005. *Paris*. New York: Viking.

Jordan, David. 1995. *Transforming Paris*. New York: Free Press.

Judge, David, et al., eds. 1995. *Theories of Urban Politics*. Thousand Oaks, Calif.: Sage.

Kabayama Kōichi and Okuda Michihiro. 1985. *Toshi no Bunka*. Tokyo: Yūhikaku.

Kaempfer, Engelbert. 1999. *Kaempfer's Japan*. Edited and translated by Beatrice Bodart-Bailey. Honolulu: University of Hawaii Press.

Kamo, Toshio. 1994 (October). "Tokyo's Economic Functioning as a Global City." Paper prepared for the SSRC (Social Science Research Council) Global Cities Meeting, New York.

Kaplan, Steven. 1984. *Provisioning Paris*. Ithaca: Cornell University Press.

———. 1995. *Farewell, Revolution*. Ithaca: Cornell University Press.

Karan, P. P., and Kristen Stapleton, eds. 1997. *The Japanese City*. Lexington: University of Kentucky Press.

Katō Masaaki. 1965. "Toshi to Seishin Fuan." *Toshi Mondai* 56, no. 11:47.

Katō, Shūichi. 1983. *A History of Japanese Literature*, vol. 3. Translated by Don Sanderson. Tokyo: Kodansha.

Katz, Richard. 1998. *Japan: The System That Soured*. Armonk, N.Y.: Sharpe.

Kawabata, Yasunari. 2005. *The Scarlet Gang of Asakusa*. Translated by Alisa Freedman. Berkeley and Los Angeles: University of California Press.

Kawamoto Saburō. 1996. *Kafū to Tokyo*. Tokyo: Toshi Shuppan.

Kawazoe Noboru. 1979. *Tokyo no Gen-Fūkei*. Tokyo: NHK (Nihon Hōsō Kyōkai).

Keating, Michael. 1991. *Comparative Urban Politics*. Brookfield, Vt.: Edward Elgar.

Keene, Donald. 1984. *Dawn to the West*. New York: Holt, Rinehart, Winston.

———. 1988. *The Pleasures of Japanese Literature*. New York: Columbia University Press.

———. 2002. *Emperor of Japan*. New York: Columbia University Press.

Keisatsu-chō, Sōgō Taisaku Iinkai. 1971 (July). *1970 Nendai no Keisatsu no Arikata*. Tokyo.

Kerr, Alex. 2001. *Dogs and Demons*. New York: Hill and Wang.

Kertzer, David. 1988. *Ritual, Politics, and Power*. New Haven: Yale University Press.

Kim, Won Bae, et al., eds. 1997. *Culture and the City in East Asia*. Oxford: Clarendon Press.

Kodama Kōta and Sugiyama Hiroshi, eds. 1969. *Tokyo-to no Rekishi*. Tokyo: Yamakawa.

Koizumi, Kishio. 2003. *Tokyo, The Imperial Capital*. Miami, Fla.: The Wolfsonian.

Kokudo Kōtsū-shō. 1998 (31 March). *Shin Zenkoku Sōgō Kaihatsu Keikaku*. Tokyo: Kokudo Kōtsū-shō.

Kokudo Kōtsū-shō, ed. n.d. *"Zenkoku Sōgō Kaihatsu Keikaku" no Hikaku*. www.mlit.go.jp/kokudokeikaku/zs5/hikaku.html.

Kokudo-chō Keikaku Chōsei-kyoku, ed. 1994. *Yonzensō Sōgōteki Tenken Chōsa-bukai Hōkoku*. Tokyo: Okura-shō.

Komiya Shōkei and Yoshida Hideo, eds. 1979. *Tokyo Mondai.* Tokyo: Otsuki Shoten.

Kornhauser, David. 1976. *Urban Japan.* London: Longman.

Koschman, J. Victor. 1978. *Authority and the Individual in Japan.* Tokyo: University of Tokyo Press.

Kurasawa Susumu. 1967. "Danchi Jūmin to Jimoto Jūmin." *Toshi Mondai* 58, no. 12 (December).

———. 1968. *Nihon no Toshi Shakai.* Tokyo: Fukumura.

Kurasawa Susumu and Machimura Takashi, eds. 1992. *Toshi Shakaigaku no Furontia.* Vol. 1. Tokyo: Nihon Hyōron Sha.

Kurata Washio. 1970. *Toshika no Shakaigaku.* Tokyo: Hōritsu Bunka-sha.

Lacaze, Jean-Paul. 1994. *Paris: Urbanisme d'état et destin d'une ville.* Paris: Flammarion.

LaFleur, William, to the author. February 15, 1999.

Lang, Robert. 2003. *Edgeless Cities.* Washington, D.C.: Brookings Institution.

Lavedan, Pierre. 1975. *Histoire de l'urbanisme à Paris.* Paris: Hachette.

LeClère, Marcel. 1985. *Paris.* Saint-Jean-d'Angély: Bordessoules.

Lefebvre, Henri. 1970. *La révolution urbaine.* Paris: Gallimard.

———. 1991. *The Production of Space.* Translated by Donald Nicholson-Smith. Cambridge, Mass.: Blackwell.

———. 1996. *Writings on Cities.* Translated by Eleonor Kofman and Elizabeth Lebas. Cambridge, Mass.: Blackwell.

Le Galès, Patrick. 2002. *European Cities.* Oxford: Oxford University Press.

Lehan, Richard. 1998. *The City in Literature.* Berkeley and Los Angeles: University of California Press.

Le Monde. Paris, daily. www.lemonde.fr.

Le Parisien. Paris, daily. www.leparisien.fr.

Levine, Myron. 1994. "The Transformation of Urban Politics in France." *Urban Affairs Quarterly* 29, no. 3 (March).

Lewis, Michael. 1990. *Rioters and Citizens.* Berkeley and Los Angeles: University of California Press.

Lienesch, Michael. 1999 (21 January). Interview by the author.

Lynch, Kevin. 1960. *The Image of the City.* Cambridge: MIT Press; Harvard University Press.

Mabileau, Albert. 1994. *Le système local en France.* Paris: Montchrestien.

Maeda Ai. 1989. *Toshi Kūkan no naka no Bungaku.* Tokyo: Chikuma.

———. 2004. *Text and the City.* Edited by James Fujii. Durham, N.C.: Duke University Press.

Maeda Shinjirō. 1957. *Hanzai no Toshika.* Tokyo: Yūhikaku.

Maki Fumihiko. 1987. *Miegakure suru Toshi.* Tokyo: Kajima.

———. 2008. *Nurturing Dreams.* Edited by Mark Mulligan. Cambridge: MIT Press.

Mansfield, Stephen. 2009. *Tokyo*. New York: Oxford University Press.

Marchand, Bernard. 1993. *Paris: Histoire d'une ville*. Paris: Seuil.

Masai, Yasuo. 1975. *Urban Land Use Map of Edo, ca. 1860*. Tokyo: Midorikawa Chizu Insatsu, 1975.

Masai Yasuo. 1989. *Jōkamachi Tokyo*. Tokyo: Hara Shobō.

Maspero, Francois. 1994. *Roissy Express*. London: Verso.

Matsumoto Michiharu. 1971. "Toshi ni okeru 'Gisei-son' no Mondai." *Hyōron: Shakai Kagaku*, no. 1 (February).

Matsumoto, Shigeru. 1970. *Motoori Norinaga*. Cambridge: Harvard University Press.

Mazey, Sonia. 1990. "Power outside Paris." In *Developments in French Politics*, edited by Peter Hall et al. New York: St. Martin's.

McCargo, Duncan. 2000. *Contemporary Japan*. New York: St. Martin's.

McClain, James, et al., eds. 1994. *Edo and Paris*. Ithaca: Cornell University Press.

McEwan, J. R. 1962. *The Political Writings of Ogyū Sorai*. Cambridge: Cambridge University Press.

McKean, Margaret. 1981. *Environmental Protest and Citizen Politics in Japan*. Berkeley and Los Angeles: University of California Press.

Merlin, Pierre. 1991. *Les villes nouvelles en France*. Paris: Presses Universitaires de France, 1991.

Merriman, John. 1991. *The Margins of City Life*. New York: Oxford University Press.

———. 1994. *Aux marges de la ville*. Paris: Seuil.

Miao, Pu, ed. 2001. *Public Places in Asia Pacific Cities*. Boston: Kluwer.

Michalski, Sergiusz. 1998. *Public Monuments*. London: Reaktion.

Mikuriya Takashi, ed. 1994. *Tosei no Gojūnen*. Tokyo: Toshi Shuppan.

———. 1996. *Tokyo*. Tokyo: Yomiuri.

Milgram, Stanley. 1976. "Psychological Maps of Paris." In Environmental Psychology, edited by Harold Proshansky et al. New York: Holt, Rinehart, Winston.

Minami Kazuo. 1978. *Bakumatsu Edo Shakai no Kenkyū*. Tokyo: Yoshikawa Kōbunkan.

Ministry of Land, Infrastructure, and Transport [Japan]. 1998 (March). *The Fifth Comprehensive National Development Plan*. www.mlit.go.jp/kokudokeikaku/zs5-e/index.html.

Mittelman, James, ed. 1996. *Globalization: Critical Reflections*. Boulder: Lynne Rienner.

Mollat, Michel. 1971. *Histoire de l'Île-de-France et de Paris*. Toulouse: Privat.

Mosher, Michael. 1997 (August). "Liberation and the Seductive Possibility of Avoiding Its Costs: Dilemmas of Globalization in Tokyo and Paris." Paper prepared for the annual meeting of the International Political Science Association, Seoul.

Mumford, Lewis. 1938. *The Culture of Cities*. New York: Harcourt, Brace.

———. 1961. *The City in History*. New York: Harcourt, Brace, World.

Murai Masuo. 1964. *Edo-jō*. Tokyo: Chūō Kōron.

Murakami, Yasusuke. 1982. "The Age of New Middle Mass Politics." *Journal of Japanese Studies* 8, no. 1.

Muramatsu, Michio. 1991. *Chihō Jichi*. Tokyo: Tokyo Daigaku Shuppan Kai.

Naimu-shō, Shakai-kyoku. 1922. *Saimin Chōsa Tōkei Hyō*. Tokyo.

Naitō Akira. 1979. *Shiro no Nihon Shi*. Tokyo: NHK (Nihon Hōsō Kyōkai).

———. 1985. *Edo to Edo-jō*. Tokyo: Kajima.

———. 2003. *Edo, the City that Became Tokyo*. Translated by H. Mack Horton. Tokyo: Kōdansha.

Najita, Tetsuo. 1987. *Visions of Virtue in Tokugawa Japan*. Chicago: University of Chicago Press.

Nakamura, Akira. 1996. "The 'Tokyo Problem' and the Development of Urban Issues in Japan." In *Globalization and Decentralization*, edited by Jong Jun and Deil Wright. Washington, D.C.: Georgetown University Press.

Nakamura Satoru. 1968. *Meiji Ishin no Kiso Kōzō*. Tokyo: Mirai Sha.

Nasu Sōichi and Hashimoto Jūzaburō. 1968. *Hanzai Shakaigaku*. Tokyo: Kawashima.

New York Times. New York, daily. nytimes.com.

Nishikawa Kōji. 1972. *Nihon Toshi-shi Kenkyū*. Tokyo: NHK (NHK Broadcasting Co.).

———. 1973. *Toshi no Shisō*. Tokyo: NHK (NHK Broadcasting Co.).

Nishio, Kanji. 1990. "The Danger of an Open-Door Policy." *Japan Echo* 17, no. 1:51.

Nishiyama, Matsunosuke. 1997. *Edo Culture*. Translated by Gerald Groemer. Honolulu: University of Hawaii Press.

Noin, Daniel, and Paul White. 1997. *Paris*. New York: John Wiley.

Nora, Pierre, ed. 1992. *Les lieux de mémoire*. Pt. 3, vol. 3. Paris: Gallimard.

———. 1996. *Realms of Memory*. Vol. 1. Translated by Arthur Goldhammer. New York: Columbia University Press.

Nosco, Peter. 1990. *Remembering Paradise*. Cambridge: Harvard University Press.

Nouët, Noël. 1990. *The Shogun's City*. Translated by John Mills and Michele Mills. Sandgate, U.K.: Paul Norbury.

Ogi Shinzō and Jinnai Hidenobu, eds. 1995. *Edo Tokyogaku e no Shōtai*. Tokyo: Nihon Hōsō Shuppan Kyōkai.

Ohashi Kaoru. 1973. *Toshi Byōri no Kōzō*. Tokyo: Kawashima.

———. 1976. *Toshi Byōri no Shakaigaku*. Tokyo: Kakiuchi.

Oka, Hideyuki. 1967. *How to Wrap Five Eggs*. Translated by Atsuko Nii and Ralph Friedrich. New York: Harper and Row.

Olsen, Donald. 1986. *The City as a Work of Art*. New Haven: Yale University Press.

Ozaki, Kōyō. 1919. *The Gold Demon*. Translated by A. Lloyd and M. Lloyd. Tokyo: Seibundō.

Ozawa, Ichirō. 1994. *Blueprint for a New Japan*. Tokyo: Kōdansha.

Pagano, Michael, and Ann Bowman. 1995. *Cityscapes and Capital.* Baltimore: Johns Hopkins University Press.

Parker, Geoffrey. 1996. *The Military Revolution.* Cambridge: Cambridge University Press.

Perrin, Noel. 1979. *Giving up the Gun.* Boston: Godine.

Piggott, Joan. 1997. *The Emergence of Japanese Kingship.* Stanford: Stanford University Press.

Pinchemel, Philippe. 1979. *La région parisienne.* Paris: Presses Universitaires de France.

Pinon, Pierre. 1999. *Paris: Biographie d'une capitale.* Paris: Hazan.

Piore, Michael, and Charles Sabel. 1984. *The Second Industrial Divide.* New York: Basic Books.

Pirenne, Henri. 1952. *Medieval Cities.* Translated by Frank Halsey. Princeton: Princeton University Press.

Ponsonby-Fane, Richard. 1979. *Imperial Cities: The Capitals of Japan from the Oldest Times until 1229.* Washington, D.C.: University Publications.

Popham, Peter. 1985. *Tokyo.* Tokyo: Kōdansha.

Préfecture Île-de-France (Paris). 1995. *Schéma directeur de la région d'Île-de-France.* www.ile-de-france.equipement.gouv.fr.

Preston, Peter, and Paul Simpson-Housley, eds. 1994. *Writing the City.* New York: Routledge.

Reiber, Beth, and Janie Spencer. 2004. *Frommer's Japan.* Hoboken, N.J.: Wiley.

Reischauer, Edwin, and Marius Jansen. 1995. *The Japanese Today.* Cambridge: Harvard University Press.

Renaud, Jean-Pierre. 1993. *Paris: Un état dans l'état?* Paris: Harmattan.

Rey, Henri. 1996. *La peur des banlieues.* Paris: Presses de Sciences Po.

Richie, Donald. 1999. *Tokyo.* London: Reaktion.

Robb, Graham. 2007. *The Discovery of France.* London: Picador.

Roche, Daniel. 1987. *The People of Paris.* Translated by Marie Evans. Leamington Spa, U.K.: Berg.

Roncayolo, Marcel. 1990. *La ville et ses territoires.* Paris: Gallimard.

Rouleau, Bernard. 1985. *Villages et faubourgs de l'ancien Paris.* Paris: Seuil.

———. 1997. *Paris: Histoire d'un espace.* Paris: Seuil.

Roullier, Jean-Eudes, ed. 1989. *Villes nouvelles en France.* Paris: Economica.

Rozman, Gilbert. 1973. *Urban Networks in Ching China and Tokugawa Japan.* Princeton: Princeton University Press.

Russell, John. 1983. *Paris.* New York: Henry Abrams.

Rustow, Dankwart. 1969 (September). "Transitions to Democracy." Paper prepared for the annual meeting of the American Political Science Association, New York.

Sacchi, Livio. 2004. *Tokyo: City and Architecture.* New York: Universe.

Samuels, Richard. 1983. *The Politics of Regional Policy in Japan.* Princeton: Princeton University Press.

Sansom, George. 1961. *A History of Japan 1334–1615*. Stanford: Stanford University Press.

Sassen, Saskia. 1991. *The Global City*. Princeton: Princeton University Press.

———. 1994a. "La ville globale." *Le Débat*, no. 80 (May).

———. 1994b. *Cities in a World Economy*. Thousand Oaks, Calif.: Pine Forge.

Satō Yasuko. 1965a. "Ryūnyū Shōnen no Hikō ni kansuru Kenkyū." *Hōmu Sōgō Kenkyū-jo Kenkyū-bu Kiyō*, no. 1.

———. 1965b. "Toshika to Hanzai: Hikō no Shūchū." *Toshi Mondai* 56, no. 11 (November): 31.

Sautter, Christian. 1994. "Paris et le dessein français." *Le Débat*, no. 80 (May): 76.

Savitch, H. V. 1988. *Post-Industrial Cities*. Princeton: Princeton University Press.

Savitch, H. V., and Paul Kantor. 2002. *Cities in the International Marketplace*. Princeton: Princeton University Press.

Scalapino, Robert. 1962. *Democracy and the Party Movement in Prewar Japan*. Berkeley and Los Angeles: University of California Press.

Scargill, D. I. 1979. *The Form of Cities*. New York: St. Martin's.

Scheiner, Ethan. 2006. *Democracy without Competition in Japan*. Cambridge: Cambridge University Press.

Screech, Timon. 2000. *The Shogun's Painted Culture*. London: Reaktion.

Secretariat to the Summit Conference of Major Cities of the World. 1991. *Major Cities of the World 1991*. Montreal.

Seidensticker, Edward. 1965. *Kafū the Scribbler*. Stanford: Stanford University Press.

———. 1983. *Low City, High City*. New York: Knopf.

———. 1991. *Tokyo Rising*. Cambridge: Harvard University Press.

Sekiyama Naotarō. 1958. *Kinsei Nihon no Jinkō Kōzō*. Tokyo: Yoshikawa Kōbunkan.

Sennett, Richard. 1977. *The Fall of Public Man*. New York: Knopf.

———. 1990. *The Conscience of the Eye*. New York: Knopf.

Senneville, Gérard de. 1992. *La Défense: Le pouvoir et l'argent*. Paris: Albin Michel.

Sharpe, William, and Leonard Wallock, eds. 1983. *Visions of the Modern City*. New York: Heyman Center for the Humanities, Columbia University.

Shibata, Tokue, ed. 1993. *Japan's Public Sector*. Tokyo: University of Tokyo Press.

Shigematsu Kazuyoshi. 1986. *Edo no Hanzai Hakusho*. Tokyo: PHP.

Shimmura Izuru. 1983. *Kōjien*. 3rd ed. Tokyo: Iwanami.

Shinohara Hajime. 1977. *Shimin Sanka*. Tokyo: Iwanami.

Sibley, David. 1995. *Geographies of Exclusion*. New York: Routledge.

Silver, Hilary. 1993. "National Conceptions of the New Urban Poverty: Social Structure Change in Britain, France, and the United States." *International Journal of Urban and Regional Research* 17, no. 3 (September): 336–54.

Skinner, G. William, ed. 1977. *The City in Late Imperial China*. Stanford: Stanford University Press.

Smethurst, Richard. 1974. *A Social Basis for Japanese Militarism.* Berkeley and Los Angeles: University of California Press.

Smith, Henry. 1978. "Tokyo as an Idea." *Journal of Japanese Studies* 4, no. 1 (Winter).

———. 1979. "Tokyo and London: Comparative Conceptions of the City." In *Japan: A Comparative View,* edited by Albert Craig. Princeton: Princeton University Press.

———. 1988. *Kiyochika, Artist of Meiji Japan.* Santa Barbara: Santa Barbara Museum of Art.

———. 2001. *A Time of Crisis.* Cambridge: Harvard University Press, 2001.

Smith, Robert. 1978. *Kurusu.* Stanford: Stanford University Press.

Smith, Thomas C. 1961. "Japan's Aristocratic Revolution." *Yale Review* 50, no. 3 (spring).

———. 1977. *Nakahara.* Stanford: Stanford University Press.

Sōmu-shō Tōkei-kyoku. [annual]. *Nihon Tōkei Nenkan.* Tokyo: Nihon Tōkei Kyōkai.

Sorensen, Andre. 2002. *The Making of Urban Japan.* London: Routledge.

Soulignac, Françoise. 1993. *La banlieue parisienne.* Notes et Études Documentaires no. 4978. Paris: Documentation Française.

Steiner, Kurt. 1965. *Local Government in Japan.* Stanford: Stanford University Press.

Stewart, David. 2002. *The Making of a Modern Japanese Architecture.* Tokyo: Kodansha.

Stovall, Tyler. 1990. *The Rise of the Paris Red Belt.* Berkeley and Los Angeles: University of California Press.

Sturken, Marita. 2001. "Memorializing Absence." www.ssrc.org/sept11/essays/sturken.

Sudjic, Deyan. 1992. *The 100 Mile City.* New York: Harcourt Brace.

Sundquist, James. 1975. *Dispersing Population.* Washington, D.C.: Brookings Institution.

Sutcliffe, Anthony. 1971. *The Autumn of Central Paris.* Montreal: McGill-Queen's University Press.

———, ed. 1984. *Metropolis 1890–1940.* Chicago: University of Chicago Press.

Suzuki Masao. 1988. *Edo no Toshi Keikaku.* Tokyo: Sanseidō.

Swan, James. 1991. *The Power of Place.* Wheaton, Ill.: Quest.

Tajbakhsh, Kian. 2000. *The Promise of the City.* Berkeley and Los Angeles: University of California Press.

Takahashi Yasuo and Yoshida Nobuyuki, eds. 1990. *Nihon Toshi-shi Nyūmon.* 3 vols. Tokyo: Tokyo Daigaku Shuppan Kai.

Takenaka, Akiko. 2004. "The Emperor, War Victory Celebrations and Spectacles." University of Chicago. Draft manuscript in author's files, Department of Political Science, University of North Carolina.

Tamai Tetsuo. 1987. *Edo*. Tokyo: Heibonsha.

Tamanoi, Mariko. 1998. *Under the Shadow of Nationalism*. Honolulu: University of Hawaii Press.

Tanizaki, Junichiro. 1977. *In Praise of Shadows*. Translated by Thomas Harper and Edward Seidensticker. New Haven: Leete's Island.

Tarrow, Sidney. 1994. *Power in Movement*. Cambridge: Cambridge University Press.

Terry, T. Philip. 1920. *Terry's Guide to the Japanese Empire*. Boston: Houghton Mifflin.

Tilly, Charles. 1990. *Coercion, Capital, and European States, A.D. 990–1990*. Cambridge, Mass.: Blackwell.

Tilly, Charles, and Wim Blockmans, eds. 1994. *Cities and the Rise of States in Europe, A.D. 1000 to 1800*. Boulder: Westview.

Tokyo Katei Saibansho. [annual]. *Tokyo no Hikō Shōnen*. Tokyo.

Tokyo Shisei Chōsa Kai. 1992. *Dai-toshi Mondai e no Chōsen: Tokyo to Nyū Yōku*. Tokyo: Nihon Hyōron Sha.

Tokyo-to. [annual]. *Tokyo-to Tōkei Nenkan*. Tokyo: Tokyo-to.

Tokyo-to, Minami-Tama Shintoshi Kaihatsu Hombu. 1972. *Tama Nyū Taun Kyojūsha no Jū-Seikatsu to Ishiki ni kansuru Hōkoku Sho*. Tokyo: Tokyo-to.

Tokyo-to, Toshi Keikaku-Kyoku, Sōmu-bu, Sōdan Jōhō-ka. 1991. *Tokyo no Toshi Keikaku Hyakunen*. Tokyo: Tokyo-to.

Tombs, Robert. 1981. *The War against Paris, 1871*. Cambridge: Cambridge University Press.

Totman, Conrad. 1983. *Tokugawa Ieyasu: Shogun*. South San Francisco: Heian.

———. 1995. *The Lumber Industry in Early Modern Japan*. Honolulu: University of Hawaii Press.

Tracy, James, ed. 2000. *City Walls*. Cambridge: Cambridge University Press.

Tsuji Tatsuya. 1966. *Edo Kaifu*. Tokyo: Chūō Kōron, 1966.

Umesao, Tadao, et al., eds. 1986. *Japanese Civilization in the Modern World*. Senri Ethnological Studies no. 19. Osaka: National Museum of Ethnology.

Unno Hiroshi. 1983. *Modan Toshi Tokyo*. Tokyo: Chūō Kōron.

Vale, Lawrence. 1992. *Architecture, Power, and National Identity*. New Haven: Yale University Press.

Vlastos, Stephen, ed. 1998. *Mirror of Modernity*. Berkeley and Los Angeles: University of California Press.

Wakabayashi, Bob, ed. 1998. *Modern Japanese Thought*. Cambridge: Cambridge University Press.

Wakita Osamu. 1994. *Nihon Kinsei Toshi Shi no Kenkyū*. Tokyo: Tokyo Daigaku Shuppan Kai.

Ward, Philip. 1985. *Japanese Capitals*. Cambridge, U.K.: Oleander.

Waterhouse, Alan. 1993. *Boundaries of the City*. Toronto: University of Toronto Press.

Weber, Eugen. 1976. *Peasants into Frenchmen.* Stanford: Stanford University Press.

Weber, Max. 1958. *The City.* Translated by Don Martindale and Gertrud Neuwirth. Glencoe, Ill.: Free Press.

Wheatley, Paul. 1971. *The Pivot of the Four Quarters.* Chicago: Aldine.

Wheatley, Paul, and Thomas See. 1978. *From Court to Capital.* Chicago: University of Chicago Press.

White, James. 1973. *Political Implications of Cityward Migration.* Beverly Hills: Sage.

———. 1982. *Migration in Metropolitan Japan.* Berkeley: Institute of East Asian Studies.

———. 1984. "Protest and Change in Contemporary Japan." In *Institutions for Change in Japanese Society,* edited by George DeVos. Berkeley: Institute of East Asian Studies.

———. 1988. "State Growth and Popular Protest in Tokugawa Japan." *Journal of Japanese Studies* 14, no. 1.

———. 1992. "Core, Periphery, and Popular Contention in the Tokugawa City." *Meijō Hōgaku* 42 (May).

———. 1995. *Ikki.* Ithaca: Cornell University Press.

———. 1998. "Old Wine, Cracked Bottle?: Tokyo, Paris and the Global City Hypothesis." *Urban Affairs Review* 33, no. 4 (March).

White, James, and Frank Munger, eds. 1976. *Social Change and Community Politics in Urban Japan.* Chapel Hill: Institute for Research in the Social Sciences.

Wilkinson, Thomas. 1965. *The Urbanization of Japanese Labor 1868–1955.* Amherst: University of Massachusetts Press.

Wylie, Lawrence. 1964. *Village in the Vaucluse.* New York: Harper and Row.

Yamakawa Toshio. 1931. "Tokai Sensei Jidai." *Nōson Kenkyū* 1, no. 1 (January).

Yamamoto Eiji. 1970. "Seisaku Kettei Katei to Jūmin Undō." *Toshi Mondai* 61, no. 5 (May).

Yano Tsuneta Kinen Kai, ed. [annual]. *Nihon Kokusei Zue.* Tokyo: Kokusei Sha.

Yazaki, Takeo. 1968. *Social Change and the City in Japan.* Translated by David Swain. Tokyo: Japan Publications.

———. 1970. *The Socioeconomic Structure of the Tokyo Metropolitan Complex.* Translated by Mitsugu Matsuda. Honolulu: University of Hawaii Social Science Research Institute.

Yokoyama Shōichi. 1991. *Shuto.* Tokyo: Taimeidō.

Yonemoto, Marcia. 2003. *Mapping Early Modern Japan.* Berkeley and Los Angeles: University of California Press.

Zerubavel, Yael. 1995. *Recovered Roots.* Chicago: University of Chicago Press.

Zukin, Sharon. 1995. *The Cultures of Cities.* Cambridge, Mass.: Blackwell.

INDEX

religion (*continued*)
—Japanese: in organization of Edo, 50–51; subservience to state, 134. *See also* Buddhism; Shinto
Restif de la Bretonne, Nicolas, 89
Revolution of 1848, 9, 161, 164
Robert the Pious (king of France), 160, 189
Rome, margins of, 84
Roppongi Hills (Tokyo), 201, 245n114
Russell, John, 107

Sacré-Coeur (Paris), 50, 134, 142, *206*
Saitama Prefecture, *81*
Sanya (slum, Tokyo), 86, 256n15
Sarkozy, Nicolas, 131, 167, 191; on suburbs, 221, 257n54
Sautter, Christian, 221–22
Seidensticker, Edward, 174
Seine, role in Parisian development, 71, 79
SEMs (public-private corporations, France), 110, 111, 126; of municipalities, 245n110
Shiba Park, temple complex of, 248n85
Shinto: mana in, 88; shrines, 35, 237n94; view of death, 134; worldview of, 50
shogunate, Japanese, 12, 15; authority of, 52; goals for capital, 41; Kyoto palaces of, 145; planning under, 129. *See also* Tokugawa era
Smith, Thomas C., 216
social control: in Edo, 54, 74; in Meiji restoration, 163; as ordering principle, 211; in Paris, 224; in Tokyo, 214
society, effect of place on, 20
statuary. *See* monuments
suburbs. *See under* Paris *and* Tokyo
Suzuki Shunichi, 66, 120–21, 254n55; free-market views of, 192; monumentalism of, 148

taille (land tax), 84
Tama New Town (Tokyo), 117, 123, 124, 198; state initiation of, 215
Tange Kenzō, 148
Thélème, Abbey of, 26
Thiers, Adolphe, wall of (Paris), 9, 70, 72, 91–92, 95
Third Republic: monuments of, 141–42; Paris during, 109, 110
Tilly, Charles, 183
tobichi (land), administrative status of, 239n17
Tōdai temple, 246n46
Tokugawa era: agrarianism of, 37; Edo in, 15, 30, 63–64, 74, 189; end of, 63; land tax in, 84; material power in, 144–45; urbanism of, 212. *See also* shogunate, Japanese
Tokugawa Ieyasu, 56; Edo under, 12, 55, 63–64, 67–68, 113, 226; vassals of, 89
Tokyo: administration of, 83, 194–96; American occupation of, 101; amorphous quality of, 27, 210; anticapital narratives concerning, 157; antisocial behavior in, 167; attitude toward past, 36; autonomy of, 16, 182, 191–92; as Buddhist capital, 51; Buddhist temples of, 237n94; built environment of, 22–23, 29; capitalism in, 1, 24, 51–52, 154, 179, 213, 214; Capital Region Development Law, 116; as City of Light, 26; city planning in, 29, 32, 64, *65*, 66, 113–19, 196–98, 213–14; class hostility in, 159; commercial development in, 119–21, 215; commercial districts, 100–101; consumption in, 32–33; continuity in, 29; corporate presence in, 18, 180, 217; cost of living in, 32; crime in, 168–69; decentralization in, 117; defenders of, 156; detractors of, 38, 173, 175–76; dirigisme in, 15, 176; divisions within,